THE VOICE, T

A Life in Broadcasting

by

Martin Muncaster

AUSTIN MACAULEY PUBLISHERS™

LONDON * CAMBRIDGE * NEW YORK * SHARJAH

A CIP catalogue record for this title is available from the British Library.

ISBN 9781528933513 (Paperback)
ISBN 9781528933520 (Hardback)
ISBN 9781528967501 (ePub e-book)

www.austinmacauley.com

Published by Martin Muncaster
And
The Claude Muncaster Estate
November, 2017

First Published 2021
Austin Macauley Publishers Ltd®
1 Canada Square
Canary Wharf
London
E14 5AA

For Sara

To Say 'Thank You'

"You most certainly have a story to tell!"

So said David Learner, editor in Macauley's production department. It was fortunate that my manuscript landed on his desk, as he is one of the more senior staff at the publishers. He told me that he had recognised the name at once and remembered well my work on television and radio. I owe him a huge debt of gratitude for considering my story to be ripe for publication and for passing it forward for production.

There are many people I need to thank for their assistance in getting my book in print. First, I particularly want to thank my dear brother, Clive, who trawled through my chapters with infinite care. He gave me many important additions and corrections, especially about family matters. There is an awful lot I would have missed without his knowledge of the many elements of my story. In that, I include my dear cousin, Tessa Atley. My daughter, Miranda, too, gave me much useful advice.

There have been a number of friends to whom I sent my self-published version for their 'feedback'. My long-time friend, Robert Gussman was particularly taken by, and helpful with, the 'Jura Living' chapter. Others include Margaret Meikle, who has much editing experience, and our joint dear friend, Jean Lyster-Binns. There were several others too, who were most encouraging and offered useful reactions.

But I really must give my heartfelt thanks to Sue Clegg who, with consummate professionalism and speed, typed out many chapters from my wiggly handwriting, with hardly a mistake! Then assisted me in the important business of proofreading.

Another who typed out my drafts with hardly a mistake was Dan Brown at 'Print it', the excellent printing establishment at Liphook, in Hampshire. I spent many hours alongside Dan as we worked on the book together. Indeed, it was Dan who created the self-published edition which I produced first as a record for the family.

Yet another I want most warmly to thank is Julie Brealey, who worked with me for hours, first turning the whole book from a PDF file into 'Word' to enable me to edit what I had written; then typing out my manuscript at lightning speed. She almost had the words on the page before I'd spoken them! She calls her business 'Type Like the Wind' – a fitting title.

I would also like specially to thank David McAlpine for allowing me to have photographed his superb Claude Muncaster oil painting of the London skyline originally commissioned by his brother, Sir William around 1960. My warm thanks also to Sir William's widow, Lady Judy McAlpine, for permission to print the photograph of my father's magnificent oil painting of 'Olivebank' approaching the Horn.

I am also much indebted to the Archivist of the Cayzer Family Archive, Susan Scott, who kindly arranged for me to include a photograph of the superb Claude Muncaster oil painting of the 'Southampton Castle' entering Durban, originally commissioned by Sir Nicholas Cayzer.

I also want specially to thank my dear friend and business colleague, Roden Richardson who, very kindly with great skill and imagination, designed the cover of my book for me. It looks really great.

Finally, but by no means least, I wish to thank the staff of the Imperial War Museum, for finding me the flotilla of 'ton' minesweepers which included the ship in which I served, HMS Essington.

I do sincerely trust I have not missed anyone whom I should have included in this list of helpers. I have no doubt that there are one or two, in which case my apologies to them as I celebrate with no small excitement the final published volume. I do hope that all those who read and share my story will enjoy the experience.

I've had a most enjoyable time putting it together.

Table of Contents

Foreword

It was during some six or seven long weeks of uncharacteristic rest, following a nearly disastrous road accident in Brussels that I began to reflect on my 80-plus years with its wide variety of personal experiences.

The result is this account of my full and busy life, recalling the highlights and lowlights, the ups and downs, of my professional and family life, together with my travel experiences in three continents and my encounters with many remarkable people I have been fortunate enough to meet.

After relating some stories from my sometimes unhappy schooldays, I recall happier times at drama school. Next, it was time for National Service in the Royal Navy, culminating in a much-coveted commission as an officer. And then I was 'free' to pursue my ambition to enter the world of broadcasting with the General Overseas Service of the BBC, then gaining experience in Canada before returning to the UK. Over many years, I worked with the BBC in both radio and TV, and also had a spell in commercial television. I went on to make documentary programmes, write books and appear in films – allowing some time for the family, plus my hobbies of fishing, sailing and golf. It has been quite a kaleidoscopic life!

As I also discovered, living in the public eye and being instantly recognisable has its advantages – and disadvantages, which provide some interesting anecdotes!

Beneath my more visible memories from those eight decades, there is also the more private life which I have tried to describe in as much detail as possible (notably, perhaps, my father's career as a famous artist). This is mainly to provide a family 'archive' for my children, grandchildren and generations still to come. I hope them – and all other readers – will appreciate and understand the candour with which I have related some very personal episodes in my life.

In closing, I would like here to pay special tribute to my dear friend Peter Marshall, who most kindly offered to edit my book for me. He has been a brilliant and most professional help, offering some excellent ideas and additions. I certainly couldn't have done it without him.

Martin Muncaster
Steep, Hampshire, 2019.

Chapter 1

A Step Too Far and a Dance with Death!

BOOM!! The explosion was thunderous, ear-splitting, devastating, all in less than a split instant. It was as if a bomb had gone off close by with a massive blast.

Shattered and stunned, I staggered to my feet wondering what on earth had hit me. I had just stepped out on to a pedestrian crossing – but with not a moment for a second step. At the kerb, I had looked right and saw a clear road – but in Brussels, they drive on the right and I'd looked the wrong way. As I moved out I was struck. A speeding motor bike had smashed into my left side, hurling me to the tarmac.

I looked around to see a motor bike on the ground, its handlebars weirdly bent. The rider, thoroughly shaken, had come over to check me out. Somebody across the road had obviously witnessed the smash and resounding crash, and had immediately phoned the police. The 'emergency' team was there in moments and now I was sitting in their car answering a bunch of questions – "should I go to hospital?" – "should they call an ambulance?" I refused these offers, as politely and calmly as I could. I was determined to get home to my local hospital instead of being stuck for days in a strange place surrounded by a team of strange medics and having to account for myself. It was not a comfortable option.

Sitting in the back seat beside me was the driver of the motor bike. Happily for him, he had only sustained a sprained wrist. In good English, he said to me: "You must be very strong!" It was not precisely how I felt at that moment. But I did feel lucky to be alive. By now, blood was oozing from my chin and my right hand; and perhaps my leg would soon be bleeding too.

I have decided to relate this story rather fully as it was hugely dramatic, extremely scary and stressful at the time, even more than two other events you will read about later in which I could well have met my end, but on neither occasions was I actually injured. In that sense, this accident was very different. Being incredibly fortunate still to be alive, I wondered as the day wore on how this event in Brussels might affect my future career. Was I going to be able freely to move about? I was pretty badly damaged.

I might so easily have been killed outright, in which case, the passion of my life, broadcasting, would have come very suddenly to an untimely end. I was lucky I wasn't struck by a large truck or bus. I have made many mistakes in my broadcasting life, but my mistake today was surely the most serious. They drive on the right in Brussels, and I had looked the wrong way! I prayed that I might in due course fully recover. It was extraordinary what fears ran through my head that day. For one thing, I now found myself devoid of a passport and in the hands of the police in a strange country. Scary enough of itself.

Having been brought up during wartime, I was minded of the years of the last war, and what it must have been like for a British spy, for instance, discovered and picked up to be horribly interrogated at length by the Gestapo. Terrifying in a city overrun by the German invaders.

Fortunately, for me, it was now at least peacetime, while I was being questioned in minute detail by one policeman, with the other taking copious notes.

But, dear reader, what had brought me to this sorry plight? In fact, this unbelievable scenario was completely unnecessary, created by the fact that I had set out for my trip to Belgium without my passport; when I left home, I had forgotten to pick it up and take it with me. Somehow, at St Pancras, by showing my picture driving licence at the gate and by dint of much assiduous explaining, I was eventually permitted to pass through to the Eurostar train with strict instructions from a friendly French immigration officer to obtain an emergency passport from the British Embassy when I got to Brussels. He really should not have let me through.

This was my first mistake! I should have missed my train, gone home, collected my passport and taken a later train. But it was too late now as, somewhat relieved, I took my seat and comfortably headed to the continent.

The reason for my trip to Brussels had been to attend a major meeting of NEWAYS (the health supplements business for which the family had become top distributors). It was a highly significant and important occasion – but even so, I should simply have missed it. The meeting was held in a packed hall in a large hotel just outside Brussels and in fact I made the meeting in good time. So there was some feeling of relief.

After long sessions and many presentations, trying my best to pick up at least some of the French, I wondered why the presenters had to speak so fast. But I suppose we British may tend to speak fast, too.

In the evening, I went on to stay with Patrick Quanten and his wife, Martine, at their home at Hasselt, half an hour away by train. My beloved partner, Sara, had driven over with them the day before. She had been working with Patrick for quite some time, generously allowing him and Martine to stay in her house for two days each month while Patrick gave patients the benefit of his unique (and often painful!) massage. This particular weekend, he was giving a workshop explaining his alternative approach to health. Many years before, he had been a GP in the Channel Islands and Sara liked the fact that he had medical training.

This weekend, though, she was working with a serious impediment as Patrick gave the whole two days of his presentation in Dutch. I was with them and, unsurprisingly, totally lost! After the workshop, Sara and I stayed the night with Patrick and Martine and were hoping to spend the Monday enjoying the sights of Brussels before returning home on the Eurostar that evening. But it was not to be…

Mistake Number Two!

Patrick had explained to me how to leave Brussels railway station by the best exit for a short walk to the Embassy to obtain my 'emergency' passport. However, when we arrived the station was in chaos due to reconstruction work and the exit I thought to be the correct one turned out to be completely wrong. The second mistake!

I left Sara with our luggage and walked the streets of Brussels, on and on, endeavouring to find the Embassy. Surely it was close? But evidently not; I had been walking away from it. The passers-by I asked hadn't a clue and after nearly half an hour of frustration I was relieved to spot a taxi, waved it down and asked for the British Embassy. I could relax at last. Well, not quite; the smartly suited commissionaire at the door informed me that they didn't issue emergency passports at the Embassy, they were issued at the Consulate. He said I would find it, an inconsequential building some way down the road. Writing it down, he gave me the code for entering the Consulate door.

I arrived to find the place deserted, save for a security porter sitting in a small, glass-protected bureau. I explained my problem and he then said, in quite good English: "Oh, sorry sir. We're closed on Mondays!"

Now what?

I must have looked sorry for myself as, eventually, after a lengthy discussion, he said: "I do have a colleague upstairs who is in today. He may be able to help. There's a waiting area over there," and he vanished into a lift.

I waited and waited more… three quarters of an hour went by and nature was beginning to make itself felt. Was there a loo… somewhere, anywhere? Soon, a lady came through the door and told me she had made an appointment to get an emergency passport. At this point, at long last, the porter returned to tell her that the Consulate was closed and to come back the next day.

But he then turned to me and apologised for the long delay and it appeared that I might possibly be more fortunate. Apparently, the civil servant upstairs on the 8th floor had taken an age, only to understand that I couldn't be found. He had checked with the passport office in London and realised that my passport had been recorded with an incorrect name – there was no 'e' at the end of my middle name, Grahame, so the computers were completely foxed and didn't recognise me. At least, though, I had eventually been, as it were, 'discovered'. But now came further unwelcome news. The porter told me that applicants for emergency passports needed three things – a special police pass, a new passport photo and the Euro ticket for that day to prove I was actually leaving the country. "Come back at five," he said.

HELP!

The porter explained to me how to get to the police station but advised me to be quick as the police could take ages issuing the necessary pass. Before I left him, he took me to the loo – much relief! By now, I admit, I was far from relaxed but, luckily, I found the police station easily, to see there was only one person in front of me. Eventually, a policewoman came to the desk and I explained my situation… and she disappeared into an office… for a long time. The minutes were running out and the Consulate would be minus even a porter at 5 o'clock. With deep relief, after she had questioned me at length about my UK address, the policewoman came back bearing the vital paperwork.

Now for the photo. I asked where this could be done and found there was a shop in a nearby street where passport photos could be obtained and I soon had one in my pocket. Next, I needed to return to find Sara, who was watching over our luggage in a huge EU Commission building next to the station. There had been nowhere for her to sit and wait in a station smothered by an array of building materials and scaffolding – and my train ticket was in one of the bags with Sara. So then came the NEXT mistake.

I was by now nervously eyeing my watch, realising that there was only just enough time to get to Sara for the Euro ticket and then back to the Consulate before 5 o'clock. I was, understandably, in considerable stress and hurry, half running down the pavements, to the EU building which, I had been told, was only a short walk from the station…

I stepped out at the pedestrian crossing and… BANG! I WAS ON THE GROUND…

A Fractured Leg

All this time, poor Sara had been wondering what on earth was happening? Where was I? Was I even alive? At length, the policemen managed to reach Sara on their mobile phone, explained the situation to her and then drove me to the Commission building. It was a huge relief to see her and she was so good about it, having waited such an age. It had been particularly awful for her as she had been unable to get to a loo. Nobody on the EU's reception desk would help her, saying she could only get into the building's toilets bearing a key with the proper code.

I had limped from the car and as we met, she said: "Darling, you've broken something."

I replied: "No, I don't think so. I'm fine."

Then I tried to take a step… and crumpled in a heap to the floor. Sara was correct; my left leg was clearly fractured. She helped me to my feet, then managed to get a taxi to take us and our luggage to the station – WITHOUT an emergency passport.

We joined the queue for people taking the Eurostar and I waited while Sara dashed to the loo. Heaven knows how she had managed to hold on for so long – and without any information from me. I had been so completely tied up with my dreadful passport predicament and in deep shock that I had failed to at least get a message to her on my mobile phone. That was really awful.

She now came back to me saying: "Gosh, that was a relief!" She then found a wheelchair and at last we were both in better comfort.

By now, with a dry mouth after the day's exhausting traumas, I badly needed something else for a bit of comfort. Quite simply, a drink. A brief cup of tea at breakfast now seemed a lifetime away. Luckily Sara, sensibly, had always carried a bottle of water with her and now offered me some. I was extremely grateful. I took two or three most welcome mouthfuls and felt much better.

Working our way to the front of the queue, a young fellow who was helping people through immigration suddenly spotted our predicament. He came over and chatted, asking what had happened. "Don't worry," he said. "We'll get you through." He pulled us out of the queue, then went off to explain our situation to the other officers. Quite soon he returned with bandages. He was clearly a bit of a 'first aider' and he patched me up. I was glad to have a cover to hold back the bleeding of my hand. My scarf was already soaking up the blood on my chin.

This young fellow from the immigration office was as good as his word. He went away with my driving licence, obviously it checked with the passport office in London, then came back and just wheeled me through, meanwhile helping Sara with the cases.

Thus, I finally got out of Belgium without the need of a passport anyway!

By now, the side of my right foot was becoming very painful as we boarded the train and found our seats. My little toe was obviously broken. However, we had an uneventful journey and at St Pancras we were impressed to see a man waiting with a wheelchair, right by our carriage. Then it was by taxi to Waterloo with a very helpful driver (Dutch, I think) steering us into the Control Room to find out the next best train to Liss and Sara's home.

Then another surprise! There had been a massive storm in England that day and the railways were badly disrupted. So we now had to wait until after 11pm for a train that was actually running. Sara called Misha (her son-in-law) hoping he would hear the phone, asking him to meet us at Liss station. It was a delight to see him on the platform, it now being well past midnight, and he took my arm to help me to his car. Walking had become a real problem for me.

Back home to Sara's house at last; but how to get up the stairs to the bedroom? Eventually, I had to work my way up the stairs backwards on my behind, one step at a time! Next morning, Sara drove me to A&E at St Richard's Hospital in Chichester, where X-rays proved that I had fractures of my left leg and right toe.

With me in plaster, we now had a long haul ahead!

A few days before our Brussels trip, Sara had exclaimed that she'd had enough, after years of painstaking caring and healing work. She was going to give it all up and look after herself for a change. Ironic…

But now she had to start looking after me and caring me back to health. It took many days, which dragged into weeks, with her giving my leg the most gentle and helpful healing massage. I was hugely grateful. I quickly found myself loving my beloved Sara ever more deeply and with unending gratitude. With her massage she had a wonderfully healing touch.

I think the angels were with me that day in Brussels. I was incredibly lucky and have given thanks ever since…

During those long weeks of uncharacteristic rest, I began to reflect on my 80-plus years with its variety of personal experiences and decided not only to write about my 'dance with death' in Brussels, but also to start chronicling my life story. So here goes…

As I mentioned in the Foreword, the result is this account of my full and busy life, recalling the highlights and lowlights, the ups and downs of my professional and family life, together with my travel experiences in three continents and my encounters with many remarkable people I have been fortunate enough to meet – ranging from Harry Secombe and Sir Laurence Olivier to Peter Sellers, Sir Alec Douglas Home (when prime minister), and even Lord Mountbatten.

Back in 1951, home from an Irish family holiday with schooling completed, I had to decide what I was going to do with my life. I was pretty sure I wanted to be an actor, but at the same time I had dreams of becoming a BBC newsreader. I even went up to the attic with my father's Daily Telegraph and read it aloud to myself for practise. I knew that the BBC newsreaders, like Alvar Lidell and Frank Phillips, never made a mistake; so, if I went wrong, I had to make myself go back to the beginning and start again.

Little did I know then the varied path I would actually take to follow in the footsteps of those famous BBC newsreaders.

There was National Service in the Royal Navy, the first steps in broadcasting in Canada, then back to the UK – with commercial TV and the BBC – before arriving at the portals of BH as a newsreader, originally with the old BBC Home Service, then Radio 4. Then there came other duties; presenting 'Songs of Praise' and 'Come Dancing', first with Peter West, then Terry Wogan. I recorded many TV and radio commercials, made documentary programmes, and more recently

I have been actin in movies for the silver screen. To repeat myself, it has been quite a kaleidoscopic life!

Chapter 2

Audition for the Guildhall

But it began in an unexpected way. The first step on the ladder came as a result of my brother, Clive, being taught the violin by a charming lady called Kit Firth and it turned out that she knew the principal of The Guildhall School of Music and Drama, Edric Cundall. Would I like to go there? My answer was a definite 'yes', so Kit Firth organised an introduction for me, which was followed by an audition.

The Guildhall School of Music and Drama in John Carpenter Street.

I've always been a bit of a mimic, particularly 'taking off' the famous names on the radio. One of these was the Norfolk postman's voice which Jon Pertwee used in his sketches and this character became a household name with his much-used line in the Norfolk accent: "Oh, m' dear, oh m' dear, what does it matter what you do with them letters so long as you tear 'em up." I think I've got it pretty well right.

It so happened that one of the professors at The Guildhall was Guy Pertwee, Jon's uncle, a gentle man and greying, I found myself in his room for my audition. After a most interesting talk with him, which included him reminding me not to say 'the idea-r is'; he was very clear that this meant I was 'bridging the hiatus'! I should say, quite clearly, 'the idea is' – leaving a proper space between the words 'idea' and 'is'. This memory just happens to be one of the things in what was, for me, the most important audition.

He then suddenly said: "What do you do?" I told him that mimicry was one of my things and I told him that a particular character I 'took off' was Jon Pertwee's Norfolk postman. Guy Pertwee then said: "Let's hear a bit then?" So I launched into: 'What do you do with them letters…etc.' and Guy's reply was simply: "You're in!"

Thus, I was able to begin two fascinating years as a student at The Guildhall, then in John Carpenter Street near Blackfriars Bridge (it later moved to the Barbican). This meant a complete and detailed course, learning to be an actor. It involved all the subjects which were to be so valuable to me when I began my profession. They included voice production and 'projection' and remembering to reach 'the back wall'. We were even trained to properly produce a 'stage whisper' and how to fall without hurting ourselves. Other subjects included mime, stagecraft, how to enter and leave a stage effectively, fencing, the secrets of good production and dancing.

This latter I learned from a rather elegant, though shortish, middle-aged lady called Miss Wildblood – an engaging name we thought. She would clutch me tightly to her bosom, which was warmly ample, (though in position rather below my chest), and spin me around trying to keep up with her long backward glides and various tricky ballroom gyrations. There was a lot to learn and I was soon quite breathless!

Another most important matter for acting was learning the technique of proper breathing. This stood me in good stead for my profession in later years. It could make all the difference to one's performance to practise deep breathing, particularly just before going on stage. Good breathing helped to engender confidence and relaxation.

Some Professors

There was the darkly professional Ambrose Marriott an expert in mime. He had a deep languorous voice entreating us to follow on stage his excruciating muscle-flexing exercises vigorously shaking his arms and hands while continuing his vocal encouragements: "Come along then, move, let's get going".

There was also Danny Roberts, a smallish, greying, slim man of great charm and long dramatic teaching experience, much loved by his students.

Mr Walters, dark haired and bespectacled, always wore a smart well-tailored suit, I remember, sloping around in the shadows at the back of the darkened theatre, watching proceedings with hawk-like eye. Then sitting down with his student actors and giving extensive critical notes to their various performances.

Well after I'd retired, I taught deep breathing to my granddaughter, who was studying law. She told me it had made a great difference to her confidence in her 'Mock Trial' exam. She didn't have thoughts of becoming a barrister then. But if she ever did, I knew that barristers often came up with a bit of 'acting' when addressing the court!

The Guildhall, then, was an excellent all-round training to help us all join a profession in which there was, and still is, huge competition.

There were, actually, many nubile young maidens at The Guildhall at that time – and there were few men, largely, I suppose, because so many had been lost in the war. But I had absolutely no experience of making relationships with females. I was so green! I was mainly just interested in my work and, of course, being a man, I was frequently called upon for many of the 'scenes' which were acted from a range of different plays, and naturally a good deal of Shakespeare. It was amusing to pass by some particular 'scene' which was being used for practice and hear famous lines being spoken aloud and echoing down the corridor.

An Opportunity in Pantomime

Towards the end of the Christmas term in December 1951, I was approached by a student called Peter Johnson, tall and dark like me, who told me that he had landed a job at Stratford. At that moment, he was acting in Cyril Fletcher's pantomime. Cyril produced a pantomime every year with his stunningly beautiful, blonde actress wife, Betty Astell. Peter told me that currently they were playing at the Arts Theatre, Cambridge, and he would have to leave before the pantomime went on to Brighton in mid-January, and then Malvern. Would I like him to ask Cyril if he would take me on? If I would like to, I would not only get paid but would be getting valuable professional experience as well.

I jumped at it!

Quite soon, Peter came back to me saying Cyril would like to give me an audition. This was quickly arranged and I travelled by train to Cambridge for the audition, which was held in the front of the 'tabs' between a matinee and an evening performance. I had to re-enact a little scene that had happened to Peter one night when he was playing the part of the bailiff ejecting a young widow from her house. He had actually fallen in love with the beautiful young widow and fell on his knees asking for her hand in marriage.

"I'll have your hand or bust!" (Cyril then shouted from the wings, to much hilarity, "'ave 'em both!!!") as the bailiff appealed to the young attractive widow. But one night as Peter fell to his knees he accidentally raised his hand and caught her wig. It came off to yells of delight from the audience, so that bit of business stayed in every night. It was this little scenario which I now had to re-enact. Not easy in the cold afternoon with Cyril and his stage manager looking on. But I must have made a reasonable fist of it as Cyril took me on for the Brighton and Malvern shows.

I went back to The Guildhall to finish the term and home for a most enjoyable Christmas. In the New Year, I joined the cast for the Brighton shows which were played at the Theatre Royal and attracted pretty good audiences. Cyril Fletcher was quite a 'star' and was a brilliant comedian.

The pantomime was 'The Sleeping Beauty' and Betty was the beauty of course. I had to be Cyril's servant, 'Liquorish' done up in 18th century servant's costume. It was too tight and the legs too short. It had obviously fitted Peter better than me. I had to help Cyril, who was playing the part of a flat-footed fairy. He wore a blonde wig which kept falling off and sang the song – "When a fairy's feet are flat, she's finished…" – holding a wand with a spring in the middle and a star at the end which kept bending sideways. His timing was consummate, and we all watched from the wings laughing our heads off – every night.

The fortnight went quickly and we had to move on to Malvern. The young assistant stage manager had arranged a B&B for me. But when I got there, I found it was damp, cold and uncomfortable with only a jug for water with a bowl to wash in. The food was of the same standard! I had to explain to the old landlady as kindly as I could that it was really too far from the theatre and I would have to move. An excuse, I'm afraid, but it was true. I found a very nice small hotel in Malvern and was much more comfortable.

On the 6th February, 1952, the sad news was announced that the King had died and on that day the theatre was, of course, closed.

But all in all, I had a great time acting in Cyril's pantomime and I had some real professional experience to my name when I returned to The Guildhall.

I was assigned to Mr John Holgate, a charming, rather stocky, quiet man, going bald, who was a delight to work with. He taught me much, particularly about speaking Shakespeare's words. Incidentally, I recall that for obvious reasons, the doors of the professors' rooms were glazed at the top, so no chance of any 'hanky-panky'!

At times of study John had me speaking some famous Shakespeare lines, including *To be or not to be*. I found it incredibly hard to put my whole being into these sessions. It somehow seemed so embarrassing just to stand there spouting away to a single person. I was much more comfortable, strangely enough, addressing a large audience.

One day, after morning lectures, I decided to invite a particularly attractive blonde girl out to lunch. She readily agreed, and perhaps thought there was more in it than I did, holding my hand as we walked along. This was a 'first' for me and it felt really nice. I said I was 'green'!

In the summer term, John Holgate also ran the much favoured Music Hall, which involved numbers of keen, bright-eyed students acting their hearts out, performing sketches, enthusiastically singing songs from the shows, and generally thoroughly enjoying themselves to a delighted theatre audience mostly made up of family and friends. One of the highlights for me was doing impersonations of the Churchill voice, and that of the famous cricket commentator, John Arlott, who I was to meet and work with in years to come.

The girl I took to lunch! I wonder if she's still alive?

There were students at Guildhall who went on to become famous. Claire Bloom was one, and another was Eileen Atkins who was absolutely contemporary with me. I can honestly say I spotted Eileen as clearly a rising star. One day, she was working with a male actor on a scene from *A Streetcar Named Desire* by Tennessee Williams. I was sitting in the theatre preparing to watch this when Eileen, very much a blonde, came walking in with jet-black hair. She'd had it dyed. I was amazed to see the transformation but most impressed that she was prepared fully to look the part. Even then, I recognised a star in the making, and how right I have proved to be. Eileen is now one of the great names in the theatre and has become a Dame, a title she richly deserved after her many brilliant performances. I suppose I became quite a famous broadcaster myself and was to work in various areas of broadcasting for some 40 years. But all that is for later.

Rehearsing a scene with Eileen Atkins (seated centre) on the Guildhall Theatre stage. We all looked so young!

A hugely significant moment for me came in my last term at The Guildhall. There was, and I believe still is, a competition set up by the BBC for the various drama schools around London. One of the judges at that time was John Gielgud's brother, Val (who became the BBC Head of Drama). The competition was designed, I believe, to give a young actor and actress the chance to spend time with the BBC Drama Repertory. The prize was £25 (a reasonable amount of money in those days when you could buy a full meal for three shillings and sixpence!) together with six months with the BBC Radio Drama Rep. This was a great chance as the young winners would meet some of the top names in radio and would have the opportunity to learn their craft. I hear that now the competition is open to four entrants, so two actors and two actresses can be prize winners. However there are no cash prizes any more. So goodness knows how many noughts the BBC would have to add these days to equate with £25 in the 1950s!!!

One of these competitions came up in my final Guildhall term and I put myself in for it. To teach us the necessary microphone technique, a radio producer from Broadcasting House, Roland Hill, came over to prepare those of us who had decided to enter the competition. I can remember him setting up a microphone on a table and asking us to sit at it and read passages from Christopher Fry's 'Boy with a Cart'. When my turn came, I had a feeling of huge excitement and as I sat and read I knew immediately what I wanted to do with my life – not struggling as an actor but becoming a broadcaster. I was completely comfortable with the microphone and my passion for my profession was born right there.

I didn't win, of course, but a worthy winner was an excellent actor, Trevor Martin, from The Guildhall. I knew he was likely to win; he had a marvellous, sonorous and very deep voice. A young actress, Catherine Fleming, who won also came from Guildhall, so the school was very much to the fore that year. Trevor was at one time in love with Eileen Atkins.

All this time, I knew I would be called up for National Service – two years which would take me away from my chosen profession. Not surprisingly, I wanted to go into the Navy and I thought it would be a good idea first to join the RNVR (Royal Naval Volunteer Reserve). So I went to the London office of the RNVR and volunteered for service. I reckoned I would have a good chance of getting into the Navy if I was already wearing the right uniform, and so it proved.

The only problem was that I had to carry out naval training every Monday evening at HMS King Alfred, the RNVR training establishment in Hove. I sometimes took the Brighton bus from Petworth, but often was given a lift by a Mr Franklin, one of the clerks at the Westminster Bank in Petworth and an RNVR officer. He drove a tiny black Austin and I had to coil myself down in the cramped passenger space. The other disadvantage was that Lieutenant Franklin smoked a pretty foul pipe and I was trapped in the swirling smoke for the hour it took to drive to Hove.

Those evenings did take me away from the activities at The Guildhall, but were definitely necessary if I wanted any chance of being taken on by the Navy for my National Service. I later joined as a signalman, one step up from seaman, because I was interested in communications and, anyway, I reckoned the one place to be in a ship was on the bridge, the 'heart centre' of operations. As a signalman, I would also be credited with sixpence extra a day; of considerable worth when added over the months.

Meanwhile, I was working for my exams to enable me to complete the course as a Licentiate of The Guildhall. This I luckily managed to obtain, after taking the exams on another hot, summer afternoon. But I got through with quite good marks and received my certificate.

The Guildhall School of Music and Drama

FOUNDED BY THE CORPORATION OF LONDON IN 1880

PRINCIPAL: EDRIC CUNDELL, C.B.E., HON. R.A.M., F.G.S.M.

Diploma of Licentiateship
in
Speech and Drama (Performing)

This is to Certify that

Martin Grahame Muncaster

is declared a **Licentiate** *of*

The Guildhall School of Music and Drama

Dated this **thirtieth** *day of* **July** *19***53.**

Edric Cundell — Principal.

John Tooley — Secretary.

My Guildhall certificate.
Then I was about to embark on a very different life indeed...

Chapter 3

Claude Muncaster's Life and a Dreadful Accident

For a life at sea I was very much following in the footsteps of my father, Claude Muncaster, the famous landscape and marine painter. In 1939, my father had to join up; like many, he was sure war was looming. He joined the Navy, having so much attachment to the sea. In fact, being a very experienced artist, he was drafted in as the Admiralty's Camouflage Advisor, which took him on many missions, often in dangerous theatres of the War.

But before recounting my 'Navy Days', I must return to earlier years.

Before his marriage, my father had sailed in a beautiful old windjammer, the 'Olivebank', which he had first spotted moored in the Thames. He traced her to Australia, took a passage there and found the Olivebank at Melbourne, taking on grain for Britain. He joined her in early 1931 and sailed aboard the ship back to Britain, serving as a deckhand at minimum wages. It took over four months. He had chosen the privations of a sailing ship at sea to get closer to the various moods and weathers of the oceans so that he could paint what he experienced with greater authority. This he most certainly achieved, but nearly lost his life at least twice! He wrote a book about the passage – 'Rolling Round the Horn' – quite a gripping tale.

After this voyage, in September 1933, my parents were married at St Margaret's Church in the village of Fernhurst, near Haslemere, where my grandparents had a large family country home. My mother told me it was a very special wedding day with the villagers decorating the telegraph poles along the streets with bunches of flowers. Undoubtedly, my mother adored my father. It is still a comfort to me that I was clearly conceived in a state of deep love between them.

I remember my mother saying she fell in love with father's singing voice as it sounded like Paul Robeson. Certainly, my father had a very fine bass voice. His skin was also tanned a deep brown having spent so many months at sea. My mother was greatly attracted to this as well! He was an 'interesting' dancer however, moving rather awkwardly with sideways steps which my mother found tricky to navigate.

He was a master of his craft, though, when it came to painting – but he was never good with money. Fortunately, my grandfather had seen my mother right financially. She told me once that after Sir Arthur had met my father and my mother had told him about the man she planned to marry, Sir Arthur retorted: "He's a very nice young man, my dear, but he'll never make any money." My grandfather's innate vision was in due time to prove all too correct…

Many years later, in 1978, came a unique project. I wrote a book about my father's life and work. I was much helped by his excellent diaries and I entitled the book *The Wind in the Oak*. This little phrase came from a passage in my father's diaries describing his joy at getting back to painting after the life-threatening stresses of working in many theatres of war as the Admiralty's Camouflage Adviser. There were two editions, one, a beautiful leather-bound volume with gold titles printed on the spine, plus a slipcase of a dozen of my father's very fine etchings. A hundred copies of this version were published at a price of £80. Not surprisingly, they were all taken up by a list of enthusiasts. It was a fine piece of publishing and we launched the book with a major exhibition of Claude Muncaster's pictures and a big party at an excellent gallery in London's Cork Street. The other edition was a standard coffee-table-sized book, but again, as with the leather-bound volume, it was richly illustrated in colour with a significant number of my father's pictures. It was a tribute to his remarkable range of talent.

My father as a Lieutenant Commander.

The book was published by Robin Garton, who in later years had been impressed by my father's *Thoughts for the Day* on Radio 4. My father recorded several of these programmes and I was told by the producer, David Winter, that his Thoughts for the Day attracted the greatest number of letters; 200 in one week, I seem to remember. My father's voice was much admired and what he expressed as an artist created a very great deal of interest.

Another considerable plus for the book was the fact that I'd managed to get Prince Philip to write a 'Foreword'. This is worth repeating here. The Duke's words captured perfectly his appreciation of Claude Muncaster as an artist:

Talent seems to be one of the few human qualities which still defy scientific or statistical explanation. The talent of an artist is the most mysterious of all. The coordination of hand and eye and brain required to create an illusion on paper or canvas would appear to be such a normal human ability, yet the fortunate few can produce results which are unmistakably more pleasurable and impressive.

I do not think this quality will ever be explained satisfactorily, but for anyone interested in the creation of pictures, there is a fascination in reading about the lives of artists. There is always the hope that somewhere a small clue may be discovered to explain their success. All I can say is that I look at Claude Muncaster's landscape watercolours at Sandringham and Balmoral and the one big landscape in oils and I wonder in hopeless mystification just how he managed to do it. It is not that he just had a talent for applying paint; he had an unerring instinct for a subject and with some sort of secret antenna, he was able to sense the atmosphere and then to incorporate it into the picture in a way which was uniquely his. Technique and observation obviously played their parts but there is more to it than that: attitude, experience, application certainly, but in the end there is no other word for it than sheer talent.

A while after publication, I showed the book to John Frost, a most creative producer working in BBC South. He could see at once the potential of producing a documentary of Claude Muncaster's life. So John and I got to work. He'd been successful in selling the idea and there was some wonderful material for the film. My father had a full and fascinating life. It was to be a half-hour documentary, including several people who knew, or had known, my father. One was Sir Peter Scott who knew my father from the War days. He gave a wonderful tribute, including the words: 'When I look at a work by Claude Muncaster, I realise I can't paint.'

We went to various places that had meant a lot to my father, including Littlehampton where the River Arun runs out to the sea. As a young boy, he'd watched a sailing ship moving slowly down the river and away into the distance. He'd said to himself: 'I want to be aboard a ship like that and sail away to exciting places.'

My mother and brother Clive were filmed sitting around a table in the garden of my mother's home at Sutton, near Petworth, which had been my father's boyhood home. They both gave delightful descriptions of the artist who, as husband and father, had meant so much to them.

I presented the programme, explaining a lot about certain pictures and describing how he had come to paint various subjects which we visited. Looking at it now, I rather wonder how I managed it! All in all, the documentary turned out well and was a considerable success. It was given a second showing on BBC-2. Since my father died at only 71 in 1974, we have held a number of exhibitions of his work with much success.

One of the major works was a large oil painting of the skyline of London, commissioned by Sir William McAlpine. It was a view taken from the top of the Shell Building, which McAlpines were constructing near Waterloo in the early 60s.

This was a fantastic painting almost in the style of a Canaletto. I found it is held by one of the McAlpine family and, of course, is now historic as the skyline of London is so dramatically changed, but St Paul's and Tower Bridge remain and, as you will see, are clearly featured in the painting. Again, I have told the story in full in my book *The Wind in the Oak*.

The detail in this huge painting, 8 ft. long, is astounding and I wondered how on earth my father managed to do it.

In 1965, father was in New Zealand judging a major exhibition sponsored by Sir Henry Kelliher, a rich brewer whom my parents had met on a cruise. Kelliher had asked my father to judge the exhibition he had sponsored to find the best painting to win the Kelliher Art Prize.

My father had already been commissioned by the Chairman of the Union Castle Line, Sir Nicholas Cayzer, to paint an oil of the new 'Southampton Castle', sailing down the Solent off Cowes. It was a superb picture with the ship passing the Royal Yacht Britannia in the background there for Cowes Week. Princess Alexandra had launched the new 'Southampton Castle', and Sir Nicholas had given the painting to the Princess as a 'thank you', for performing the launch. Sir Nicholas now wanted a painting of the new 'pride of the fleet' entering Durban and, of course, asked my father to do this painting as well.

Claude Muncaster oil, The London skyline painting. Courtesy, The Hon. David McAlpine.

It turned out to be convenient for my father to do his research for this on his way home from New Zealand via Durban. With great generosity, Sir Nicholas had given my mother a free passage to South Africa in 'The Capetown Castle'. She was thus able to meet my father at Durban. My mother, never good at being on her own, invited Iona and me to go to South Africa with her. It was an enticing invitation and we both accepted. By then, we were married with three children so, of course, we had to organise people to look after the children. We found a very nice lady to stay at Little Crofton Cottage with Miranda and Timothy, but needed a professional 'nanny' to look after little Oliver. Big mistake! Oliver was still a tiny baby and it was really awful for him to be taken away from his mother and home at such a time. We were away nearly a month, an age to a small child.

Iona should never have gone. I should have joined my mother by myself, which would have been perfectly possible. We just didn't think things through, and Oliver told me a long time later what a deep effect being moved away had had on him, not only being taken away from home but from his mother too! The children were well used to having me away, so that's how we should have played it.

To South Africa – Again

As it was, the voyage with my mother went really well and we enjoyed it. Personally, I loved being at sea. My father flew safely to Durban from New Zealand, having judged another exhibition for Sir Henry, and I so well remember the emotional meeting we had with him when he came aboard and found us. He was greatly touched at seeing us, and there were tears in his eyes as he hugged my mother. It was, indeed, a very special moment. If only it had lasted like that. Little did we know it, but there was terrible drama to come…

We all stayed in a very comfortable and well-appointed hotel in Durban. If my memory serves me right, it was called 'The Eden Roc'. I do recall my mother buying some lovely scent at the time, Chanel No 5, and if I happen to meet a woman wearing that scent today, I am immediately wafted back to that hotel in Durban. Indeed, just recently, on the train to London, a well-dressed woman came and sat ahead of me with her husband. I was soon aware of a very memorable aroma and plucked up my courage to ask the woman about the perfume she was wearing. She was a bit surprised at being suddenly approached, but then told me she was wearing Chanel No 5! She roared with laughter when I told her the perfume meant a lot to me as it was the scent my mother used to wear!

My father now got down to the research he had to do for the picture Sir Nicholas had commissioned. One site he took us to was the 'Bluff', a spit of land on one side of the harbour which jutted out to sea. It gave a high vantage point for my father's picture and he saw the potential for painting an oil of the 'Southampton Castle' steaming past the 'Bluff', into the harbour and the docks. It really was the perfect spot.

It was great to have some time together as a family. We were all enjoying the break before my parents had to return to England. Sir Nicholas Cayzer, with continuous generosity, had arranged for my mother and father to have a free passage home in the 'Windsor Castle', so things were looking really good.

Well, they were...

To Get the View Across the Harbour – and Then!

Iona and I had fixed our flight back to England via Johannesburg. We said our 'goodbyes' and made our way home. The next day, my mother and father were treated to a 'slap up' lunch on board the 'Windsor Castle' with the Captain and one of the Union Castle directors. A good time was had by all and the wine flowed, so much so that my father began to feel guilty, that with all the wonderful hospitality he'd received he really hadn't done enough research for the commissioned painting. There was one view of the Durban harbour and docks that he felt he hadn't looked at properly and was wondering how he could obtain a really expansive sight which might be good for the painting. But it meant going ashore, and the ship would be sailing in a couple of hours. He asked the director for advice and was told there was a wonderful view across from the Union Castle offices on the other side of the harbour.

My mother was worried sick that my father wouldn't get back to the ship in time if he went ashore now, but the director told her: "Don't worry, Mrs Muncaster, it's minutes in my car and the ship won't sail without my 'say so'."

So it was agreed that the director would take my father to the offices so that he could get the view he was looking for. Off they went, confident they would be back to the ship within half an hour or so. Meantime, my mother, who was someone with great intuition, having begged my father not to go, was pacing the deck in a dreadful state of anxiety. She was terrified something would happen to prevent my father getting back to the ship in time.

She was all too right!

My father and the director, having reached the Union Castle offices in five or six minutes, climbed the stairs to an upper window which gave a wonderful view right across the harbour. There was only one snag – the Union Castle flag, which flew from a pole set on a balcony outside and below the window. The wind at that moment was flying out the flag beautifully straight, but right across the view my father was so keen to see. He suggested that if he got out of the window and dropped down to the balcony he would be standing below the flag. A good idea. The director, I gathered later, was a bit concerned, but my father retorted that he'd spent months in a sailing ship and had done an awful lot of climbing.

They opened the window for my father to sit on the sill outside and ease himself down to the balcony. But, as it happened, there was very little window sill for my father to sit on and as he prepared to jump down, he slipped and fell down to the balcony, landing heavily and very awkwardly, suddenly yelling out with pain. He'd broken his femur!

In a flash, the whole situation changed utterly. It became most urgent to get my father back up to the window and safely into the offices, but how? The director, now a very worried man, called urgently for help. Somehow, they got a chair to my father so that he could at least sit down. With extreme difficulty, I think, four strong men manhandled my father, literally screaming with pain, back up to the window.

The director now called for an ambulance and my father was rushed to hospital. By amazing good chance, the top bone surgeon happened to be on duty. He arranged for an X-ray and was able to diagnose the damage. He told my father that in a way he was lucky. The doctors had just received a new metal, titanium, I think, which would be much safer for hip joint repairs, as the body didn't reject the new metal. This was obviously comforting news.

Not for my poor mother, however…

By now the director had gone back to the ship and, white faced, had to deliver the ghastly news to my mother. She now had to leave the ship urgently before it sailed with her on board, leaving no one to look after my father.

My mother was a fastidious perfectionist and had put everything tidily away in the cabin ready for the voyage home. But the ship was now about to sail! The director told my mother to quickly gather everything she could and guided her to the crews' gangway. She got off in the nick of time. And now she had to stand watching the stately 'Windsor Castle' slowly pulling away from the dockside carrying all her main luggage with it!

Now what?

There was, however, a modicum of 'silver lining'. My parents had been introduced by my mother's best friend (Betty Connolly) to her sister, Sheila Perry and her husband who lived just outside Durban. Indeed, while my parents were in Durban, they had been to see the Perrys. My mother, in desperation, now made contact with Sheila, asking if she could stay with the family while my father was in hospital. Of course, Sheila was very happy to help, a huge relief to my mother. She was able to relax a little, giving her time to get over the appalling shock, and to be with my father as much as possible. It hardly needs to be said that Sheila was a godsend and was most sympathetic about my parents' awful situation.

My mother now had to plan how to get my father home. It was going to be at least a fortnight before the hospital would release her husband and allow him to fly.

"Come Back and Help"

Meantime, after a long flight, Iona and I had reached home and were delighted to see the children again. All had been well while we'd been away. I was in the house for a bare twenty minutes when the phone rang. It was my mother. She told me the dreadful news. "Darling," she said, "your father has had the most frightful accident and is in hospital. Can you possibly come back and help me get Father home?"

This was a bit of a bombshell and it took me some minutes to take it all in as my mother gave me more detail. I was immediately concerned that the BBC wouldn't allow me to be away again. I had already been on holiday for nearly a month. I decided it would be best to see Andrew Timothy, the Chief Assistant, Presentation (Sound), personally. I felt I could tell the story better face to face than on the phone. I had to go to the BBC anyway, to find out what my duties would be now that I was back. Thankfully, Tim (as we knew him) was most sympathetic and told me at once to take 'compassionate leave', as long as I needed to. That was good news and a great relief.

I had rather wondered why my mother needed me to help her travel home with my father, but she was not good at being left alone. I had always needed to be with her as much as possible while my father was away. For one thing, she was quite scared of sleeping alone, but did have a friend living in the bungalow near the house. We knew her as 'Betty Bung', and she was a most helpful companion to my mother, helping with the shopping and various chores around the house.

So, relieved that my mother had at least some companionship with the Perrys, I realised that my own presence for her was going to be important. So I arranged a flight, turned around and went immediately back to South Africa. Needless to say, my mother was delighted to see me. The Perrys were equally generous to me and insisted that I stayed at their home for as long as was needed.

On the flight back, there was a nasty occurrence, which could have been extremely serious. We had to make a stop at Khartoum to refuel and as the aircraft lost height, it ran into a violent black storm with thunder and heavy rain which buffeted the plane. As we flew through the storm, we heard a sudden huge bang and there was some shuddering. I heard afterwards the plane had been struck by lightning. Indeed, as I walked away (we were allowed a break in the terminal) I saw the pilot examining the fuselage at the front of the aircraft. There was a large area where the paint had been burnt off. Another situation in which I could have met my end!

So, I made the best of another 'holiday', enjoying the South African sun, warm but not too hot and visiting my father with my mother as much as we could. Thus, the weeks went by, and at last my father was released from hospital and we all three flew home, with my mother most uncomfortable as she hated flying.

For father, it was necessary for him to be moved by wheelchair. A chauffeur-driven car had been arranged and we were safely met at Heathrow. I remember my father talking animatedly to our driver, even telling jokes, until we finally reached home, 'Whitelocks', in the village of Sutton, near the South Downs. My father was delighted to be home but was now faced with the considerable problem of painting the large oil of the 'Southampton Castle' entering Durban. This proved to be a huge effort for him, as his movements were much impaired.

'Whitelocks' at Sutton, now modernised and improved, had been the family home for decades. It was my father's home until he married.

In the studio, he set up his easel and made a little platform on the table by him on which to set up his brushes and paints. Some of this homemade platform was put together by an ingenious fabrication of 'Meccano', I remember, and was constructed to help him reach his tools, oil paints and brushes, more easily without having to turn his body too much.

Somehow, with great effort, he managed to start the painting. He was determined to deliver it at the time that had been arranged by Union Castle. For my father, it was an extremely difficult deadline. But gradually, over many days, taking breaks to regain his strength, the painting began to take shape, and my father had the admiration of us all. The work progressed, despite him often being in much pain, as it was so difficult for him to turn to the side to pick up a brush or mix his paints.

I really don't think it's an exaggeration to say that it was by superhuman efforts that the Claude Muncaster oil painting of the 'Southampton Castle' entering Durban was finally completed and delivered on time. We all thought it was an incredible achievement. It was a stunning painting, a masterpiece; Sir

Nicholas was very pleased and I believe the painting took pride of place in the Union Castle boardroom. It now hangs on the wall of a very senior office indeed in the Cayzer Family Archive.

My father, we felt, really should have been awarded a medal!

Later, I was told the family were happy with the painting but were sorry there were so many dead whales in the picture! In my father's defence, he was only painting what he saw, and it has to be remembered that at that time there was nothing like the widespread and very public emotional opposition to the whaling industry which has come later. Actually, if the Cayzer family had asked my father to tone down the sight of the whales, or even paint them out altogether, he would have been happy do so. The King, after all, had asked him to alter a watercolour! (As I describe in more detail later!)

Luckily, I think most viewer's focus will be taken by the ship, including mine, by the way!

The Claude Muncaster oil, of the 'Southampton Castle' entering Durban. © The Cayzer Family Archive

Chapter 4

Back to the Beginning

(L) My mother as a teenager. (R) My mother and father on their wedding day, September 1933.

I was born on the 17th July 1934 in a bungalow in the small village of Tillington, high on a hill near Petworth in Sussex. From their home, my parents enjoyed a panoramic view over the cornfields and away to the sleeping South Downs, shimmering in the heat. The corn was ripe and golden.

My mother had given birth in a heatwave and water for dirty nappies was scarce. It was around 5 o'clock in the morning. Apparently, my mother was cross; the Petworth doctor, Dr Druitt, had come to attend her without his teeth in! My mother was fastidious about such things. My father was ecstatic at my birth. He told me many years later that shortly after I'd come into the world he had walked up the road saying to himself: "I've got a son. I've got a son."

The two tiny Claude Muncaster watercolours together.

Then he painted two delightful miniature watercolours of the view across the village with the church and cornfields backed by the South Downs. One of these tiny paintings was a present to me; the other, slightly larger one was for my mother as a 'thank you' for delivering a son. A little later, the nanny my mother had engaged picked me up exclaiming: "Madam, he's the image of Sir Arthur!" How she had managed to discern this when I was barely three days old was remarkable. But it was a nice compliment for my mother to hear.

(L) My paternal grandfather, Oliver Hall. (R) 'He's the image of Sir Arthur'.

My father having been born Oliver Grahame Hall, my mother, therefore, became Primrose Hall, her maiden name having been Primrose Balfour (of which more later). She now had to set up home in a pretty basic bungalow – perhaps 'modest' would be a fairer description, but it was all my father could afford at the time.

My dear mother, after her marriage, had moved from the stylish and imposing Riverdale Grange, situated in the more salubrious sector of Sheffield, away from the smoke, grime and scorching fiery furnaces of the steelworks, to a life very different from the one she had been used to. My grandfather and grandmother, Sir Arthur and Lady Balfour, enjoyed the services of a sizeable staff – a butler, cook and under cook, housemaids and two gardeners. My granny also had a private secretary. My grandfather was a visionary businessman; he must have been a workaholic. He not only ran the family steelworks, 'Balfour's Capital Steelworks' in Sheffield, he was also chairman of several companies and Government Commissions. His children – two boys and three girls – were lucky if they saw him at weekends. Even then he was often not there, being away in foreign parts selling steel. He later joked that he didn't know how the heck he was going to manufacture all the steel he'd sold! He retired just before the war but had to return to work in the family business as his two sons had to join up – Robin in the Navy and Francis in the Army. This played heavily on my grandfather's health.

Lord Riverdale's remarkable career is fully described in 'Burke's Peerage'.

My maternal grandparents, at the time of my grandfather's investiture as Lord Riverdale in 1935.

But, returning to my earlier years, we were in the bungalow for a relatively short time before my mother became pregnant again. Meantime, I believe I was on the Cow and Gate dried milk – my mother clearly didn't like breast-feeding. Indeed, years later she told me she found it 'a messy business'!

My brother Clive turned out to be a huge baby. When women were told that he was eleven pounds when he was born, they turned pale! This fact, unfortunately, was dreadful for my mother. She became seriously ill and was sent to a special hospital in Hove, Sussex. She had such a hard time with the birth that my father thought she might die. The pain for my mother became intensive. She was given one of the very early Caesarean-section births and when she was sewn up afterwards, the surgeons had trapped a lot of wind inside her and she spent days in agony. Not surprisingly, my father became extremely anxious. But at last, my mother pulled through, almost certainly because she was so young. She was only 20 when she had me, and then Clive a bare 18 months later. But sadly, after the operation, she could never have another child.

I was growing up quite fast, and here on the lawn by our modest bungalow I was trying to catch up with father's prowess on the golf course! (Before the War my father was a 'scratch' golfer).

My parents were inspired to call their second son Clive, having been impressed by a film they saw about Clive of India. But Clive's name was in due course to create much questioning, particularly when he went to school. On my father's side, his mother (my granny) had an aged aunt relative who was the last of the Muncaster line. She lived to be over 100 and received a congratulatory telegram from Queen Mary. I discovered the telegram among my father's effects after he died. Clive, therefore, by parental choice became Clive Muncaster Hall – of which more later.

Moving to 'Four Winds'

While all this was going on, my parents were having built a modern family home on a hillside outside Petworth with, again, a panoramic view of the Downs to the South. In fact, they had an almost 360-degree view from their lofty position which overlooked the little village of Byworth across the valley. My grandfather, Sir Arthur, generously helped out financially with the new home which my father named 'Four-Winds' – it was buffeted in all directions! It became a really happy home for the four of us. Indeed, my father dubbed us a 'four-square family'. Amazingly, Clive told me recently, that he remembered being taken to visit the new house when it was being built.

A 'happy family', though not quite "four-square" in this shot.

And a little later, two happy fellows at "Four-Winds" with father's devoted collie, Meg.

I certainly enjoyed an idyllic childhood of great freedom, though my mother kept a beady eye on me when I set off down the drive on my little bicycle! One sunny morning, however, she took her eye off me. I escaped and rattled off down the drive to the farmyard next door. There was a steep track down into the yard and I was able to pick up some pretty good speed down it on my smart new 'trike'. Unhappily, I had got the navigation a bit wrong and didn't see the large boulder ahead of me at the bottom. I rammed this with considerable energy and was flung over the handlebars into sticky mud! I had not bargained for this and immediately suffered terrifying panic and shock! Deserting the 'trike', and with a liberal amount of mud plastered all over my face, I raced home yelling my head off. Our next-door neighbour was certain I was being attacked! Fortunately, my mother was excellent in an emergency and soon calmed me down and cleaned me up. Such are the unexpected moments of life with small children!

By now, my father was having to go up to the Admiralty every day and he used to leave for Pulborough Station each morning on his motorbike. I always watched him set off down the drive to wave him goodbye. One morning as I listened to the noise of the bike fading away into the distance, I heard a sudden resounding crash. We were at war and I was sure my father had been killed! Screaming with shock, I tore off down to drive as fast as my little legs would carry me, only to find my father extricating himself from the rolls of barbed wire which had been laid along the lane to discourage the Germans. Actually, my father had hit the milkman who, turning the corner, had been blinded by the sun, then rising brightly in the east! Luckily, my father had been wearing his thick flying suit so only suffered some scratches. Though Clive told me only recently that he remembered father having hurt his leg quite badly in the accident.

The bike that hit the milkman!

Schooldays – and War!

But the time came for school and my parents signed me (and later Clive) into a nursery school, North End House, by a main road leading out of Petworth. Even then, school was not to my liking. I wanted to be at home. My mother was a wonderful cook and the school dinners were of a very different standard. Indeed, so appalled was I at the hunky cheese affair put in front of me one day that I refused to eat it! This did not go down well and I was sent upstairs to explain myself to the Headmaster, an ex-Army man, and husband of the lady who ran the school. He treated me to a scary interrogation: "Why wouldn't you eat a perfectly good lunch?" I ended up plodding my way through the ghastly cheesy concoction, overlooked by the voluminous dinner lady!

Clive, not yet at the school, was still a chubby little chap at home.

In Granny Hall's garden at Sutton

But life was made bearable by Miss Bracewell, an excellent teacher who understood the needs of small boys. She used to write delightful, inventive stories about little characters called 'Boots and Shoes' and we listened in rapt silence as she read them to us when she was taking the class. Many years later, Betty Bracewell married my uncle Leslie, my father's elder brother. His first wife, Ruth, had been seriously ill and died very young, having presented my uncle with five children. Diana, the eldest, turned out to be gorgeously attractive.

After my enjoyable times in Granny's garden at Sutton, I well remember going into Petworth and being attracted by the blacksmith's shop at the bottom of the street (Grove Lane), and listening to the ringing of the anvil, ting! ting! ting! The rhymical sound of his hammering.

I used to lean up on the stable door and watch as the old blacksmith fashioned short rods of red hot steel in to the shapes of horse shoes, while the puff of his blower heated up his fiery furnace behind him.

That historic smoky shop has since been converted in to a frightfully smart stone walled cottage.

How things change ….

My cousin, Diana.

It was at North End House that I had my first introduction to acting. We were performing a little play about life in the countryside and I had the part of a local farmer. Some nasty man had wandered on to my land and I remember rushing at him (another rather surprised small boy) shaking a stick and yelling: "Get off my land, get off my land." It felt rather good, creating such a scene, especially in the Sussex dialect taught to me by my father. It's certainly my earliest memory of performing.

By the time Clive had joined me at North End House World War Two was well under way. I can remember lying in bed and hearing the German bombers groaning overhead. At other times, it was our own squadrons of bombers braving their way to Berlin. I can still hear the sounds of those planes in my head to this day and I knew the different rumble of the German engines from the steady roar of the British Rolls Royce engines. And all this in our house in the Sussex country.

Before a raid from German planes, the siren on the local police station used to echo its awful wail around the town, up and down, up and down. We then just waited for the 'all clear', hoping to be spared the bombing. Strange how certain things can stay with you, sounds or scents – even the memory of my mother's expensive Chanel No 5. But in the little art class at North End House, all I could draw was planes crashing down out of the sky, bombs, bullets and streaks of smoke.

Murder from the Skies

Then, on one dreadful day for the whole of Petworth in 1942, murder came from the skies without any siren. My little brother (who became a very fine musician) was at the time daydreaming, he thinks, of the Royal Albert Hall. As he peered out of the school window, he suddenly spotted a German plane streaking over Petworth. Beneath it, he saw a yellow-looking object dropping through the air. Bomb! It bounced on the road, then into the wall surrounding Petworth Park and was flung back, smashing into the local village school, exploding in a huge ball of flame and smoke, completely destroying the school building. That one afternoon, Petworth lost the flower of its youth in a ghastly instant – 28 were killed and many injured. The headmaster and his assistant also lost their lives.

The village school was at least a hundred yards up the road from the private North End House, so the blast was contained in a relatively small area. I had already moved on to Prep School by then, but my brother Clive was still there and he was incredibly lucky. He was sitting by a plate glass window and the blast blew the glass outwards, away from him – a strange phenomenon which may have saved Clive's life.

Somebody rang my mother: "They've bombed the school." In wild panic, imagining her precious Clive dead, she grabbed her bicycle and raced to the town, clambering over the smoking rubble as she saw with huge relief that North End House still stood. Though she was appalled to imagine the carnage that awaited the rescue services as they arrived behind her. There is a memorial graveyard in Petworth to all those poor children who perished.

Then Prep School – and Sergeant!

When I was seven, it was time for Prep School. My mother knew the headmaster of Fernden, Charles Brownrigg – she used to play tennis with him and his sisters. The school, near Haslemere, was reached up a long drive to the building which stood at the top of a steep hill. And so, one afternoon, my mother took me to see the school and meet 'Mr Brownrigg'. I clearly remember him guiding us around the school, the extensive grounds and the playing fields at the bottom of the hill.

Charles Brownrigg.

Aerial shot of Fernden School.

I joined Fernden as a boarder in the summer term of 1942 and so began six years of my young life in a place I was far from keen to be. So homesick was I at the beginning of each term that I always wanted to sleep facing home. I suppose it gave me some sort of comfort for being forced from life with my parents and particularly my mother, whom I adored. Life at Fernden was certainly regimented, with gym before breakfast, interminable lessons before lunch, soccer in the afternoons, more lessons before supper, then a period of homework and bed.

Cricket in the summer gave me some solace as I very much enjoyed the game and developed some skill as a fast bowler. I hated the swimming, however, which was carried out in an outside pool which, very soon after being filled with fresh water, became a home for newts and toads in water which had turned a smudgy green. At swimming lessons, we were looked over by Sergeant King, the games and gym master. He was something of a tyrant and if we were in some way guilty of a misdemeanour, we were bent over by Sergeant to receive a painful 'biff' on a bare leg. We wore shorts then, of course, and it was a simple matter for him to pull up a trouser, usually the right leg, to expose the flesh for him to thwack with his hand. Not surprisingly, we nicknamed him 'Biffer Sergeant'. For some reason, we never questioned this dire punishment. Today, such treatment would put him in prison!

I remember when I was a senior, Charles Brownrigg brought me into his confidence and told me that he had asked Sergeant to 'back off a bit' – although the Headmaster himself over the years delivered many a beating. Unthinkable today, but there was quite often a sorry little queue of boys outside his study door after lunch awaiting punishment for some terrible crime, such as not gaining enough good 'house points'.

'Mr Charles' at Fernden, however, was an excellent teacher; he had his very own patient methods of teaching French and Latin and I doubt if I could ever have got through my Common Entrance exams without him. He could, on occasion though, let fly a terrifying temper. On a day in class, one small boy called Cuff was late, and the Headmaster, a strong man, thrashed him hard with a gym shoe in front of us all. I can still see a mental picture of that occurrence, even today. I wonder what happened to Cuff in later years.

Again, we took all this for granted. It was part of the system in those days. Personally, I did everything possible to be a 'good citizen', thus to avoid trouble! I certainly tried hard at sport. Mr Charles was extremely keen on sport. During matches against rival schools, he couldn't bear to witness our side **losing**! If, from the touchline he judged we were exhibiting less than the proper prowess on the playing field, he would shout out loudly and in vocal tone as if in excruciating pain (ably supported by sundry parents): **"COME ALONG FERNDEN!"**

I can hear that 'touchline voice' to this very day!

One time, I got on the wrong 'side' of Sergeant. In the summer, we all traipsed down to the playing fields to arrange each of the houses (I was in Grenville House) in circles for Sergeant's strenuous exercises. That morning, I had lost a gym shoe. Probably some rascal had lost his so borrowed mine. This made me late for 'circles'. Of course, one just didn't arrive late for Sergeant and I, with another poor miscreant called Malcolm Gage, did our very best to join our circles without Sergeant seeing. Not possible! In the end, I had to own up and explain my problem to him. Clearly this was not acceptable to our 'games master'. He was not impressed and he hit me hard about the head on both sides, making me reel. I had a headache for the rest of the day. I never did find out what happened to poor Malcolm Gage – I was too busy recovering from my own pain as I joined my house circle.

After matches, Sergeant used to hold in the gym a kind of 'post mortem', telling us in detail what we'd got wrong and also what we'd got right. It was a great feeling if he praised you, maybe for a particularly good pass, or even better if you'd scored a goal! An exciting highlight came when we were awarded our 'colours', a green, frilly fern design, which we wore with pride. I clearly was awarded mine when I reached the soccer 1st eleven in 1947.

1947 1st Eleven Team. We were all lined up for a celebration photograph proudly showing our colours - I'm standing second from the left back row.

Another time, I got on the wrong side of Sergeant for a different reason. It all happened because after rising to the dizzy height of 'sixer' in the Wolf Cubs, with an armful of badges, I had refused to join the Scouts, which was Sergeant's well-honed expertise. On Fridays, he always wore his Scouts uniform, with the specially designed hat, to take the Scout group.

Somehow, my darling mother had persuaded 'Mr Charles' to release me from the Friday afternoon Scouting time, and I don't think Sergeant ever forgave me. But after the summer term, there was always a week arranged for a Scout camp during which the boys learned all manner of knots, how to fashion enclosures from sundry wooden poles and how to build bonfires. None of this attracted me! Far from it, at the end of term I wanted to get home with my parents as fast as possible. No way was I going to spend another precious week still, as it were, at school.

On another day, Sergeant scared the living daylights out of me. A small group of us were 'excused Scouts' and worked with the gardener doing our bit for the war effort, endlessly digging potatoes or cleaning out the goose shed. On this particular afternoon, we had obviously worked with unusual enthusiasm and the gardener let us off 20 minutes early. Somehow, Sergeant heard of this and as we lined up in the yard to go into tea, he called me out saying: "You little rotter. I'll deal with you later." I imagined I was in for a terrific 'biffing' – but it never happened and I spent the next fortnight terrified of meeting Sergeant. Clearly, and thank goodness for me, he had forgotten all about it.

But such were the moments that became long lasting memories.

Another, just a brief moment perhaps, but which nevertheless stayed with me, again involved Sergeant. He had us playing soccer in all weathers and it could be biting cold up on that hill. We would even be out on the field in what I remember as 'horizontal sleet'! One day in the cold, Sergeant blew his nose between his fingers, not using a handkerchief. Several of us thought this was rather disgusting as the 'snot' went flying in the wind. I was careful to avoid that area of grass afterwards... strange how little things can make such a lasting impression. Another was the winter use of the loos, which were set in partitions outside the main building. Flickering, smoky paraffin lamps were laid beside them in a vain attempt to stop them freezing up!

Perhaps the worst of these memories for me, though, which has lasted me for life, was occasioned by a swimming lesson in the gym. Sergeant would line us up, lying on benches, to learn the breaststroke. I was actually quite athletic and good at coordination. Sergeant was so impressed with my breaststroke movement that he singled me out, saying: "Now watch Hall." This did a lot for my confidence. But not so, however, later on in the swimming pool. Obviously, Sergeant imagined I would make a strong swimmer and he pushed me in at the deep end. I sank like a sack of potatoes, thrashing to get to the top and gasping for air! Eventually, Sergeant had to hold out a pole on which there was a canvas strap for me to haul myself back to safety. That day, I caused Sergeant to 'lose face'. But I was left with a deeply felt scare of entering water which, as I say, lasted for a very long time.

I mustn't leave you with the idea that Sergeant was awful all of the time. He displayed quite a sense of humour at times. There was a large beam in the gym with a flat edge and we had to walk along it with arms outstretched to keep our balance. One young fellow found this a bit of a challenge. He kept falling off and having to try again. Sergeant would then pipe up with a loud and sonorous voice, singing the old patriotic song: 'Old Soldiers Never Die', to much laughter from the other lads! The song actually ends "they just fade away". But Sergeant never sang that bit. Actually, Sergeant did teach us some worthy things. As a good gymnast himself, he gave us very good instruction in the gym which he kept pristinely clean. We were never allowed in the gym without wearing clean gym shoes. He also taught us about good manners and how to lose in good heart as well as being generous winners. He also had an impish sense of humour!

Being completely taken up with life at Fernden, we'd no idea whether we were winning the War against Germany!

But away at school, we missed being at Four-Winds one terrifying night for my parents. In early summer, 1944, my father awoke to hear the deadly sound of a V1 flying bomb (Doodlebug) coming towards the house. Then seconds later the engine of the Doodlebug cut out. It had run out of fuel.

Knowing the likely devastation when it landed, in horror, my father quickly pushed my mother under the bed in case the ceiling came down! Moments later there was a massive explosion, shaking the house as the bomb hit the ground but, fortunately, in some low lying land away from the house and just missing the local waterworks nearby. It was a close shave!

A few days later, back from school, my father took Clive and me down to see the huge crater, so we could search for shrapnel. I well remember the scene. But not whether we found any trophies! Only recently, brother Clive told me he remembered seeing the twisted wreckage of the Doddlebug under some trees many yards from the crater.

However, on school walks up on Marley Heights, a lofty hill opposite Fernden, we occasionally found trophies – odd bits of 'chaff' or 'window'. These were strips of silver aluminium foil scattered by the Luftwaffe, to float down and interfere with our radar frequencies.

You were a bit of a hero if you went back to school with one of your silver 'finds' from German aircraft! But little did we know that the enemy material we were handling was TOP SECRET!!

FRANK OWEN SALISBURY, R.I., R.O.I. (1874-1962)
Intercepting Doodlebugs over the South Coast, 1944.
Courtesy The Rountree Tryon Galleries.

It was being sent a copy of the above painting of Doddlebugs over the South Coast that reminded me of the terrifying night for my parents in the summer of 1944.

Discovering Music

But before I leave the subject of Fernden, its sometimes strange happenings and the well-mannered gentlemen we were taught to be there (we were never allowed to swear), there is one other matter which has also lasted my life. This had to do with learning music and particularly piano lessons. I forget the age at which I started piano, I think I was eight or nine.

Fernden was not a particularly musical school, though my dear brother Clive – who followed me there a year or so later from North End House – was a natural. He started learning the violin at eleven, having been inspired by a concert at the Royal Albert Hall with our parents. He was entranced by the playing of Yehudi Menuhin and afterwards he badgered my mother to get him a violin. After much entreating over several weeks, my mother gave in and Clive had his violin. He went on to be a brilliant musician and after Public School, he spent three years at the Royal Academy of Music, studying the violin, composition and music theory.

This natural ability for music passed me by, though I did, and still have, a very good 'ear' for music. Unhappily, this did not help me in learning how to **read** music. My teacher was a man of considerable years who was not known for his patience with small boys struggling at the keyboard. He just could not understand why I was such a dunce at transferring the notes on the page to the keys under my fingers. In the end, he shouted at me, saying: "You donkey, can't you see boy?" as he endeavoured to teach me the notes on the lines and spaces of the stave. "Can't you see, boy, F.A.C.E – face?"

I just cannot be shouted at. When this happens, the blackboard of my mind is wiped clean and I'm left in hopeless desperation. It is not surprising, then, that I gave up the piano, feeling terrified by all those black notes, sharps and flats. They left me cold.

Very sadly, this dreadful beginning stayed with me until later years when I started singing in the local choir at Haslemere. At the time, from the late sixties to the new century, we were living at Lynchmere, near Haslemere.

But I really mustn't give the impression that all things at Fernden were dreadful. There were many good times, too. One was an evening when some boys were giving their fellows an hour or two of entertainment. I was asked to tell some of my Sussex stories in the old West Sussex dialect, which – as I said earlier – were taught to me by my father from the days when, as a young man, he worked in the fields with the farm hands. This occasion gave me another chance to do a bit of acting. As I related the stories, there were gales of laughter from the boys sitting in rows on the floor of the hall. I began to realise what a joy it was to me to be able to make people laugh, a kind of elixir, which was to serve me well in years to come in my broadcasting profession.

Another time, my father was invited to give one of his lectures about his journey in the sailing ship, complete with large black and white slides of his paintings. This obviously went down well, as many years later boys told me how much they remembered and enjoyed my father's lecture. But on one occasion, his lecture at a large girls' school didn't go quite as intended. As he was speaking, he took a step backwards and disappeared behind the stage to shrieks of laughter from the assembled girls! Luckily he wasn't hurt.

There were great and special days at Fernden too, among them, the sports and gym displays. Parents flocked to the school for these events to see their beloved children show off their various athletic skills, overlooked by Charles Brownrigg and, of course, Sergeant, who'd taught us just about everything in sport and gymnastics.

One of Sergeant's complicated tableaux!

One year, for the Gym Display, things didn't go too well for me. I had worked assiduously at grasping Sergeant's tortuous exercises, and was judged good enough to head one of the teams with a line of chaps behind me following my lead.

Things went fine; for me anyway, until a couple of days before the Gym Display I contracted a nasty dose of German measles and was sent to the 'San'.

I remember lying in a darkened room listening to the distant thumps of Sousa Marches as Mrs Charles hammered them out on the piano for the teams to follow in strict order.

Thus, my poor mother was denied the joy (sitting among the serried ranks of parents) of watching her beloved son doing his bit for this important Fernden spectacle!

In the late summer term we all enjoyed the fathers' match, which was a lot of fun. I was so proud of my father as he went in to bat, knowing that he would make at least 50. Not so. Thinking he was only playing with small boys, he didn't want to show off and sent an easy catch to the man at point. He only made a couple of runs. I was devastated.

Many years later, there was a story about Ollie who had followed his brother, Tim, to Fernden and became a weekly boarder. He was particularly good at sport. In the summer 'sports display' he did very well in most of the sports and won the Victor Ludorum (winner of games) Cup. Naturally, he was mighty pleased at winning such a top award, and so were we.

*10 June 1978, Ollie proudly displays his cup, the 'Victor Ludorum', meaning
'Winner of the Games'.*

But I return to my own time at Fernden around summer 1947 and further memories of the sports display and the fathers' cricket match which was such a highlight, even though I was upset my father didn't make lots of runs.

Sergeant. 'An impish sense of humour', and dressed for scouting.

However, before, finally, leaving tales of Fernden and Sergeant 's commanding disciplines, I have to say that we enjoyed amazing freedoms there. On Sundays, for example, in the afternoons, we could spend inventive time lighting fires in the woods. We somehow acquired large potatoes for baking and cooked them (often to a cinder!) in the hot embers. Imagine such freedoms today. Health and Safety hadn't been thought of in the early '40s. We could have set fire to the entire Fernden estate!

But we were at least watched over by a master of memorable character, Mr Pym, a tall, stately-looking man with white receding hair, who stalked about keeping a 'beady eye', then eventually calling 'time!' by blowing 'hoots' like a steam train through his cupped hands. I remember trying to mimic him, but without much success!

Personally, I used some of these freedoms in a quiet, secretive and rather extraordinary way.

Chapter 4a

The Fernden Spy

I don't really know why, but from a tender age, I was always fascinated by spy stories. This began, I suppose, as far distant as the antics of Enid Blyton's 'Famous Five'. Later, I devoured the gripping adventures of Sherlock Holmes, the world's most famous detective.

Still at Fernden, I think I was about 10, I dreamed up a plan. How about instituting a secret 'Spy Club'? Just the thing for young lads with inventive minds to get up to.

I put the idea to my best friend (whose name shall remain a secret), and it wasn't long before he was drawn in. I assured him that developing espionage would engender heightened powers of observation. This actually worked quite well.

The idea was not so much to spy on the other boys, many were my friends, but to target the masters. One or two of them were 'odd bods' anyway and, we thought, ripe for investigation and undercover work.

Both my best friend and I were excited at the prospect of secretly finding out more of the infamous workings of our band of ancient teachers (in age, they were at least twenty-five or thirty). I suppose they enjoyed something of a reserved occupation, or were simply not well enough to go to war. A couple had been called back from retirement.

We didn't find out much in our espionage endeavours, of course, we were somewhat lacking in 'spy experience'. But one day, in a Divinity Class, I was riveted to realise that the master teaching us was wearing different makes of shiny brown brogues, one design on his left foot and quite another (though slightly similar), on his right. With my 'spy' hat on, I was sure something was afoot, or perhaps some kind of clandestine biblical intelligence. Following the lesson I quickly passed on this exciting discovery to my best friend. It made him even keener to unearth other hidden secrets.

One such involved Sergeant (who, I remember, smoked like the proverbial chimney). On a particular day, for instance, during an hour of Sergeant's invigorating morning exercises on Fernden's beautifully mown playing field, we detected that he'd suddenly shifted his smoking habit from the rather low grade 'Woodbines', his favourite cigarettes, to another. Cigarettes were scarce during the War, and we wondered if Sergeant had somehow 'purloined' some. He was now flicking the ash off a classy filter tip – 'Craven A'. Surely, we thought, an underhand, secret 'smoke-and-mirrors style' message for our club members to spot.

Actually, we always thought Sergeant was preparing us for soldiery. There was a war on, after all, and he had us marching about smartly whenever we were on the move – left, right, left, right, left!

Talking of war, feeding us at Fernden during all those years, must have been quite a challenge for the kitchen! Small boys are often hungry and I have a memory of the time when I was in the dormitory next to the dining room which had steps up to a door which opened on to the top table. The staff always had their supper at this table and there were often some 'goodies' left behind. In the dead of night, I recall sneaking in through the door and stealing some roast potatoes, cold of course, but jolly good if you're hungry! I felt I'd done a bit of errant spying! We were rationed, remember.

If I'd been caught, I would have been in for some pretty serious punishment. But luckily for me, I got away with it.

Stealing, at Fernden? Never. Unheard of! Well, not quite…

My good friend Graham Prain, himself a Fernden old boy, told me the story recently of a time when a large portion of some fine Stilton cheese went missing. Somebody important noticed and in the Chapel during Evening Prayers, Mr Charles announced that if anyone wanted more food they only had to ask. But items of food must **never** be stolen. Graham Prain went bright red and the culprit was clear, especially as everyone was looking at him! I even felt guilty myself!

So, life trundled on…

Sadly, I have to admit that our 'Spy Club' didn't last that long. The packed programme of daily school life left us little spare time for our 'spy' hobby; cricket and sports, football, as well as sweaty lengthy sessions in Sergeant's pristinely clean gym, and endless lessons. They all kept us well occupied it seemed in every hour.

But still, our spying and undercover amateur espionage was fun while it lasted…

Believe it or not, some of this story is perfectly true, some less so – the memory fades after seventy to eighty years.

To this day, however, I find myself still absorbed by spy stories, the most recent being 'Agent Jack', by Robert Hutton; 'The True Story of MI5's Secret Nazi Hunter'. A real page-turner! I owe him the warmest of thanks. It has reminded me of a singular experiential schoolboy exploit.

A Bit More School

Now came the time for Common Entrance to a public school. My parents chose Stowe as they were much impressed by the Headmaster, Mr J.F. Roxburgh. The approach of Common Entrance meant a good deal of hard work in preparation for this change in school life. It would mean experiencing the difference between being a senior, and therefore a big fish in a smallish pool, and a small fish in a very large pool. The number of boys at Fernden, even during the War, reached around 120 – and there were some 500 boys at Stowe.

And so came the agonising wait for the results. I hoped I would be OK in French, Latin and English. I enjoyed English and had a natural bent for it, never finding spelling to be a problem for me. Maths and Geometry, however, were quite a different matter. I was hopeless at both, probably following my father who told us dreadful stories about his maths master at school who would stand behind the boys, thumping down a heavy form book on the head of any boy who gave a wrong answer. My father was an easy victim and I often wondered if it had something to do with the headaches he suffered in later life?

My geometry result gave people much glee! I was given just TWO marks – one for charity and one for neatness, as there was practically nothing on the page. No one had *ever* left Fernden with such a dismal showing. But my French, Latin and English answers in the exams must have been reasonable enough as they got me into Stowe, thereby setting my course in a very different direction indeed.

Chapter 5

Abandoning Britain

As I have intimated, holidays from school were sacrosanct! I wasn't joining Stowe until the winter, Michaelmas term, so had eight wonderful weeks of summer holidays ahead of me. A most welcome break after all the exams.

I had left Fernden at the end of the summer term in 1947 at the age of 13, having spent almost six years of my young days mainly 'entombed' at school. Maybe that's a bit 'over the top', but that was how it had often felt. With a new freedom, I enjoyed my time at 'Four-Winds' and also a fortnight's family holiday in the west country, where my father did some painting. We spent a very happy Christmas with the family; it was all very festive and for me, warmly welcoming.

It was about this time, after the War, that my father decided to change the family name by Deed Poll. He had already changed his professional name to Claude Muncaster. Claude, because he was a great admirer of the work of the old master, Claude Lorrain, and Muncaster to revive the name after his aged aunt who, at the age of a hundred, had been the last of his family in the Muncaster line. Neither Clive nor I much wanted to have our name changed, but we were persuaded by both our parents that it was a good idea to tidy things up. In any case, when my mother went to the village, her husband already being Claude Muncaster, the village folk didn't know whether she was Mrs. Muncaster or Mrs 'All!

Therefore, having been Martin and Clive Hall (Hall 1 and Hall 2 at Fernden) when we got to Stowe, we were both known as Muncaster. For Clive, this was later to be queried by a bemused Bursar at Stowe. Why was he recorded as Clive Muncaster Muncaster? I had to explain the reason when my brother came to join me at his public school.

During the summer of 1947, my father had the most prestigious commission of his whole professional life. The King's Private Secretary had been to an exhibition in London of Claude Muncaster paintings. He was most impressed with what he saw and at the time he happened to be looking for a birthday present for the King, which the Household presented to the King each year. The Private Secretary suggested that a painting would be an appropriate gift for His Majesty and purchased a fine Claude Muncaster watercolour. The King was delighted with his gift and then commissioned my father to paint a watercolour of the *Long Walk at Windsor*. The elm trees along the walk had been killed by disease and had to be felled. With the avenue of magnificent elms gone, this opened up a staggering view of the Castle which had been hidden by the trees for generations.

Again, the King was pleased with the picture, but was concerned that my father had made the felled trees look too healthy. He asked my father to go back to his studio to paint in some black on the ends of the trunks to make them look diseased!

The Queen was a great collector of pictures and invited my father to join the family at Balmoral and Sandringham to do a number of paintings around the surrounding countryside. At Balmoral, the King actually took my father up the hill above the Castle to show him His Majesty's favourite view of the valley and magnificent distant hills. This resulted in the huge oil which Prince Philip mentions in his Foreword to my book about my father's life and work *The Wind in the Oak*, which I referred to in Chapter 3.

Balmoral Castle.

71

However, as 1948 approached, my enrolment at Stowe was put on hold. I had wondered why I was not already there, but by the New Year things were suddenly going to change in a most unexpected way. It became clear that my parents had other ideas. Thoroughly fed up with existing in a socialist, grey and dismal bankrupt Britain, they, like many others, had been thinking of emigrating. After several months of deliberating, the idea took root and they decided to take off for South Africa.

By April 1948, all was arranged. 'Four-Winds' had been rented to a friend and we all stayed, as I remembered it, at the Mayfair Hotel in London on the night before sailing. My father was particularly attracted to the Ellerman Shipping Line, with its buff funnels, which had a white band topped by black. The ships were all named after cities and my father had booked us aboard the old 'City of Exeter'. Built in 1914, she had survived two world wars and was probably one of the last 'coal burners' in the Ellerman fleet.

It was all very exciting… Until I awoke in the middle of the night with raging earache! My poor parents were suddenly presented with a most unwelcome drama. Should they go after all? I clearly needed some pretty rapid doctoring. This was no easy matter. It was Easter and there were no doctors to be found until, fortunately, the hotel made contact with one who came to diagnose my problem. It was certainly serious as he informed my parents that I was suffering from 'acute middle-ear infection' – medication was urgent.

Somehow, my mother discovered that there would be a doctor on board the ship to inject me with penicillin and this enabled them to carry on. And so we all joined the ship together at Tilbury docks, but with my parents still extremely worried about my condition. Very soon, they had talked to the ship's doctor, a friendly Scot, who began my treatment straight away. He injected my buttock, which turned out to be a very painful exercise. It took some time for the pain to wear off! But my parents could at least relax, realising that they had taken the right decision. My treatment went on for some days and thanks to my mother's quick action, my ear was saved.

It took a fortnight to reach Cape Town, and I noticed that the Indian crew were relegated to the stern, surrounded by cages of chickens, which mysteriously lessened as the voyage progressed. We suffered a storm in the Bay of Biscay and the ship surged up and down as it met the big 'rollers' amid huge clouds of flying spray over the bow. When we were through the Bay at last, after some family seasickness, the sun shone and things greatly improved. Off Finisterre, I stood with my father 'up for'ard' watching a large tanker plying north, passing us at a steady speed. He later painted a fine oil of the scene.

Claude Muncaster oil, tanker 'plying north'.

A Picture in His Mind

As we progressed, at 4.45 one morning, my father called me and Clive from our bunks telling us to 'Come and look at this'. We followed him up to the for'ard area of decking, ahead of the saloon, peering into the dark in a cooling breeze. We watched for some time, only seeing what seemed to be a large, dark cloud ahead. Before long, however, I began to discern sparkling lights weaving into the heights of this great cloud. What I was actually seeing as the dawn slowly came up behind the cloud was the island of Madeira. It was a most romantic scene as we all saw a winking red light from a lighthouse on a point at the northeast end of the island, and the blue-green colour of the dawn etching the sharp lines of the land in silhouette as we approached, riding a steady swell. My father was entranced, as I was. He could see a picture in his mind. Indeed, he painted a watercolour of the scene and later a magnificent oil which hangs in my cottage today. Every time I look at it, I am reminded of that early morning with the breeze in my face as Madeira gradually loomed clear.

Claude Muncaster oil, Madeira at dawn.

We had a grand day ashore at Funchal, being guided around cellars filled with casks of Madeira wine. It tasted good, even to a 13-year-old! We were taken back to the ship by open boat before sailing, to stand at the ship's side to watch small boys diving for coins. They particularly liked the silver ones, sixpences and even shillings. They never missed, though would sometimes tease us, waving as if they'd found nothing, but then picking a coin from their toes!

There were also the most colourful boats offering us all manner of wares as well as songbirds in cages, fashioned out of old orange boxes. One such offering was a beautiful yacht with attractive sails. Both Clive and I fell in love with this and with much entreating, persuaded my father to buy it. The little yacht was brought aboard with much ceremony and beaming smiles from the boatman who had just made an extremely good sale! The ship's carpenter made a strong crate for our purchase, which went round South Africa with us. It was certainly an awkward addition to our luggage, but I must say our parents were most patient about it, and it was fun to watch it being swung ashore by derrick when the ship was alongside.

In the tropics, the heat of the boilers below and the shovelling of coal became unbearable, even for the Indians, and we quite often saw one of them who had fainted in the heat being carried by his companions back aft to recover. We were very sorry for the poor souls who were helping the ship speed on for the sake of the 'well-heeled' passengers on the upper decks, sunning themselves, at least in places where they could find a bit of welcome breeze. Our cabins, I remember, were pretty basic, with water in open scuppers running up and down to the ship's movement. Clive and I slept in cramped bunks. It was so different from the comfort and space of modern carpeted ships' cabins but the food was good, I remember. At home and at school, with rationing, we were only allowed a small pat of butter once a week. Onboard the ship for breakfast, we had lashings of butter and hot rolls. What a treat!

When we arrived in Cape Town, I recall watching all the teams of local dockworkers piling up huge bags of sugar as these were brought ashore by derrick. The bags had survived quite well in the holds but some had split open as they came ashore and the dockside was strewn white with crunching sugar.

My father was feted when we arrived – 'Famous British artist comes to Africa to exhibit his paintings'. He was also interviewed on Cape Radio by a young presenter called (I'm almost certain) Meryl O'Keeffe, whom I was to meet in very different circumstances many years later.

Claude Muncaster oil, Olivebank on its way to the Horn.
Courtesy The Hon. Sir William McAlpine.

Radio by Crystal Set

While we were at Cape Town, we stayed at a Dutch-style mansion house, set behind Table Mountain. A young boy on the ship had showed me how to construct a crystal set, by winding a long wire around an old coffee tin. I made the set work quite well by festooning a nearby wattle tree with a long aerial. I spent much time fiddling with the cat's whisker, trying to get a good signal from the radio station. I'm sure it was the voice of Meryl O'Keeffe which I heard clearly when I found the right spot on the crystal.

'High Constantia', behind Table Mountain.

The time at Constantia was, sadly, not good for my mother who suffered badly from asthma. It was rather damp behind the mountain and it affected her breathing. She had a large 'puffer' thing with a bowl for the medication, attached to a bulb below which she squeezed to spray the liquid into her mouth. It certainly helped her, but the effect didn't last very long, I remember. Today, of course, there are much smaller and more effective 'puffers' for people with breathing difficulties.

On board the ship there was a young woman passenger for whom the 'City of Exeter' had not been a happy home. She was seasick much of the way and was also exhausted with attacks of asthma. Very naturally, my mother was sorry for her and decided one afternoon to pay her a comforting visit, driving us round the coast to where this poor lady was staying in a hotel at the beautiful Camps

Bay. My mother went in to see her while Clive and I played on the sandy beach. After a while, my mother came back to us looking pale and shocked. She had gone into the woman's bedroom to find her dead in bed! We had no idea she had become so ill. The constant bad asthma attacks had obviously, in the end, killed her.

But, on the whole, we enjoyed our time at Cape Town and I was excited to find the marvellous Hornby OO trains in the shops, which had been exported from Britain. A very kind young man we'd met in the ship and who had taken quite a shine to my tall and blonde beautiful mother, bought Clive and myself several stretches of rail, wagons and carriages and even the most magnificent and perfect model of the famous Sir Nigel Gresley engine – very smart in its blue livery with shining silver wheels. We were in our seventh heaven! Not quite on one dark night in the War, however.

At around the same time that my mother had bought us boxes of Hornby 00 trains, she also bought me, as a birthday present, a smart green army lorry that housed a silver grey barrage balloon – just like the real ones! I was very proud of this and screwed an eye hook into the ceiling so that from a drum of string on the truck I could wind the balloon up in to the 'sky'. Great fun!

One night, our nanny came in to the bedroom to check us, stepped heavily on my army truck with a crunch, and wrecked in an instant my carefully arranged mechanism. I was most upset. No way of replacing toys during the War!

Odd how young memories can last a lifetime.

But back to South Africa ….

After a while in Cape Town, we sailed on via Port Elizabeth and East London, to Durban, where we were met by my uncle Philip (my father's younger brother) and his wife Anne. It was marvellous to see them waving to us from the dockside. Philip was a housemaster at Michaelhouse, a famous public school at Pietermaritzburg, in Natal, not far from Durban. Being there, reminded me of the story father had told me about meeting his brother, Philip, during the War when by chance their two ships were visiting Durban at the same time.

My Uncle Philip at a wedding.

Actually, Philip was very homesick, and he asked my father if, from memory, he would paint him a watercolour of the view from their old home in Sutton. After the War, Philip took the picture to check it against the view and he told me himself that when he looked at the painting he could only find one thing wrong. One of the trees was slightly too much to the left! Such was my father's photographic memory.

Having landed up in Durban after our voyage, Philip and Anne offered us a bit of a holiday in a farmhouse at Mooi River, belonging to friends of theirs while they were away. On the first morning, I remember enjoying a most delicious bowl of porridge, cooked by a broadly smiling young African boy who gave us a large jug of fresh cream from the farm to go with it. Yum, yum! I'm sure I took too much!

There was a huge water tank near the farm buildings and Clive and I had a great time sailing our Madeira yacht on it. I found the farm rather attractive and painted a small watercolour of it. My father was really impressed and presented me with ten shillings! "That's your first commission," he said. I have that picture hanging in my cottage today.

My little watercolour of the farm at Mooi River.

After our holiday, we had to journey to Johannesburg for my father's next exhibition. During our voyage onboard the ship, my parents had made good friends with a newly married couple, Jeff Slemick and his very attractive blonde wife, Diana. We arrived in Jo'burg to be invited to stay with Diana's parents in their large country home near Vreeniging, not far from the city and on the banks of the expansive Vaal River. We wondered if there were any crocodiles. Clive and I had a great time taking rides along a small railway system in the gardens. How the rails and trucks got there we never knew, but the sloping rails gave us good speed!

My father's exhibitions, both in Cape Town and Jo'burg where extremely successful and he sold a lot of his works. He was pretty sure his success was boosted by ex-pats who were homesick for Britain, and father's sensitive watercolours reminded them of the green English countryside.

We travelled back to Cape Town in the famous 'Blue Train' with its carriages of great class and comfort. It meant a long journey by day and night through the Transvaal and Orange Free State. I remember lying in my bunk as the train swept smoothly through the night feeling much attracted to Diana even though I was only 13. Imagining a sense of her stroking my face, must have been my very first loving feeling towards a woman. It was quite difficult to get off to sleep.

And Then 'NO' to Emigration

Clive's and my own education were a problem for our parents as we were missing many months of schooling. They arranged for some tutoring, but this never made up for what we were losing in scholastic education. Eventually, my parents decided that emigration was not for them and in the late summer, they booked a passage aboard the 'City of New York', a new and very modern liner, smart and comfortable, one of the latest ships in the Ellerman fleet. My friend, Richard Woodman, Master Mariner and Elder Brother of Trinity House, did a bit of research for me. In his personal library of maritime books, he checked an entry for August, 1948, and found that the 'City of New York' was the 'class vessel' of five brand new post-war passenger cargo liners for the Ellerman Line. No wonder we found her so smart and comfortable!

On the back cover of his book 'Fiddler's Green', a History of the British Merchant Navy, my friend Richard Woodman, used a colour print of my father's oil painting of the tanker we had watched 'plying north'. Sadly, after much research of funnel markings, Richard was never able to establish the tanker's shipping line. He couldn't find a funnel marking like the one my father had painted on the tanker! So, my father obviously created his own version!

One evening onboard the 'City of New York', a tall and rather gangly man with wavy fair hair invited me astern, ostensibly to watch the sparkling fluorescence in the frothy wake behind the ship.

After a while, we both needed the 'heads' and there were toilets nearby. As we stood at the urinals, my companion said: "Let's get it out then." I didn't at all like the sound of this and pushed off pretty smartish. I told my father about the incident and he was furious. He tore the man 'off a strip' in no uncertain terms and the fellow never bothered me again.

Otherwise, it was an enjoyable, though not particularly eventful passage home. There were, however, the ship's concerts and various entertainments, and one evening, my father performed his very own version of the song *Oh, agony, pain!*

He had made friends during the voyage with a Mr Spain, who wore a dicky little moustache. One morning, he appeared at breakfast without his moustache; he had shaved it off. At the evening concert, my father with his 'squeezebox' sang the song, '*Oh! Agony Pain*' famous at the time, but he'd given it different words and sang, "Oh! Agony Spain, Oh! Agony Spain; life is so harsh without a moustache, Oh! Agony Spain!!" We all thought this was rather clever and inventive of my father. Meanwhile, I had to play the part of 'the village idiot', lolling about stupidly, but I enjoyed performing again.

And Home Again…

We arrived back in the Thames after a fortnight at sea and I remember, after the sandy dusts of Africa, being delighted and almost 'moved' by seeing the green of England again. Also, on shore, we saw the tall, upstanding Metropolitan policemen, which somehow gave us a sense of security and safety. London, too, looked welcoming after our many months away.

As we left the ship and went on to the docks, we had – of course – to pass through Customs; more governmental control. My father was careful to declare items we were bringing into Britain that might attract duty because they were cheaper or even much easier to acquire in South Africa. Father mentioned to the 'beady-eyed' customs officer two or three things he thought necessary, including our precious trains and some African diamond jewellery my mother had bought, when suddenly Clive piped up: "What about our watches?"

We were both wearing fine Swiss Rotary watches, far cheaper to buy in South Africa, which my father assumed would be treated as the watches we would have been wearing anyway. But 'the beans were now spilt' and the watches were added to the Duty we had to pay! Clive certainly lost a few 'brownie points' that day.

Life back in Britain, however, was still pretty grim and dismal with a Labour government having been voted in with a massive majority after the War in 1945. But even now, in 1948, the government still had to keep administering rationing and coupons, spending from an empty purse and a substantial national debt!

Father had always said – 'Travel is the great university'. But we had been away from the disciplines of regular time at school. Both Clive and I suffered from this, particularly me when I found myself at Stowe – in the bottom form. I did not look forward with any easy mind to the future in my new and completely strange environment…

Chapter 6

Stowe at Last

Finally, on Monday 14th September 1948 all was ready for Stowe. My dear mother had packed my trunk and filled my tuck box with good things. I think we had a meal on the way, aiming to arrive at Stowe in the early afternoon. All this time, I can remember being racked with dreadful anticipation, almost feeling sick. So, for me, it was a pretty horrible journey.

At last we approached the school along a very long drive with fields of potatoes on either side. As we reached the school, driving beneath rows of fine elm trees, I began to appreciate the huge building which was now to be my home with its tall stone columns and adjoining colonnades. This was the North Front, very imposing with a flight of wide stone steps leading up to the impressive front door. We'd arrived.

My memory fails me at this point, but I presume we found out which dormitory I was in, and I'm sure my father would have helped me get there along corridors with my luggage. Now it was 'goodbye' with my father wanting to get away.

He hated long drawn out departures. My mother, though, was hanging on, checking that I was "all right?" Soon my father got her in to the car, and I watched as they drove away, disappearing under the column of elms. I felt completely abandoned; standing there for some time wondering what to do next.

At this stage, my memory lets me down again, I think in a way, I was somewhat traumatised, and nothing has stayed with me in any detail until the school assembly next morning, when the Headmaster spoke to us, raised up on a podium. J.F. Roxburgh was a tall, upstanding man of great culture. He wore glasses with light, translucent frames, his grey hair tidily combed back. He had a powerful voice which echoed around the domed Assembly Hall. He commanded immediate attention. "Good morning, gentlemen," he said and went on to say he hoped we'd all had good holidays and to offer us his best wishes for the coming term. I could see why my parents had been so impressed by him. This, then, was my introduction to the Headmaster of this famous school. Some months later, he was to call me in to his study for a strange reason!

In many ways, I feel almost reluctant to relate my time at Stowe. I was so unhappy there. Nevertheless, I will recount the story, as it played a major part in my young life and teenage years. I also feel it may be helpful to many, many others who suffered similarly at school. They would realise they were not alone. Not all found school the happiest days of their lives.

However, before I do set out on the Stowe years I must make it clear that later, on reflection, I realised that much of the bad treatment I received was my own fault. You could say I almost allowed it to happen because I was simply not confident enough to deal with it. I have a pretty strong voice and I could have used it to good effect!

Although I was nervous at the start of my time at Stowe, there was a good tradition that was very helpful. Every new boy was assigned an older pupil to show him the ropes and the various corridors, classrooms, dining room etc. and the Junior House Room in my case, (strangely following on from Fernden), the Grenville House Room. This was in the main buildings. Gradually, I became familiar with the environs of this massive place. I became familiar, too, with my companions in the dormitory, a rather cramped environment, and cold as winter came close. Down the corridor, there was a bath and shower room, all rather basic. None of this did much for the feeling of homesickness. It took some time for that to die down.

In the House Room, we all had our own steel lockers in which we could stow the various books and equipment we needed for lessons. In my case, anyway, these lessons were not held in the main building, but away in classrooms in other separate areas.

Ice Cream – Against the Rules

Thus, the terms went on and not being academic I found learning the various different subjects and rules pretty challenging.

One day, for a particular reason, I most certainly was challenged. To eat ice cream when walking on the North Front after a visit to the Tuck Shop, was firmly against the rules. As I walked along (it sounds almost a silly detail now), I took a very quick, and it was a very quick, scrape just with my front teeth. I suddenly realised I had committed a terrible crime. A crafty Monitor peering from the window of his study in Temple House, one of those in the main building, yelled at me: "Muncaster! Come and see me!" I knew I was standing into danger (to use a naval term). He gave me a real dressing down, reminding me of the unbreakable rule of 'not eating while on the North Front'. He then put me on to 'Defaulters'. This meant at least an hour, sometimes more, of painful P.T. exercises on Saturday afternoons. There was usually quite a 'clutch' of defaulters every Saturday. I regarded this as a complete waste of precious free time and determined never to be caught out again. Defaulters happened in the gym, to me a cultural shock after Sergeant's pristine one at Fernden. It was pretty filthy and hadn't, I thought, seen a broom for quite some time.

Stowe Tuck Shop, source of the illegally 'toothed' ice cream!

Another culture shock for me was the dreadful swearing that went on at Stowe, with liberal use of the 'f' word. Anyone caught using a swear word at Fernden, even a gentle 'damn', would live in fear of his life! Thus, the terms plodded on. I was so longing to be home, indeed, that each term I drew out a calendar of all the days of the term, crossing them off as the days passed by.

The time arrived when Clive was due to be accepted as a pupil at Stowe, but the Headmaster called me into his study to tell me Clive's Common Entrance had not reached the standard for entry. In fact, Clive had won a violin scholarship to Stowe, so surely had a special reason to be accepted. But not so, and the paucity of his exam results looked like his being turned down. However, J.F. Roxburgh welcomed me to his study, a place few would ever expect to enter, except for a painful beating. Such as for poor David Niven, who'd received 12, yes 12, mighty blows from J.F.'s cane for cheating in a public examination. A heinous crime which had put Stowe into serious disrepute! J.F. was apoplectic! His great school had been disgraced.

Slightly shaking having heard about J.F.'s terrifying treatment of young Niven, I was asked to sit down. J.F. now perused again, Clive's thankfully, perfectly legal, Common Entrance efforts. Putting the papers down J.F. said "We'd really like to take him you know". I wondered what was coming next. Another silence. Then suddenly Roxburgh said to me "Do you think he'd be a good citizen?"

"Of course," I quickly reassured him and thus Clive was given permission for entry and joined me at Stowe in Grenville House. I felt I must have done something right. I reckoned our Headmaster had realised the value of having a fine musician in his school.

The masters were all very different, each having their own ways of teaching. I remember the English master was very good. I liked learning English and so it was a happy thing that I liked him. He was also excellent at keeping order! Occasionally, after a lesson, I would ask him about some particular point which I hadn't quite understood. But then boys in the class accused me of 'sucking up to him'. It was difficult to learn in such circumstances. Indeed, I lived much of my life at Stowe in a state of fear. There were some good reasons for this, as the 'gang' I was forced to live with, took a serious disliking to me and could make my life extremely uncomfortable. One frosty morning, the gang set on me hauled me on the floor along the corridor to the bathroom, then dunked me bodily in to a freezing cold bath. They enjoyed that!

In due course, I think after two or three terms, we were moved to another 'dorm', high up in the main building close to the huge North Front clock, which clanged the hours, all day and through the night. I suppose we were expected to just get used to the noise.

The new 'dorm' was almost worse for me. The wooden door into the room creaked badly when it was opened or shut. One of our family failings was needing the loo in the early morning. At home, we had a potty under the bed. No such niceties at Stowe! I always awoke early at 6 or 6.30 am and badly needed to visit the bathroom. Try as I might, taking great care to move the handle quietly, that damned door creaked loudly as soon as I opened it. This obviously didn't go down well, as the other boys were woken up well before time. They made their ire very clear to me by taking away and hiding my underclothes hoping this would make me late for assembly. In that they were not successful, as I simply went down, rather uncomfortably, without vest and pants.

I've always wanted to get on with people and I had a good conversational relationship with the Master who taught us French. He was quite young and had been, I believe, a boy at Stowe himself. He had an easy and charming manner. Unfortunately, too easy.

He didn't seem to notice that most of his form were not paying attention and there was an undercurrent of talking. Again, it was a difficult environment to learn anything he was telling us. He was good at his French, but not good at all at keeping order. I found this really annoying, but there were lighter moments. One boy, Richard Cobham, I seem to remember, had a naughty sense of humour. If the Master blew his nose, or sneezed, Richard would fly back in his chair as if the wind from the sneeze or nose-blow had hit him in the chest. I can see that little scenario to this day!

Richard, in fact, had a brother at Stowe, David Cobham (well known for his 'Tarka the Otter' film), who was Head of House (Grenville, my house). Chatting to David on the phone recently he mentioned he wasn't feeling too well but went on to tell me a perfectly true and most amusing Stowe story.

One evening he had to beat in the dormitory, a young miscreant lad who'd committed some calamitous crime, so was definitely deserving of punishment. As this most senior Prefect speedily lifted the cane in preparation, it got jammed and completely stuck in a crack in the ceiling above him! The young criminal was in luck that day!

In later years, David Cobham married the famous actress Liza Goddard. Very sadly, a short while ago he died of cancer.

But I must return to our characterful masters.

Our biology master was a particularly unusual character. I remember him getting us to dissect frogs. Not my favourite pastime! He also took us out to the woods by the South Front to point out 'fairy rings' in the grass. On the whole, I don't think many boys believed in fairies.

Another memorable master was the tall Reverend Humphrey Playford. He had a deep, sonorous voice, and taught us things biblical. If he saw a boy eating his fingernails, the 'Rev' would bellow at him 'don't bite'! I particularly remember one occasion when Playford read to us the famous passage from Matthew 7, verses 24-27. I can almost recite it today:

Therefore whosoever heareth these sayings of mine, and doeth them, I will liken him unto a wise man, which built his house upon a rock: and the rain descended and the floods came, and the winds blew and beat upon that house; and it fell not: for it was founded upon a rock. And everyone that heareth these sayings of mine, and doeth them not, shall be likened unto a foolish man, which built his house upon the sand: and the rain descended, and the floods came, and the winds blew and beat upon that house; and it fell: and great was the fall of it.

I always thought that Rev Playford read that to us as an allegory for the way we should go on to live and carry out our lives.

Music, Yes – Rugger, No

One of the activities I enjoyed was the music. I sang in the choir and if I hear a recording of 'Tales from the Vienna Woods' even now, I am transported to singing it in the Stowe choir. It was good to be performing again. The music master, Dr Huggins was a fine musician and excellent organist. I used to very much enjoy his playing of what was known as 'the voluntary' after services in the Chapel. He would play music I particularly liked, such as Baroque and some of the famous choruses from the oratorios – all on the organ. Dr Huggins taught Clive when he joined me at Stowe.

And so terms went on – summer, winter, Easter…

Winter was bad for me as it meant afternoon after afternoon of rugger, a game I hated, 'loathed' would not be too strong a word. It was not good for Clive either. In one game, he broke a collarbone, on the left side, the shoulder side for his violin. I imagine he gradually got better because he was so young. On one winter afternoon, a stocky fellow from another House did his level best to show me how to tackle but I was useless. I just could not throw myself bodily at another man with the likelihood of a flying nailed boot in my face. Perhaps I had too vivid an imagination. I also reckoned you were in dire danger if you were holding the ball and I got rid of it as quickly as possible! When the actual game eventually started, my 'instructor' ran up and down the touchline, shouting: "You're yellow Muncaster, you're yellow!"

After the game, I ran off the pitch as fast as I could, to be first in, and out, of the changing room which stank strongly of hot, sweaty bodies.

The following summer we, of course, played cricket. Clive and I played in the same team. One extraordinary afternoon, the two of us bowled out the entire opposing side! As a result, we were promoted to the Colts, but never showed such prowess again! I think it was on that afternoon that I lay in the hot sun, watching the cricket with another team playing. That night I became extremely ill with sunstroke and was rushed to the 'San'. As I recovered, with much relief at the peace and quiet, I lay in bed listening to music on a small radio my parents had given me.

Later, there was, however, a much more serious reason for my being sent to the 'San'. I became badly ill with agonising stomach pains. Fortunately, Stowe had a very good and professional Matron in the Sanatorium. She diagnosed that I had appendicitis and I was rushed by ambulance in the middle the night to the Radcliffe Hospital in Oxford. The surgeon operated next morning, and after having been made dreadfully sick by the anaesthetic, I was soon beginning

 to feel a lot better. The nurses put my badly infected appendix in a bottle of water on the windowsill for me to gaze at! It was not a piece of 'art' I was particularly keen to 'gaze at'!

All this happened at the time of my birthday and I was delighted to receive from 'J.F.' (the Headmaster was always known simply as 'J.F.') a birthday card wishing me well. I thought this a really nice touch. He'd also addressed it to 'Martini', his name for me.

I was soon on my feet. I remember my first welcome bath, having been in the hospital for over a week. This meant, after my birthday on the 17th of July, it was almost the end of term. Not worth going back! So it was with a feeling of huge delight that my parents came to fetch me and take me home for an extra-long holiday. The year was 1949.

So, time went slowly on…

I don't remember much about that 'extra' holiday. I think we went for a couple of weeks to a rather smart place called Thurlestone, in Devon, where we played tennis and some golf. And at home, I also spent a good deal of time improving my homemade cinema which I had built in the attic. I even put an electric clock into a frame which lit up – just like the Regal! (the local cinema in Petworth)

Now I had interminable terms ahead during which I worked hard, using the quiet of the library for my studies. Learning the sciences, biology and Latin did not come easily for me. In fact, my housemaster called me in to his study one day and told me I was working too hard. "You should play more," he said. He also quizzed me about my use of pocket money. I was given a shilling a week, plus half a crown my father added for me. I explained that I only went to the Tuck Shop for the odd purchase, as I was saving up for a second projector (£40) for my cinema.

It was also about this time that I asked my Housemaster if I might be allowed to assist in the Projection Box when films were shown on Saturday nights, the one thing I really wanted to do at Stowe. But this request was refused. He said there was already a senior boy who worked in the Projection Box on Saturdays. He didn't need a helper. I never understood why my request was turned down. I would have been happy simply to help wind back the reels! Somehow, at school, for fear of being taken as insolent one never asked questions.

Another matter was the joining of the Corps. I wasn't in the least interested in the Army and crawling through mud and slush every Friday afternoon was not an exciting prospect. Rather naturally, I wanted to join the Naval Section and the Master who ran it was an RNVR Lieutenant. But this also was refused. Luckily, I got my mother to request that I might be released from joining the Corps, so at least I got away with that, and I seem to remember having to do 'light duties' instead, like endlessly lifting potatoes from the fields each side of the long stretch of drive.

During the summer term, we were allowed to bathe in the Lake, an expansive area of chilly water. This was another time I was set upon, when 'the gang' got together and pushed me under the water, holding me down. After my Fernden experience, this was terrifying, flailing about trying to come up for air. Young children can be really cruel at times. It put another 'nail in the coffin' as far as I was concerned for Stowe as a place of learning.

After the requisite number of terms, I was moved up to the Senior House Room which was a bit quieter and more civilised, I guess because when boys were older they were also a bit more sensible.

But there were many stresses about living all the time with the same group of people, like having one's locker next to a boy whose name also began with 'M' who was quite dreadful. He never had his own books or equipment and was constantly borrowing from me! Again, I should have been much stronger and simply told him to 'b...er off' and find someone else to borrow from. But I believe he had to be forgiven. I heard that he and his parents had been held in a Japanese prison camp during the War, so if that was true, God knows what he had experienced.

I think one of the worst stresses, though, was what happened at night in the dormitory. Young boys, of course, are pretty full of testosterone, and sex was beginning to rear its ugly head. I remember one of the monitors switching off the lights and as he shut the door, saying, "Have fun!" In no time, of course, boys were out of bed engaging in the obvious activity. Indeed, I was the only boy in the dorm who didn't join in, but just lay there feeling utterly terrified.

Thus, it was little wonder that after the summer term I was definitely on the edge of a nervous breakdown. It had never occurred to me to run away, which I believe did sometimes happen. Once home, I remember my father looking at me one morning standing by his studio. I must have appeared white, and he asked me: "Are you all right?" Then out it all came. I felt I had been given permission to tell my father everything. He was appalled and said: "We're taking you out of that place."

And so it was. I had to go through one more winter term. But now it wasn't so bad, as I could see 'light at the end of the tunnel'.

There are other things I could include in this chapter, like for instance, on another occasion in the dormitory being set upon by the gang. Also, there was a noticeable change in the school when 'J.F.' retired and we had a new headmaster. I certainly perceived a different energy in Stowe at the time. But I feel I have now said quite enough, save perhaps for my experience at the end of the winter term in December 1950. I can vividly remember the scene in the dark of the very early morning as I stood by the pillars of the North Front, watching the boys joining the coaches that would take them to the station. I don't think Clive joined me at that moment, he was probably still asleep!

But there I was, knowing that before long, our parents would be turning up in the car to carry us home. It was one of the happiest days of my life.

I would soon be out of prison...

Chapter 7

In the Navy

My parents now arranged for me to have a private tutor, an ex-Major who lived locally. He improved my English as well as my French. In later exams I managed to achieve School Certificate in English and French, unfortunately not good enough for things to come.

Now, in the summer of 1953, before I was called up for National Service, my father organised a holiday trip for the family in a small merchant ship along the coasts of Italy and North Africa.

We visited many places, including Genoa, where my father looked for likely subjects. He had, on an earlier visit, painted a remarkable watercolour of Genoa Harbour. I was astonished by all the detail in the drawing.

Claude Muncaster watercolour of Genoa Harbour
Bought at auction for me by Gordon Randall

Later, my father painted an oil of the Italian landscape and the mountains behind.

All in all, we had a grand holiday, and even went on to call in at Algiers and visited the Casbah. My mother was quite scared as our 'honking' taxi weaved us through the narrow, bustling, noisy and colourful streets. She'd been told to keep any jewellery well out of sight, as young thieves would reach through the windows and snatch away anything that shined. My mother made sure the windows of our taxi were kept well shut! Again, my father managed later to make a detailed drawing of the wide scope of that very African town.

At last the date for National Service 'call up' was upon me and on the 2nd of November, 1953, with the official service number: P/J 932682. My father drove me and a friend, Peter Farley – who was being taken away from his accountancy studies – down to Portsmouth. We entered through the impressive stone gates of Victoria Barracks wearing our brand new sailors' uniforms as recent RNVR recruits. For each of us, it was a significant moment which we both knew we would remember for many years ahead.

What awaited me in the future would be testing, to say the least. Life for Peter, however, would be taking a very different course. He had the necessary academic education behind him. I did not!

For now, though, we were both engulfed by the inevitable 'joining routine'. There were haircuts, dentistry (rather different from the gentle care we were used to in civilian life!) medical checks, together with injections and inoculations, and the naval 'fodder' we had to get used to. Actually, the food from the naval chefs was pretty good – basic, but plenty of it for hungry young matelots.

Malcolm Reynell as a Midshipman when serving in the Far East.

In the 'dining room', I happened to meet a chap called Malcolm Reynell who had joined up at the same time. I was astonished to see him; he had been the first boyfriend for Iona (the girl who in later years was to become my wife). Malcolm lived with his parents and sister locally at Bedham, near Fittleworth, where Iona's parents had a cottage in the woods, the home in which Iona was being brought up.

Later, Malcolm went on to be examined before becoming an Upper Yardman – the Navy's term for an officer cadet – as did my friend Peter Farley. The Upper Yardman course would consist of four tough months of training in all that was required to become first-class officers, most of them starting as Midshipmen.

Meanwhile, for us all, it took about a fortnight to get through the whole joining routine at Victoria Barracks. As the days went on, we were supplied with all the necessary kit, which included a kitbag, hammock, a greatcoat and a strong pair of boots. There were serge trousers and top and sailor's square rig collars and lanyards. There was a lot of stuff and most of it had to be fitted into one's kitbag!

We also had time out for an address by the RN Chaplain. I remember he spoke about the threats of VD and showed us horrifying pictures of some of the results on sailors' bodies. There were photographs of the horrible rashes in the obvious places, but also on men's mouths. I was appalled by this. As I've mentioned, I was hopelessly 'green' when it came to any sexual relationships and wondered how on earth these bloody 'wheals' could get to the mouth? It may sound simply astonishing not to know about that in these more liberal days. But my lack of understanding at the time really was the case. The Chaplain also said: "Don't be found where your parents would feel disgraced!" I presume he meant, if bombed out, don't be found in bed with a prostitute.

On one of our evenings, we enjoyed an early film of 'Oliver Twist' with Alec Guinness playing Fagin, the infamous old Jew, who ran the group of youthful thieves. I think Guinness's Fagin was the best I've seen.

After those two weeks, Peter and Malcolm went on as CW (Commissions and Warrants) candidates and both, I'm sure, passed through the Admiralty Selection Board successfully to become Midshipmen, probably with excellent exam results. But not for me! The Navy didn't consider that English and French at Ordinary level were quite enough for a budding officer and I was sent on the Signalman's course. My first drafting was to HMS Implacable, an aircraft carrier well past its prime, sitting in dry dock at Devonport Naval Base; she had been converted for the Training Squadron.

HMS Implacable. She was one of the two 'Implacable Class' carriers. The other was HMS Indefatigable, so I served in both!

I have to admit that this was not an agreeable beginning. There was no water or heating on board and one had to go ashore to wash or go to 'the heads'. These latter were basic in the extreme! They were originally built for the 'dockies' and consisted of wooden seats in exposed cubicles situated over an open drain, along which water was flushed from time to time. The smell from many 'openings of bowels' along the drain could become somewhat overpowering. There was one particular joker in my class who thought it fun to light bits of newspaper and send them down the drain as the water 'flushed' with the inevitable explosive exclamations as the flames passed below many bare behinds!

After lunch or supper, all the plates went through a huge washing machine. Unfortunately, with no heating on board, the plates were washed with cold water and came out of the end of the washer in the same state as they went in. How water was brought on board for the washer, I never knew. An especially uncomfortable situation for me was the fact that more trainees seemed to come aboard the ship than there was room for them in the mess decks. Several of us, therefore, had to sling our hammocks behind wall-bars fixed to the side deck in one of the hangars. When these aircraft carriers were in operation, the hangars were used for housing aircraft brought down by lift from the flight deck to be stored when not flying.

It was to be a cold winter and being so tall, my hammock was too short for me. I had to choose between having cold feet or a cold head! I did my best to cover myself with a spare blanket and my greatcoat. I certainly missed my warm bed at home and my mother's smooth, clean sheets. I also missed the music we used to listen to a lot at home. Clive and I played records of music, mostly classical, on our wind-up gramophone, the height of technology in those days!

On board 'Implacable' during 'stand-easy' times, popular music was played over the ship's tannoy system. There was one memorable piece played by the Mantovani Orchestra, which was a great favourite of mine: 'Charmaine'. Mantovani's cascading strings were a new sound at the time and the music used to echo around the messdecks and hangars. 'Charmaine' became famous. If I hear that music today, I am instantly wafted back to 'Implacable'; it made such a lasting impression on me. Little did I know then how music was going to play a significant role in my broadcasting life to come.

Appointed 'Class Leader'

There were other things which made a deep impression, but for quite a different reason. A tricky situation for me came about because the Irish Petty Officer Yeoman assigned to our class made me 'Class Leader'. I think he thought I was 'posh'. Anyway, it was a position of considerable responsibility without an ounce of power! One just had to direct operations as best one could without creating dissent amongst one's fellow trainees.

A particular happening which was a touch testing for myself as Class Leader occurred one morning. When ashore, sailors visit the local pubs and much beer is consumed. If chaps get really drunk, they had to be helped by a couple of their 'oppos' to ease them up the gangway and over the brow, and then stand up long enough to salute the Officer of the Watch. I think it must have been sheer training that enabled them to lift an arm enough to effect something near to a salute. Then they would go below to be dreadfully sick all over the mess deck.

However, often they would make it OK to their hammocks, but quite quickly, nature would take a hand and it became urgent to have a 'pee'. Unfortunately, the situation was far too desperate to go ashore to the heads, so they would relieve themselves on board. Being a training ship, classrooms were built in the hangar deck and it was behind one of these partitions that sailors found a reasonably hidden spot to 'let go'. After a night of this activity a huge lake of urine built up behind the chosen classroom and in the morning I was given the job of cleaning up the mess. I was Class Leader, of course, and had to encourage others to give me a hand. Luckily some of them took pity on me and with buckets and scrubbers and as many cloths as we could find, we managed to clean things up. It occurred to me afterwards that if the ship had suddenly moved as the dock was filled with water, the 'lake' would have sloshed in all directions. But fortunately, the Implacable was solidly fixed in dry dock.

A strange thing had happened to me only a day or two after joining HMS Implacable. Endeavouring to get a wash at the drinking fountain in the washroom (there were only a few basins for some 70 trainees) a fellow from Newcastle with a strong accent called to me: "What's your name, then?" Against the bustle and noise of the dockyard, I said, of course, Martin Muncaster. But he misheard and somehow mistook the name Martin for Charlie! "Oh, Charlie Mooncuster," he said, laughing… and 'Charlie' I became for the rest of my time as a Signalman.

And so the many weeks for we signalmen gradually went by as we learned to touch-type to music and were introduced to secret books containing a mass of information about signalling and the various formations that ships could be told to take up when given a particular flag signal. This was the traditional method for sending the appropriate order to the Flotilla.

We also had to learn all the different flags used to make these signals. It took some time to get all the colours and markings into one's head. There was also the inevitable need to learn semaphore and Morse code, such that the letters became second nature. Hence it was four months of intensive training before we became competent signalmen. After this, we were sent to HMS Mercury, the on-shore signal station at Clanfield in Hampshire, to pass out.

Duties at HMS Mercury

We signalmen all lived in very basic huts. The officers and their wardroom were situated in a beautiful old mansion home, Leydene House, with a fantastic staircase. The place must have been privately owned before it was commandeered by the Navy. One of our first daily duties was to lay the fires in the offices used for work by the officers. There was precious little fuel with which to build them. We had to be pretty inventive to make the office fires burn well and had to find sticks and kindling from all manner of unlikely places. I often wondered if the fires we had made with so little fuel even burned at all!

After these duties, I can remember lining up outside for the morning inspection by a duty officer. One day it happened to be a Midshipman who inspected us. I recall shivering in the cold as we waited for him to arrive. Personally, I knew the Navy was keen on smartness, so I made it my business, if possible, to be the smartest man on parade. Imagine my feelings, therefore, when this particular Midshipman appeared to me, anyway, to be a complete shambles! His uniform looked as if he had slept in it, his cap was askew and he had very long hair. Yet we were supposed to be smartly turned out for inspection. I was not impressed! Recently, I drove over to Leydene House and stood at the precise spot where over 60 years before, in line and the biting cold, I'd stood staring ahead at the beautifully polished front door. It was a strange feeling to think back over all those years.

Our draft to Mercury meant passing a series of exams. One of these involved a basic appreciation of mathematics. In this, I was utterly hopeless, as was my poor father. But somehow, my divisional officer had got wind of this and arranged for me to have extra maths instruction. Thus, I had a 'schoolie' to myself for a couple of hours every day. I must admit I wondered why this special treatment had come my way.

The possibility, I thought, may have had its birth several weeks before when I was still on board the carrier. One day, the warrant officer in charge of our course called me into his office to discuss my progress. After some conversation, he suddenly said: "I'll just go off and get a cup of tea." While he was gone, I saw that his record book listing the progress of the class lay on his desk and the page was open at my record! Naturally, I had a quick look and read a glowing report. My confidence was given quite a boost. The warrant officer came back with his mug of tea and released me, knowing full well that I would have seen his report on National Service Ordinary Signalman Muncaster! I'm pretty sure this report must have done the rounds and landed on my divisional officer's desk at HMS Mercury. He clearly thought I was worth encouraging, hence the extra maths lessons.

Also at Mercury, we spent long periods peering across the valley at a tall signal mast with a flashing light at the top. From this mast, standing in pairs usually in a chilly wind, we would read the various letters and signals sent to us by our Yeoman. One man would read the light, while telling his companion who looked the other way what to write down. After some weeks of reading flashing lights sending us Morse code, and arms waving hand flags sending us semaphore for us to decipher, we became pretty adept at getting the messages accurately.

At last we were ready for passing out.

More exams! I now knew well the signal exams and knowledge of the various books and had no difficulty answering the signals questions in the exam papers put before us. The maths paper, however, was a very different matter! I must have done so badly – probably there were an awful lot of 'noughts' – that my divisional officer, a kind and considerate man, simply binned my paper so it couldn't show on my record! I must have done really well in the other subjects…

Now came the time for drafting to a ship. Wanting to become an officer, there was another way the Navy could test my ability for gaining a commission. I had to spend three months as ship's company to be assessed before being eligible to go before an Admiralty Selection Board. I was therefore drafted to join the 'ship's company' of an Algerine ocean-going minesweeper, HMS Rinaldo. I went aboard her to take my place in the for'ard mess at Harwich, where several minesweepers were lying. Thus, the clock started ticking for my journey towards the dizzy heights of Upper Yardman. It meant lots of sea time…

As I clattered down the ladder to the for'ard messdeck, hauling with me my kitbag and hammock, I was joining what was amusingly known as 'the gash hands' – the cooks, stewards and sundry signalmen whose shipboard home was 'up for'ard'. They were a motley crowd but we all soon became friends and I just joined in with the various routines and duties that were part of the signalman's life.

I'm afraid I have rather vague memories of a minesweeper's day-to-day existence, but I do have some strong ones. One forenoon, we were anchored in formation as a Flotilla in the Thames Estuary, awaiting the Queen and Duke of Edinburgh's return from a Commonwealth tour. They were, of course, embarked aboard HMS Britannia and we were keeping our eyes 'peeled', looking into a fairly dense fog. On the bridge, I watched and watched through my binoculars until I was sure I saw the faint shadow of Britannia steaming towards us. I should have spoken and would have been pleased to be the first to spot her. But as a junior signalman, I just didn't quite have the confidence and missed the opportunity. A moment later, the Captain spoke: "There she is" – and I seem to remember that we all sounded hooters as Britannia sailed through our lines of ships.

My 'Dreadful Crime'

I think it was at about this time that we spent a period in Portsmouth Harbour, moored abreast of several other 'sweepers'. It was my duty one morning to raise the 'Jack' – the Union Flag – on the pole at the point of the bow on the fo'c's'le. I did my duty proudly. However, the pride didn't last long. I had forgotten to change into the proper 'rig' – the dark blue serge uniform complete with cap and square rig collar. It wasn't long before sundry commanding officers in other ships were appalled to see the signalman aboard Rinaldo wearing the light blue No. 8's (our dungaree-type working rig) instead of the correct uniform. Things then happened rather quickly as indignant reports reached our Captain. He then called for the Yeoman to explain how this could possibly have happened. Our Yeoman then thundered into our mess-deck calling loudly for me: "Get your cap, Charlie!"

He marched me off to appear before the Officer of the Watch, the First Lieutenant in this case, as far as I remember, who was standing, waiting at a large desk reading the report of my dreadful crime. I walked forward and stood smartly to attention. The Yeoman standing behind me then barked out: "Off caps." I obeyed the order, then listened to the report read out to me by the 'Number One'. I could give no answer other than to accept the charge; and so, there and then I was given 'stoppage of my weekend's leave'. Awful! Thus, I spent 2½ weekend days on board the ship instead of at home. To me, it felt completely unnecessary. However, it was all soon over and I just had to move on.

Soon afterwards, we were ordered to go on a duty tour of Norway and Sweden, which meant visits to Oslo and Copenhagen. When the ship was made ready, we set off into a pretty rough North Sea. I was not feeling at all well after a while and found it hard to concentrate when it was my turn to be on watch on the bridge. All I wanted was to be tucked up in my warm hammock which swung steadily to the ship's motions. Following my afternoon watch, I actually retired to the signal office where I lay stretched out on the large table there. I awoke hours later feeling quite better and ready for my duty on the Morning Watch, 4am to 8am. I remember so well how the ship was now steering towards Oslo in the light of a beautiful orange-coloured rising dawn with the marvellous aroma of the forests of pine trees reaching us as the ship steamed gently forward up the fjord.

I forget how long we stayed at Oslo. There was just time for a brief run ashore, I think, but we were soon heading for Denmark and Copenhagen to the south. Here I remember passing the sculpture of the naked maiden on a rock in the harbour. I also have somewhere a photo of me hoisting the 'Jack' as we went alongside – wearing the correct uniform this time! The flag was raised as soon as a ship was anchored, or the first line went ashore.

Time in Oslo

I had a good time myself when I went ashore, tasting a Swedish meal in a nearby restaurant. I also purchased a beautiful little silver clock.

When we returned to Britain, I had been on board for the requisite three months to enable me to go before an Admiralty Selection Board. My Divisional Officer arranged this for me and the time came for me to travel to HMS Daedalus at Gosport on the selected day. Once again, one had to wear the right 'rig' and I remember that I realised, with horror, that I'd forgotten to put on my belt. I was certain this would be noticed and would go against me for being 'improperly dressed' again! Indeed, I remember having the awful intuition that on this day, I would fail.

I did not do well on the sort of exercises given to candidates on these 'selection' days, like being told to cross an imaginary river with only a bit of plank and a piece of rope which was too short! This was supposed to test the ability to think on one's feet and to see how far one could find ingenious ways of getting to the other side of the river. Swimming was not allowed, I seem to remember. Quite possibly we were told the river was full of alligators anyway!

There were various tests we had to work through before the final interview before the Board. Here I definitely did not give a good impression. Being simply a National Service Ordinary Signalman, I felt overtaken with anxiety sitting before a brusque captain and a line of officers displaying a disarming amount of 'gold braid'. After a number of questions, the Captain of the Board suddenly asked me: "Do you know what a vector is?" Sadly, my reply was in the negative.

"Well, I tell you what," said the Captain. "There's a table over there with paper and pencil, so sit down and see if you can work it out?" At that time, I had never done any sailing and it would be many years before I had a boat and learned about navigation, taking sights with a compass and having knowledge of the effects of wind and tide. I sat at that small table with the feeling that a row of senior officers (and all that gold braid) was waiting for me to supply them with an answer. My mind was completely blank and after a while, feeling acutely nervous, I had to own up that I still knew nothing about 'vectors'. I realised that awful moment had certainly sealed my fate and I went away feeling dreadful.

Anyway, I thought afterwards, what a ghastly piece of psychology that captain had shown, designed it seemed to throw me into utter confusion. Perhaps he was testing my ingenuity. That day was a disaster for me and I had the ignominy of returning down the ladder to Rinaldo's for'ard messdeck to retorts like: "You back again?" and, "We thought you were going to the f...ing wardroom!"

But after my dreadful display of ignorance at the Admiralty Selection Board I was told the amusing story of the young candidate who was asked for the number of the taxi that had brought him to the Board. The young fellow quickly said something like: "HWZ 346, sir."

"Goodness," said the Captain, "Well done. How on earth did you remember that?"

"Well, I knew you wouldn't know it, sir." That man certainly passed.

On another occasion, quite unconnected, the Captain inspecting a line of young NSUYs threw his cap down on the deck and yelled, "Unexploded bomb! What are you going to do about it?" One quick thinking young man stepped forward and smartly kicked the cap over the side of the ship! I'm sure he passed, too.

So now I was faced with a further three months on board until I could be assessed all over again. Around this time, there was one occurrence which could have turned out to be really nasty. The Flotilla were out on exercise, being signalled into various formations. On one of these, a nearby ship read a signal incorrectly, turning to port instead of starboard and she came towards us at speed and smashed into us amidships, making quite a hole (fortunately above the waterline) reducing our wooden sea-boat, a whaler, to matchsticks! The mess was considerable and our Captain, Commander Buckeridge, a splendid 'skipper', went down the ladder abaft the bridge to view the chaos. He stood there quietly for some time, with possible witness at Courts Martial ahead and a huge amount of paperwork, and all he said in the end was: "Mm, pity!"

A typical naval understatement; I'm sure he must have trained at the Naval College at Dartmouth.

Another time, at sea on exercise, I was on duty and was sent off on some errand or other. I went down the ladder abaft the bridge, slipped on the wet deck and flew forward, landing on my eyebrow. There was suddenly a lot of blood! I took myself to the Sick Bay and the Sick Bay 'tiffies' were delighted to have a real live 'casualty' to deal with!

At this juncture, however, I had a bit of luck. My Divisional Officer was drafted to another vessel and a really friendly officer named Malcolm George came aboard to take his place. Obviously, Lieutenant George had already read my reports and took a special interest in me. He had learnt about my difficulty with maths. We were in dry dock during a very hot summer and Lieut. George managed to arrange some weeks of extra maths teaching with, again, a 'schoolie' who was asked to help me. Being in dry dock, there was plenty of opportunity for me to be released from duties and I spent hours poring over problematic maths questions during my lessons at the Royal Naval Barracks in Portsmouth.

I can remember the Education Officer being somewhat exercised at my inability to work out the many mathematical equations he set me to solve. I realised all too soon that I just didn't have the right sort of mind to grapple with, and resolve, these impenetrable problems. But at least I hoped my readiness to learn and the extra-curricular studies would serve me well in my later reports.

Life in the Messdeck

Meanwhile, there were occasions when one had to accept just about anything. The months were hot and the trays of meat delivered to the mess weren't necessarily consumed quickly. These trays were placed on the ladders, latched to the overhead deck, in case we had to evacuate through the forehatch in emergency and the meat could stay there for some time, simply going bad. On one occasion, one of the cooks went to retrieve some meat from the trays and found it was crawling with maggots and the whole lot had to be ditched. This was of acute interest to me as my hammock was slung alongside the ladder!

I don't know whether this situation had anything to do with it, but one of the cooks, a bushy rather rotund fellow, came back aboard late one evening incredibly drunk. As he arrived back in the mess, held up by the couple of his 'oppos', he proceeded to be extremely sick, which ran all over the deck, smelling dreadfully! It was some time before this was eventually cleaned up and the offending cook was hidden in the oilskin locker until he'd fully recovered, some 24 hours later. In the meantime, his good friends 'stood in' for him.

There were some lighter moments, too. One day, one of the stewards who had been in the Navy from a boy at HMS Ganges, the Boys Training Establishment near Harwich, sidled up to me with a question. He would soon be going 'outside', the term for leaving the Navy and going into 'Civvy Street'. He had heard that there was a Muncaster Castle in the Lake District and his question was simple. "Charlie," he said, "when I get outside could I cum an' be a bootler in your cassel?"

He was actually a northerner and he spoke with an unmistakably northern accent. I had to tell him that the Castle wasn't mine!

We were laid up in dry dock in Portsmouth, for quite some time and there was obviously a lot of work that had to be done on the ship. Groups of dockies came on board day after day. Even so, we had to 'clean ship'; there was lots of that, but at last there came the time for a fortnight's leave.

This was most welcome as the summer was passing all too quickly. For me, it meant a wonderful break with the family and an opportunity to spend time with Clive, still working away at learning the violin. During my time at The Guildhall for two years, Clive had started to spend three years studying at the Royal Academy of Music and gained his LRAM distinction.

When I returned to the ship from my leave, I had to take a signal to the Captain, Commander Buckeridge. He said to me: "Hello Muncaster. Have a good leave?"

For some unaccountable reason, I replied: "Exquisite, thank you, sir!" I really wondered why I'd said that, except that my granny in Sheffield used to use the term. It happened that the Captain's steward was lurking in the background at that moment. Later, he came up to me in the mess and asked me: "What was that word you used to the skipper?" I explained what I'd meant.

"Blimey, Charlie," he said. "I thought for a moment you were telling him to f... off!" He had never heard the term, of course.

It was now August and autumn was creeping on. I was beginning my extra three months before I could go before another Selection Board. There was more sea-time, more exercises to be gone through, more boring but nevertheless important shipboard routine. All this meant a great deal of responsibility for the Signalman, operating in all weathers or at night, on a cold open bridge, sending and receiving vital, often 'restricted' messages, having to be fully understood and interpreted before being passed to the Captain or Officer of the Watch.

Of course, many of these messages had to be read from a flashing light in Morse code, particularly difficult at night or in foggy conditions. On the flag-deck, too, the right flags had to be clipped on in the right order, just before being hoisted. Get them wrong and there was all hell to pay! Equally, at that time, semaphore was very much in use and peering through binoculars at a distant yeoman, leaning against the wind and sending at speed could be extremely testing, It was getting such signals incorrectly understood that could lead to the sort of collision or accident that had created a serious hole in Rinaldo's side!

So, although no one saw it as such (one was just doing one's job) the business of being a Signalman could be quite stressful, particularly being basically only a junior rating without 'officer power'.

That being said, if – as in my case – the target was to become an officer, wearing the cap badge that was often seen as the best in all the services, my record had to be excellent. It was certainly the cap badge I was determined to wear, whilst every day having to display plenty of OLQ (Officer Like Qualities) even if it meant clean fingernails having done a filthy job cleaning ship!

Yet all this time, and time after time after time, when I saw an officer wearing 'that badge', I said to myself: 'I'm going to wear that. I'm going to wear that'. I even kept a small diary of experiences, happenings and affirmations which I thought important to write down. I used to go to the Chapel when I had 'stand easy' breaks, for some peace and quiet and to write my diary and read what I had written before. Sounds a bit odd now, but it was important to me then.

The cap badge, actually, is very well designed – well, I thought so anyway – with a crown on top, set in crimson velvet, with a silver, 'fouled' anchor below and all surrounded by beautiful gold oak leaves. Wonderful.

Jane Francis

It was about now, during my leave, that I met and became very fond of Jane Francis, daughter of my mother's best friend, Betty. Jane was really my first love and we wrote letters to each other during my National Service. She was a striking girl and her loving letters helped me to get through my time as a Signalman. In fact, I gave her the little silver clock as a 'thank you'. She has it to this day.

Close up of the naval officer's cap badge.

Time for Another Selection Board

Young men, probably most, just plodded through their National Service without any particular aim. I thought I should make the best use possible of the two enforced years with a definite goal in mind. I therefore worked hard and the weeks went steadily on and I had completed my extra three months by the end of October, 1954. It was then (I cannot recall the exact dates) that Lieut. George organised my candidature for the next upcoming Admiralty Selection Board. This was to be held at Dartmouth and it was to the Board there that I now travelled.

On this occasion, things went well for me. I had no trouble with the communications questions and even did a reasonable job of crossing the imaginary river with only a short piece of rope, a barrel and a short plank – too short to be much use for anything! However, the chap before me had the basis of what I could see was a jolly good idea. Without copying, I used some of his idea for my own plan and made a pretty fair job of crossing the river without accident.

I was beginning to feel reasonably confident and made a much better impression at the interview. It seemed that I was listened to intently by the owners of all the 'gold braid', which had so taken all the stuffing out of me at the HMS Daedalus interview. Then came the time for each of us to go before one of their Lordships' most senior Admirals. On this occasion the Admiral who headed the Board, offered a kindliness and obvious understanding of our situation, having to convey a calm confidence when pretty stressed by the fact that we had to be fully prepared to become first-rate naval officers.

I must have done something right, as after a period of questioning. His Lordship said: "Well Muncaster, I'm glad to be able to tell you that you have passed."

My sense of jubilation can be imagined. I had at long last, after many weeks and months of concentrated hard work, triumphed. I would now be sent to the training ship, HMS Theseus, moored in Portland Harbour, to join the Upper Yardman class. On the train back from Dartmouth, I was hugely excited and utterly overjoyed – and that really wasn't an overstatement.

Now it was up to me…

Having already spent so much time there, I was well acquainted with Portland Harbour. In fact, I had experience of it well before my full time National Service. During my time at The Guildhall, my RNVR training included an obligatory fortnight serving on board a ship. In my case, I was drafted to the aircraft carrier, HMS Indefatigable, which lay at a large mooring buoy at Portland in company with Implacable.

When I joined the ship in the summer of my first year at The Guildhall, I somehow missed joining up with the party of RNVR sailors who were to be my companions in the mess-deck arranged for us. I was, therefore, quite alone when the MFV (Motor Fishing Vessel) set me alongside and I hadn't the foggiest idea where to go on board this huge aircraft carrier with its many long corridors and watertight doors. As it was, after a search, I ended up in the ship's company seamen's mess and a friendly fellow there helped me to find a space to sling my hammock and I spent the night wondering where I was to report? I was eventually directed next day to the right mess. Once there, I soon made friends with a delightful chap named David Richards who was learning to be an accountant. We got on really well, so well in fact that once he had qualified I asked him to be my accountant. He looked after my financial and tax affairs for many years afterwards.

David Richards joins me on the messdeck in HMS Indefatigable.

I don't remember much about that fortnight except that we were introduced to the business of seamanship, tying knots and the like, and learning the general workings of the ship. Little did I know then that in due course I was to find myself aboard Indefatigable's sister ship for the four months of my signals training.

The Upper Yardman Course Begins

Again, I don't remember the exact date, but it must have been well into the New Year before I reported aboard HMS Theseus, to join the current Upper Yardman course. The two training carriers now were Theseus and Ocean. I think Indefatigable and Implacable had been mothballed during the months I was away in the minesweeper, Rinaldo. We had four months of exacting training ahead which kept us on the run most of the time. We were expected to show aptitude for just about everything! There was lots of parade drill, mostly carried out on the flight deck in sun or snow. We were drilled how to march smartly, how to give orders to a squad, given instruction in the plethora of detail to do with good seamanship, the intricacies of ship's engines and a whole lot more. We were also given all manner of experiences, which included a day in a submerged submarine at sea (a happy thing that I didn't suffer badly from claustrophobia), an engineer officer's tour of the engine room, navigation and the correct use of a sextant... and mainly with little time to gather it all in! We had to keep a Journal too.

'Sussex Class' all set for a photo on the Theseus flight deck. I'm the tallest next to our Yeoman at the back. Note my very white shirt.

One of the continuing problems was the heat and stuffiness of those boxy classrooms, particularly after lunch. It was a Herculean effort to stay awake and offenders who fell asleep would find a hard blackboard duster flung at them with unfailing accuracy by the instructing Chief Petty Officer. This flying weapon woke us up pretty smartly!

One of the things an Upper Yardman was supposed to learn was the detail of his ship and the Divisional Officer could all too easily point out something and say: "What's that?" – Usually an obscure piece of equipment or 'part of ship', and a candidate had to come up with the answer – "I'll find out, sir!" The writing of the Journal had also to be fitted in with all the painstaking business of learning just about everything. NSUYs had to be competent in semaphore and Morse codes, too. All in all, a 'full on' course.

For me, the continuing pressure became more and more stressful, particularly as I was keeping up my personal objective of staying really smart. I reckoned that if I wasn't especially good at all the subjects, I could at least always be smart. I knew the Navy was impressed by the well turned out sailor.

I found I was always the last, often well after midnight, ironing my bell-bottom trousers in cross-creases so that they went up the leg in 'ladders'. This always gave a good impression and was actually, in sailors' terms, 'pretty tiddly'. One's boots, too, were always expected to shine. This meant long efforts working on the toecaps with, literally, spit and polish. So I was nearly always late into my hammock and badly needed a good 'kip' before we were awoken again at 5.45 by the Duty Petty Officer. One or two were pretty harsh and would walk around the mess-deck hitting our hammocks with a big stick! "Come on then, rise and shine, let's 'ave yer."

There was one I remember as being much more kindly. He just used to lean through the door and switch the lights on! There weren't enough basins for all of us so I made it my business to be first in the washroom, which gave me a bit more time than others to 'lash up and stow' my hammock before 'clean ship' duties. After this, we had to parade in line for inspection on the flight deck and to be informed of the day's duties and lessons.

Treatment for Hay Fever

It so happened that one of my health problems in life was a tendency to suffer from hay fever, sometimes badly if downwind from a field of hay. Because of this, in a period of leave, my mother had taken me to see a specialist at Harley Street in London. This particular consultant was a surly Australian, devoid it seemed, of any sense of bedside manner. He asked me a whole lot of serious questions, then got me to bare my arm on which he made a series of pricks. On to these he then dropped different medications to find out which ones I was allergic to. Hay clearly came out top and he prescribed injections to be given once a week for a number of weeks ahead.

Of course, I had to present myself each week to the sick bay to receive my injections. They weren't pleasant as they made the site of the injections tickle. One week, I completely forgot to go to the sick bay for my injection. Then, in a ghastly moment, far too late for my appointment, I rushed down to see the ship's doctor, quite expecting to receive a dressing down for my late appearance. However, this didn't happen and the doctor treated me with great kindness before the sick berth attendant was ready with the syringe.

Suddenly, I burst into floods of tears and for some time was quite unable to pull myself together. Through my tears, I could see the doctor at his desk assessing this surprise situation while the sick berth 'tiffie' stood patiently aside. Afterwards, I could only presume that my outburst was the result of a build-up of stress over many weeks, but without knowing it, there was much more serious trouble to come.

A week or so later, I began to feel terribly ill with raging ear-ache and had to present myself once again at the sick bay. From there, I was quickly sent ashore to the Portland Naval Hospital and started to receive penicillin injections. I remember the sick berth attendant advancing on me with a large syringe saying: "This'll put you f...ing right, mate!" I did not find this particularly comforting. However, the medics at Portland weren't at all sure what was wrong with me and sent me off to the Navy's main hospital at Haslar, Gosport. After examining me, the doctor there seemed similarly unsure of the nature of my problem. I must have told my mother and she determined to get a second opinion. She contacted the Admiral Surgeon at Haslar and asked if she could take me for a second opinion. She had the Admiral's immediate permission, took me home and next day I went to see a top ENT surgeon, Miles Formby, at his London clinic in Hanover Square.

He examined me and in seconds had the answer. I had another case of acute middle-ear infection. He ordered me to go to University College Hospital in Gower Street, saying he would operate first thing in the morning. He was as good as his word, and I believe he had me on his operating table by about 0730. Thank goodness, he did. He put me on a drip and extracted about half a pint of poison from my antrum. He kept me on the drip as there was a bit more still to come, but by next morning I felt hugely better. I think I was kept in hospital for three or four days. While still in hospital, the nurses had to check my pulse and write the result on a record sheet which hung at the end of my bed.

One especially attractive young nurse gently rubbed my wrist with her thumb as she felt my pulse. Not surprisingly, my heart went into overdrive! She was very naughty, and I am sure did this little action to see just what the speed of my pulse would be. Goodness knows what she recorded on the sheet at the end of my bed. I was so embarrassed I was lost for words.

I have always been eternally grateful to my mother for all the care she took for me. Her urgent action undoubtedly saved my hearing. All this might have seemed like bad luck and bad news. I was kept at home and under observation for quite a while. However, this apparent disaster turned out in fact to be a gift. Because I was taken away from my course, I was 'back-classed' which gave me another most valuable six weeks for, as it were, revision. I now joined the class which had been coming up behind me – Sussex class. There could have been no better name for me, having been born and brought up in Sussex. I felt it was a good omen.

I was now back with a familiar routine. Back to the ironing late at night by the low level lighting that remained after the main lights were out and again the 5.45 awakening. I seem to remember the same petty officers were in charge, some wielding those big sticks to whack our hammocks. Or the quiet one who simply put his head round the door and switched on the lights. It was rather a case of Deja vu!

But the bunch of chaps I now joined were delightful and we all took on the training as a lot of fun, though at the same time much concentrated work. We were under the not-so-tender care, however, of one Chief who was pretty tough and it was best not to cross him. One fellow who did, and I don't remember why, was David Patterson, a tall, elegant and disarming chap, who this particular CPO thought should be taught a lesson. He was, therefore, ordered to run round the flight deck for an hour with a rifle on his shoulder, which bounced up and down as he ran along. Even now, I have a clear memory of seeing poor lonely Patterson jogging round the flight deck. I was so sorry for him, knowing what dreadful bruising would result from this torture. But we were all young and bodily hurts healed fairly quickly.

There was a group of Upper Yardmen who looked after one of the whalers and whose job it was to smarten it up. They took infinite care with every detail of varnish, brass polish and paint work and after this treatment, that boat looked brand new, actually even better than that.

One of the activities with which I had not been involved in my earlier class was a morning's sailing in one of the ship's whalers – not the one the Upper Yardmen had spruced up. Now, as I had intimated earlier (in my first dreadful experience of the selection board at Daedalus) I had never until now done any small boat sailing. In fact, I had no experience of sailing at all, surprising really being in the Navy. I was therefore, very much struggling to understand the various instructions being given by our class Petty Officer who was at the helm. One such order came when he suddenly yelled at me: "Back the jib… back the jib!" I hadn't a clue what this meant and hovered hopelessly wondering what to do. Luckily, however, up in the bows with me was a companion who had done quite a lot of dinghy sailing on the Staines reservoirs and he quickly showed me what to do.

'Backing the jib', as any yachtsman will know, meant pushing the jib sail by hand out into the wind. This helped to fill the sail, thus easing the bow round to 'go about' and get it moving on the other tack. Whalers could be pretty sluggish 'going about' when there wasn't much wind.

Another thing we all had to learn was how to climb up a rope ladder. If you simply put your foot straight on to it, the ladder swung away from you which made it impossible to climb. You just hung there, more or less on your back! The ladders were fixed on to a long boom which was swung out from the side of the ship. One of the motor boats was often tied up to the end of one of these ladders. The trick for us, when climbing up to the boom from a boat, was to work one's way up the side of the ladder thus ensuring that it didn't swing away from you. When done a few times, we got used to the ladder trick and were soon shinning up with ease. Once up on to the boom, there was a safety line to help us walk along the boom and back on board.

This was just one of the many things we Upper Yardmen had to learn. There was, again, the awful struggle to stay awake in those stuffy, tin box classrooms trying to avoid the board duster treatment! But I got a lot of help from lads who were good at maths and navigation. In turn, I gave others a lot of help with Morse code and semaphore, both of which of course were second nature to me.

There was one charming and rather laid-back member of the class, George Beatty, who didn't seem to take much care about looking smart, but who had a fine brain and, in fact, went on to become a QC and rose to the ranks of RNVR Commander. He stayed on the reserve for many years and eventually became Captain of HMS President, moored alongside the Thames Embankment near Blackfriars Bridge. She was the ship which became the RNVR London headquarters. Many years later, I had occasion to go aboard for a special evening reception arranged by the Maritime Foundation of which I was, and am still, a Vice President. That evening we were addressed by Admiral West (now Lord West) and I had a nice chat with him.

For now, though, it was the day-by-day education of the Upper Yardmen class, and the days of passing out exams came ever closer. Meantime, there were various activities, some amusing, which took us away for a while from the serious business of working to show we were good officer material. OLQ (as mentioned before) became extremely important.

I remember on one occasion I was marching the squad towards another one with men lined up in smart formation learning about the methods of good rifle drill. As I marched my squad towards them, I realised I would have to give the order to 'wheel' my chaps around the other squad lined up in a square. I gave the order: "Right Wheel" – then, "Left Wheel," thus marching clear of the other squad. The Chief Petty Officer, teaching the details of proper drill, was the very man who had ordered Patterson, shouldering his rifle, to run for an hour round the flight deck. As a complete surprise to me, as I marched my men on past him, the Chief said loudly: "There you are, that's good manners. Remember that when you are in charge of a squad." I was absolutely astonished.

A side-line which gave us a break from the hard graft was the Squadron Concert. I dressed up as a Commander (I must have borrowed a uniform) and it was all arranged by one of the actual Theseus Commanders, who was very musical and wrote the songs using Gilbert and Sullivan tunes. The whole thing was made up of a number of songs and sketches, mostly at the Navy's expense! I had to sing: "I am Commander of Impossible…etc. etc." It was all a lot of fun and I got one of the friends in my class to film it with my 9.5mm camera. (I wonder what happened to that.) It was another occasion which reminded me what I really wanted to do with my life – be a broadcaster.

At one point in a break from rehearsals I was standing at the edge of the stage when round the corner came the Captain of Theseus, Capt Anthony Miers (always known as 'crap' Miers – I never knew why) and I saluted him smartly. I remember him looking at me rather quizzically. He had never seen that particular Commander before!

So at last, after these many weeks, months indeed, of going through illness, yet another hospital 'rescue', and careful revision, it was time for exams again. I gave much thanks for the extra time I had perforce been given. This had been so useful.

Would I Pass?

I got through the communications and seamanship exams without difficulty, but the navigation exam which involved knowledge of star sights, caused me great grief. I thought I was getting on OK until I made a particular mistake which worked me clean off the page of star sights! I could, literally, go no further. In the end, I appealed to the invigilator, and it took him quite some time to see where I had gone wrong. This was another moment when I worried if I would pass.

A few days later, the entire class was assembled in a classroom to be addressed by the top brass and our Divisional Officer who then read out the names of each individual and whether he had made the grade. In our case, there was just one poor unfortunate chap who was told that he had failed and after a few kind words of encouragement, he left the room – and later we saw him leave the ship in a small motor boat looking utterly lonely and disconsolate.

For the rest of us, the Captain made a very warm speech of congratulations and emphasised the responsibilities of the role we had now taken on as commissioned officers. For me, having passed was A HUGE RELIEF! And I had that feeling of jubilation again.

All the others in my class became Midshipmen, but being over 21 (because of my year's deferment) I was too old to be a Midshipman, so I passed out as a Sub-Lieutenant and had one gold stripe on a beautifully, Gieves-tailored arm of my uniform. I was very proud of that stripe. I can honestly say that the day I put on that uniform and wore that cap was the happiest day of my life so far, even better than leaving Stowe…

Me in officer's uniform, proudly showing the one gold stripe!

I was taken ashore from HMS Theseus in the MFV to see my mother waiting for me in Weymouth to take me home in her car. She had a rather smart Sunbeam Talbot. It was wonderful to meet her wearing my brand new uniform, which had been delivered to me by Gieves, the traditional naval tailors. I was feeling very proud; my mother was so glad that I had made it to officer. It was summer 1955.

I now had some leave after passing out and it was one of the best leaves to look forward to. At long last I could relax for a while and simply wait for my posting as a Sub-Lieutenant. On the way home, we stopped for some lunch at the West Meon Hut on the A272 and to this day, I have a memory of standing at the bar as a naval officer. Indeed, that now distinct picture comes back to me every time I drive by, which I often do on the way to the Upper Hamble, a river I have fished for trout for some 50 years.

I have little memory of that particular leave but I know I would have spent some time in my cinema. I do remember painting posters for films I hired from Wallace Heaton in London. I placed these posters up the stairs leading to the attic room. I also made a little box with 'thank you' in a window which lit up when a shilling or sixpence was dropped into the slot. The movement of the coin pressed on a tin plate which completed a circuit linked to a battery. It was a bit unreliable, but when it worked visitors who came to see my films were highly amused to see the 'thank you' sign light up.

When at last my 'call up' came, I was posted to a coastal minesweeper named HMS Essington. She was one of the 'ton' class, and I was to join her at Hythe on the Solent near Southampton. However, when I arrived there, I found Essington had already sailed for Harwich. I therefore waited for a couple of days and when my orders came, I was told to go to Harwich to join the ship there. So, it meant a train journey (First Class as an officer!) to find Essington moored with other 'sweepers' opposite HMS Ganges, the Boys Training Establishment mentioned earlier.

HMS Essington. The second in line of the Flotilla. © Crown Copyright IWM

The 'Third Hand'

There were only three officers on board, the Captain (ex-lower deck), the First Lieutenant, an excellent officer who trained at Dartmouth and became a good friend, and myself as the 'third hand'. I was quite excited to have a real job as an officer, and soon got to know the lads of the ship's company. It was a small ship with a small team and was much more enjoyable for me than my time in Rinaldo.

We went out on exercise a few times into the North Sea, rough again, and I was none too well on the first day. These little wooden minesweepers bounced about all over the place, but luckily I soon got used to the movement and felt fine. On one occasion, we were sent to Sheerness and 'Number One' was having difficulty getting the ship alongside in a tricky cross wind. From the bridge, he started yelling at us on the fo'c's'le, myself and a leading seaman, to 'do something'. I could see that the headrope we had got ashore wasn't strong enough for the job. We had to use a wire wound up on the fo'c's'le. But the leading hand, an experienced seaman, refused to use it. We both knew that this particular wire had seen better days. I could see that the bow was moving pretty quickly away from the jetty, so taking a considerable risk I got down to the job of uncoiling the wire to get the end ashore to a waiting 'dockie' and get the ship safely moored. Since I got stuck in myself, the leading hand relented and gave me some help. We both knew that if we weren't quick and too much strain was taken up by the wire as the ship was blown away from the shore, the wire could part, flying back dangerously. In fact, had that happened it could have killed us both!! Fortunately, we got the wire ashore in time and all was well. For me, as the fo'c's'le officer, it was a nasty moment.

In another situation, on duty on the bridge when we were in company with other ships of our Flotilla, I had to stand back, rather than get stuck in, or even show off because I was able to read messages flashed to us quicker than our own signalman. I felt it was only right and proper to let him do the job, so waited for him to report signals to me which I already knew! I repeat that the Navy's signal training was truly excellent. I didn't want to be doing National Service, but at least I had opted for something in which I was interested – communications.

There was another situation which, quite unexpected by me, I believe endeared me to Essington's ship's company. When I got involved with work that had to be done on board, I would wear my 'number eights' working rig, which had been through so many washes on board Rinaldo that they were now a very light blue indeed. New trainees always looked new, because their 'number eights' would still be dark blue! Thus, the lads aboard Essington could instantly see that I was a bit of an old hand. I think that fact went down well.

My Own Cabin

One wonderful comfort for me was having my own cabin and a bunk rather than a hammock. I could retire to my cabin if I wanted to rest or have a bit of peace. The First Lieutenant (I wish I could remember his name) had made me the Wardroom Wine Officer. Now this was not in the least my interest. A glass of wine with a meal was about as far as I wanted to go but, of course, the Navy is known for its hard drinking! Just not my style. Further, I had never had even the slightest training in how to keep the books or proper accounts. I therefore found this duty pretty difficult. I often had to appeal to the First Lieutenant, who was wonderfully patient, to help me get the figures right.

Then of course, there was 'Up Spirits', the daily issue of a tot of rum to the sailors on board. It was my duty to oversee this traditional 'ceremony' performed by a petty officer who ladled out the precise measure of rum and water to the sailors lined up with their mugs. This reminded me that when I was in Rinaldo on the receiving end of my rum ration, I could even use it as 'currency' for some favour or other from my 'oppos'.

Talking of rum, one major difficulty was that our captain in Essington was almost an alcoholic. He was on the 'horse's necks' (brandy and ginger ale) by about 11 in the morning. I never asked, but I believe he had been a Chief Petty Officer before gaining a commission and was not really cut out to be a commanding officer. Though, I have to say, he really knew his minesweeping and was fully in control when we carried out sweeping exercises. I knew hardly anything of those skills.

Another tricky one for me was replying to AFO's (Admiralty Fleet Orders). I have never been good at filling in forms and quite often find I have made some silly mistake so the form looks all 'messed up'. On one occasion, I got it wrong twice and the poor officer reading it at the other end had to send it back to me to be corrected. Even worse, I got it wrong again! This time I was given a frightful 'bottle' for being so stupid. I was hugely embarrassed.

After some time, and a number of exercises and sea-time, we were ordered to Cyprus to be a guardship with the duty of stopping the gunrunning that was going on. The Turks and Cypriots were at 'daggers drawn' with General Grivas and Archbishop Makarios very much in the frame. This, of course, meant a long haul for our little vessel, all the way down through the Bay of Biscay, past Spain and Portugal and on to Gibraltar to turn into the Med. We were, in fact, making for Malta where the ship would wait for further orders.

The Mediterranean can be very rough and it certainly was for us as we headed for Malta. Most of the ship's company were laid low with seasickness, but thank goodness I was fine and went round the deck to chat to the lads sitting out to get fresh air. I was pleased to be able to have a chat to cheer them up as best I could.

As it happened, I only had about four months of National Service to complete when I became an officer and my time ran out while we were in Malta. My end date was the beginning of November, but after two years we were given a month's 'demob' leave and a civilian suit. There was another 'extra' – I would be seeing Jane again!

So in early October, I was sent home without even getting to Cyprus. But of course, I had to pack my bags and leave Essington saying goodbye to the men with whom I had become so friendly. In fact, as I was leaving I was most touched to receive a pewter mug from the ship's company. It was inscribed – 'To the Subby from the lads'. I have it to this day.

I had to wait a few days living in the wardroom of the shore base in Malta. I was even brought a cup of tea in the morning by a steward. Luxury! Quite soon, I was found a berth in a large cruise ship. The journey home in a first-class cabin was most comfortable and hugely enjoyable for me and I can remember one evening standing on deck watching the going down of the sun in a warm, orange glow as it slid slowly behind the horizon.

It felt to me like another ending…

Chapter 8
Radio Luxembourg and G.O.S

After a spell of leave and hanging up my uniform (though it would be used again for my fortnights of training while in the Reserve), I decided to concentrate on building up my career. Getting myself before a microphone was now a priority. But how to do it?

My father happened to have met and got to know Max Robertson, the famous radio commentator for the Wimbledon tennis matches. It always amazed me how he managed to follow the ball and give clear and concise commentary shot after shot. It was a considerable skill. I reckon the television commentators, though they have great knowledge, do have it a bit easier, at least to a degree, since in vision, the tennis speaks for itself.

But for now, thanks to my father, it was definitely Max Robertson to whom I wrote. It was a careful letter, or so I thought, asking for his advice as to how best to approach the BBC as a potential narrator. Quite soon, I received a reply from him, a kind letter, but containing some valuable criticism. He said: "When writing to important people, it's a good idea carefully to check your letter before you send it. Yours included three spelling mistakes!" One of the culprits, I remember, was the word 'acquire' without the letter 'c'. I realised he was giving me sound advice and I wrote to thank him, even though he had also said that he was sorry but couldn't really help me get into the BBC.

So, I reckoned I'd better get started finding some contacts. It was interesting, because years before when the family were on a holiday at Sennen Cove in Cornwall, we had met Ted Kavanagh, writer of the hugely popular ITMA radio series. My father had told him of my aim, of becoming a BBC announcer. Much later, my father remembered to tell me what Ted Kavanagh had said: "Tell him, never to give up developing contacts." I was now doing just that!

I started walking around Soho, going into every agency, film studio and commercial radio and TV production house I could find, offering my services as a 'voice' and narrator. I even braved the portals of Broadcasting House and was given a form to write up my interests, which would go to the Admin Department which kept files of such requests. I would even be happy to be taken on as a humble studio manager. On and on I went, until one day I walked into the offices of Bensons, already the producer of TV commercials for the new commercial television stations, Rediffusion in London and ATV in Birmingham. I just walked in, talked to the Commissionaire on the Reception desk and told him what I was looking for. He thought for a moment, then said: "There's a producer upstairs who may be able to help. I'll see if he'll talk to you."

He soon returned and told me to 'go up to see Peter Fox'. I went up and found Peter Fox at his desk. He stood up and welcomed me with a warm smile. We chatted for a bit, after which he suddenly said: "I'm looking for someone to voice a series I'm working on for Radio Luxembourg and we don't have a sponsor yet for the programmes. It's a series of thirteen, all about the famous American composers, Irving Berlin, Richard Rodgers, Cole Porter, George Gershwin, Jerome Kern, people like that. Not much money, I'm afraid, but would you be interested?"

I jumped at it! And I was soon joining Peter in the Radio Luxembourg studios in a backstreet in W1.

This was a strange development for me, as I'd really disliked the music that was played from Radio Luxembourg, very loudly (!) on the speakers on board the Rinaldo mess deck. It was all very much the 'pop' music of the day. Now, here I was working for the very Radio Station which had given me such unwelcome 'noise' in the Navy, booming out around the ship!

Radio Luxembourg was actually beamed out to the Midlands where there was a considerable population. Down south, where we were living in Sussex, the signal was weak and would come and go, sometimes fading away almost completely. I can remember, literally lying on the floor next to my parents' old radiogram, listening to the recordings I was now working on with Peter Fox. It could be really maddening hearing my carefully couched introductions disappearing into the night before coming back in stages, with much of the music fading too!

In fact, I found the series I worked on most enjoyable. It was music including great melodies which I found extremely good listening. In those days, the programmes were recorded on huge reels of tape, and I found it fascinating watching Peter editing the music and speech we'd recorded on large 15 ips (inches per second) machines.

Strangely enough, there was another Peter I met in the studios, Peter Pritchett-Brown, whom I was to meet again much later, in completely different circumstances.

Meeting Richard Murdoch

One day, I followed on from a series which Richard (Dicky) Murdoch was presenting. I had a most interesting chat with him and told him how much I enjoyed listening to *Much Binding in the March* with him and Kenneth Horne. I found 'Dicky' a delightful chap to talk to.

Amid all my activities, I happened to have a conversation with my cousin, Diana Hall. She was working as a secretary for a man who was manager of a 'film-strip' company called Unicorn Head Visual Aids Ltd. Her boss was a man named Tim Leigh-Pemberton and, apparently, he needed a Production Assistant. Diana suggested I get in touch. I did so, and soon found myself in the office of the Chairman of the company, smartly suited, his grey hair balding, who offered me the job. To say I was thrilled would not be an exaggeration. In a way, it put me on the 'ladder' towards contacts I wanted to make and to have a continuing professional job. It was a really exciting step forward. The offices were in Aldersgate, and I soon got involved in the making of the filmstrips, which were mainly aimed at schools and the education market in general.

Of course, these filmstrips needed pictures and the company used a particularly excellent young photographer who took super photographs for the various subjects covered in the 'strips'. It would seem archaic today but it was the top technology of the time! The pictures and script were all produced on film, which the users – often teachers in schools – would click on, frame by frame, to tell the particular story and subject in question.

One week I was deputed to join the young photographer (I forget his name) at a Fry's chocolate factory for a filmstrip telling the story of chocolate production. I found this assignment really fascinating and the photographer set up his tripod at the various stages as the trays of hot liquid chocolate moved along the production line. Sometimes, the warm chocolate being shaken to make it settle in the trays didn't quite level properly, and the operator would use a finger to fiddle it into place. Imagine that today! 'Health and Safety' wasn't even heard of in those days, the 1950s.

My job gradually developed and I became more useful as a production assistant. I was paid just £3-ten shillings a week, which was a meagre salary when top-trained secretaries were getting up to £15! But I had negotiated a deal which allowed me a lot of flexibility, and I could also perform 'voice-overs' and narrations which could pay pretty well, especially for commercials with all the 'residuals'.

The first TV commercial I was booked for was an 'ad' for 'Coty Lipstick'! I certainly thought it strange that the producers had decided to use a male voice to expound on the special values of this unique lipstick. Perhaps they were of the opinion that young (and older!) women would find a male voice more flattering and alluring for this particular product? Strangely enough, I was to record this TV commercial for Bensons, through which I'd had the introduction to Peter Fox and Radio Luxembourg. The fee was 15-guineas plus the extras, so it seemed like a fortune to me!

However, one day, I believe over a weekend, tragedy struck the Unicorn Head Visual Aids Company. It suffered a serious fire which roared up through the centre of the offices, ruining, and in many cases destroying, the small tin cans in which the rolls of film were kept and, indeed, sold. The whole place was in chaos with most of the stock blackened and useless. It certainly was a setback for the Company and Dr Michael Hooker, our Managing Director, having dealt with insurance and all the mounds of paperwork involved, now had to set about looking for new premises.

After a considerable amount of searching, he found a nice office in Weymouth Mews just around the corner from Broadcasting House. It all meant a huge amount of reorganisation. After a time, though, things were settled and we got on again with the business of filmstrip production. Here I will relate a story which is really quite strange; anyway, it was a strange thing that I did. Every morning as I walked to the company office, now in Weymouth Mews, I passed the Langham, once a smart hotel, but now containing BBC recording studios, offices and bedrooms for the overnight announcing staff. As I walked by the large front doors, I saw a tall ex-guardsman Commissionaire, white gloves and all, welcoming BBC top brass entering the Langham and wishing them 'good morning'. He didn't know me, of course, so I wasn't treated to a 'good morning'. One day I decided to wish a 'good morning' to the Commissionaire. He looked a bit puzzled the first time but when I kept doing it, he at last wished me a cheery 'good morning, sir'. I really felt I'd started to make my way in to the BBC! It may sound odd, but it's a perfectly true story.

The Langham.

A BBC Appointments Board

Then one morning, the phone rang on my desk. I picked it up. It was a woman at the BBC! She told me there was shortly to be a Board held to take on studio managers. Somebody had fallen out, and would I like to take their place? Imagine my total surprise! My original request for a job at the BBC had obviously surfaced in the Admin Department. It took me precisely a second to accept the invitation! But there was a slight caveat. The Board was to be held at midday on exactly the date I had been booked by Bensons for my first commercial. That was to be recorded at 1.30pm on that very day. I reckoned that if the Board ran a bit late, I would still have time for both.

And so, a couple of days later, I presented myself at the BBC studios at 5 Portland Place, and waited to be called... I waited and waited more. By 12.30 I was certainly getting worried and asked the secretary who'd welcomed me in, how long the Board was going to be? She confirmed that it was running late, but that I shouldn't have to wait too much longer. In the event, it was 5-minutes to one before I was asked to go down to a basement studio for a microphone test. I was asked over the intercom to please read some pages of news which lay on the table by the microphone. My readings would be linked up and heard by the members of the Board sitting in a room above.

By the time I'd finished the 'test', and been led up to the Boardroom, it was five past one. By now, I was not in the least relaxed! There were six Board members sitting around a long, very polished, mahogany table, with the Chairman sitting at the other end. There was a fog of smoke.

He gave me a searching look over his gold-rimmed half glasses. Then, turning over some papers, he slowly began the interrogation. "I see, Mr Muncaster, you were educated at Stowe. Do you have any languages?"

"Well, obviously sir, English, some French and I think I could get away with German pronunciation." This did not go down well.

"It is not BBC policy," he retorted with undisguised contumely, "to get away with things!" I didn't feel I was making much positive headway. He asked me one or two other things which I completely forget, and he passed me on to the man next to him on his left.

On the wall, there was a huge BBC clock, and in a state of rising panic, I watched the big red second hand which ticked regularly round. It was now well past 1.15 and the next interrogator having lit up another cigarette with a dying match, took an age to begin his questioning. By 20 past, I could stand it no longer, knowing that not only would I miss my chance of getting in to the BBC, but was in dire danger of being dreadfully late for my commercial recording. I was between a rock and a hard place!!

Eventually, I plucked up my courage and said to the Chairman: "Please forgive me, sir, but I'm afraid I have another appointment." I'm sure he thought I was meeting my girlfriend…

All he said was: "I expect, Mr Muncaster, the members of the Board also have appointments! Thank you very much."

I quickly gathered up some books I had with me and my mackintosh, brought against the rain, turned and was faced with two doors. Now, which one had I come in through? I chose one, in the event the wrong one, and walked straight in to a broom cupboard. Covered in confusion, I left the room, raced down the stairs and out in to the street. Thank heavens, the universe was with me and a taxi came by at that precise moment. I gave the driver urgent instructions. Fortunately, the recording studios happened to be pretty near and I arrived bang on 1.30. By a whisker I had secured my 15 guineas.

In all the historic annals of the Corporation, I doubt if there is anyone who has got in to the BBC by actually failing a Board! I think I created something of a record. I, of course, received the inevitable slip of paper, thanking me for attending the Board, but telling me that, unfortunately, I did not meet the standard required of the BBC but I at least had my 15 guineas from the 'Coty Lipstick' TV commercial

Sadly, however, I did not secure my job at the filmstrip Company. After the fire, it was necessary to cut costs while the Company got back on its feet. I was called in to see the Chairman, again at his office in the City (another name I forget, I'm afraid). I sat down and listened to him as he gave me some unwelcome news. "I'm afraid, Mr Muncaster," he said, "we are having to cut down, and since you were the last in, I'm sorry to say, you have to be the first out!" He gave me a short time to try to find another job, but I left his office with the knowledge that I had been given 'the sack'.

However, an extraordinary thing happened. A day or two later, again quite unexpectedly, the phone rang on my desk. I picked it up. "Martin Muncaster?" the voice enquired.

"Yes," I said.

"My name's Aidan MacDermot, I'm Head of Presentation at G.O.S. (The General Overseas Service of the BBC) and I was most impressed by your microphone test at the Board the other day. I wondered if you'd like to come and do some holiday announcing for us."

As the saying goes – you could have knocked me down with a feather! What a turnaround. I, of course, accepted with alacrity and within a couple of days was sitting in Aidan MacDermot's office at 200 Oxford Street, where the GOS studios were situated.

We had a talk and he told me what would be needed. He organised for me to start several days later. I would be in the studio trailing (i.e. sitting with) an old hand, Jack de Manio. Jack was an extraordinary character, an ex-Guards Officer who had been announcing for the BBC for quite some time. In fact, he was also the presenter of the morning 'Today' programme and became famous for getting the time wrong when he read the clock incorrectly. He was more or less accurate until the hands got down to the half hour, after that his maths, or more likely his subtraction, let him down!

Learning from Jack de Manio

It was Jack who I was now going to learn from. After about half an hour with him in the studio, during which he explained the duties of the announcer, he suddenly stood up and went off to the canteen. I'd no idea when he would be back, so I sat there knowing I was certainly going to have to give the closing announcement for the programme then on the air. Jack had at least pointed out the red button that had to be pressed to bring the microphone alive, but I stared at all the technology with which I was surrounded in mystification, and had not the faintest idea what, or who, was at the end of the lines of three telephones, one red, by my side. Fortunately, Jack came breezing back with a cup of coffee, so I was released from my very first duty of speaking to the world via a BBC microphone.

For my next duty, I was booked for a very early morning announcing shift. It was several days later, and I stayed in a room at Lexham Gardens, which my friend Malcolm Reynell had rented. He had passed it on to me, as he had decided 'to spend time in Canada. His father was a stockbroker and Malcolm wanted to join him and had decided to go to a stockbroking business in Montreal to get some overseas experience. He told me later that in Canada for some adventure, he'd done a bit of lumber jacking for a few weeks first. But when he left the job, he'd had all his lumber jacking wages stolen!

But now I'd taken over the room at a few shillings a week, since I was obviously going to spend a lot of time in London, I hoped with the BBC.

On this particular morning, for my shift in Oxford Street, the BBC were going to send a car to pick me up at 5 am to take me to the studios. I got up early, of course, and waited outside on the pavement so the driver could see me and pick me up. I seem to remember my shift started at 5.45, so to be picked up at 5 would give me plenty of time to settle in. But this was another occasion when I did a lot of waiting, getting more and more anxious as the time went by. It seemed like an age before the car eventually arrived and by now, about 5.25, I was in a terrible state. I can remember wondering what on earth I would do if I was late for my shift. But I made it in the end, managed to gather my wits and got through the job without any disaster.

On another occasion, however, I came quite a cropper. I was working a shift in a studio announcing a record programme for various foreign countries. These records had to be carefully timed to be played on air in the right order. I should explain here that when the announcer pushes the button on his desk that activates the microphone, the speakers in the studio are automatically switched off so that the announcer speaks in a silent environment.

I was very pleased with myself this particular morning, as I'd timed the relevant record to come on and end at precisely the right moment before the chimes of Big Ben. I started to spin the record and all was well, except that I heard no music from the speakers. I wondered what had happened. I pressed the 'talk back' to speak to the engineer behind the glass separating him from the announcer's studio, saying: "Is this thing working?" He frantically pointed to the microphone button, waving at me to switch it off. It was a blessing I hadn't used a swear word, which would not have been popular, but my little question to the engineer went out across the world to all manner of foreign places!

By now, the girlfriend who had been Malcolm's had become mine. It was surprising that I had not met Iona long before, as she lived quite close to my parents in a cottage in the woods at Bedham, not far from Petworth. Her father, Donald Gilbert, was a very fine sculptor, so we both had fathers who were artists. I took Iona out a lot, and we often met at a wood on top of the hill overlooking Petworth, known as the Gog and Magog. I would cycle up the hill and Iona would walk through the woods to meet me. She was also carrying out a domestic science course at Queen Elizabeth College in Kensington, so we saw a good deal of each other in London too.

Iona. Our engagement photo.

I now wanted to get in to the domestic side of BBC radio and went to ask advice from a contact I'd been given who was Head of the Light Programme, Sandy Grandison. I arranged to see him and he was helpful, except he said: "We really only take on people who can offer some experience. They'd run a station in Malta, for instance, or spent time with BFBS (British Forces Broadcasting Service) in Germany. I suggest you go away and get some experience."

This got me thinking and I wondered if I should go abroad. Others who'd come to the BBC had experience with Australian and New Zealand broadcasting and personalities like Cliff Michelmore had become known for their considerable broadcasting experience with BFBS in Germany.

I thought Australia was too far, the States certainly didn't attract me, nor Europe for that matter. So I took a pin and it hovered over various countries on the map; then I suddenly stuck it into Canada, and that felt right. I would be meeting Malcolm, too, which would be a bonus. So, I took myself to the Canadian Embassy in London to get myself a visa, and opted for Montreal.

The die was cast…

Chapter 9

To Canada

King's Cross was bustling with large holiday crowds (it was Easter) as Iona and I looked for the platform for my train to Hull. I was going there to join the ship which would be carrying me across the Atlantic to Canada, along the coast of Newfoundland into the Gulf of St Lawrence and all the way along the river past Quebec and finally to Montreal. I had opted for a two-year stay in Canada to allow me to settle down and hopefully to find the sort of work which would give me the needed broadcasting experience so strongly recommended by Sandy Grandison.

Once we had found the right train, I took my luggage on board and found myself a seat. Iona, meanwhile, was waiting on the platform and we had a few minutes for a loving 'goodbye'. I then joined the train and stood at a door to be able to wave to Iona as the train pulled out. A Guard's shrill whistle sounded and we were off; but not realising it, I was standing in the Guard's door and as the train began to move, he stepped on board, giving me a heavy push to get me out of his way! I nearly lost my balance, but quickly got to a window, just in time to catch Iona waving at me as she faded into the distance. I then lost sight of her and went to my seat, feeling strangely sad and already a bit homesick.

I enjoy trains and we had a good, uneventful journey to Hull, watching the passing green landscapes as the train rattled on. At Hull, I took a taxi to the docks and found my ship lying alongside in one of the dock basins. I had chosen an Ellerman's vessel, almost for old time's sake. We sailed next morning in beautiful, calm sunshine and made our way up the coast to Scotland, then turning to port into the Pentland Firth. The Scottish landscape looked green and inviting, the detail of rocks and moorland standing out in clear focus. Scotland in such weather can be tantalisingly beautiful and I have to say that a sense of homesickness made itself all too evident as I now felt pretty lonely.

It took nearly all day to clear the land, with the rocky outcrops of the Isle of St Kilda to the South slowly vanishing from sight as it drew away to a mere shadow. I was acutely aware that through my binoculars I was losing my last contact with home, possibly for some time to come.

I don't remember meeting much bad weather on the way but there was always the Atlantic swell, which our little ship rode happily. During the voyage, I read the whole of Dickens's 'Oliver Twist', which, as it happened, would come in very useful in the weeks to come. As we neared the coast, we ran into the famed Grand Banks fog and it would be some time before we came out into clear weather as we reached the Gulf of St Lawrence, with the melting ice floes drifting down on the current.

I had told Malcolm Reynell of my intention to have some time in Canada and when we at last reached Montreal, after the long journey up the St Lawrence River and passing Quebec, there was Malcolm on the dockside waiting to greet me. I was delighted to see him, was soon ashore and he drove me to his apartment. As he drove, we chatted of course, and he wanted to know about my trip and how things were at home, amongst other matters. He then most generously gave me a month free of rent in his apartment while I looked for a job, or even achieved some broadcasting work. This turned out to be a most valuable offer.

So, what next?

Malcolm had a client to see 'out in the sticks' so next morning he drove me out to a country house and I walked around, thinking of home, while he spent time with his client. Everything seemed rather grey, I remember. I suppose that was because it wasn't long before that the countryside had been under a blanket of snow – it was now the end of April. I scanned the sky, wondering about the difference between this and an English sky? Actually, it looked much the same with clouds moving steadily on the wind.

Then my first night in Malcolm's room, which was sparsely furnished with just a bed and two or three orange boxes! But I was very grateful to have somewhere to stay. Malcolm shared his flat with a young fellow who was keen on the Army and I think was in the Reserve. He always seemed to be polishing something!

The Search for Work

I now thought it was high time I did some investigating, so I set off on foot to find my way into town. It was a case of looking around for likely places where I could walk in and present myself as a 'voice' for narration or 'voice-overs'. It brought back memories of plodding the Soho streets in London all over again. I was looking for production houses, radio stations, TV and film studios and agencies. People had warned me that Montreal would be a difficult place to find work for an English voice, as there was a considerable French influence, being so close to Quebec.

I realised it was going to be a long haul, as it had been in London. But even so, there were many possibilities and I gained the impression that there was a lot of media activity in Montreal and plenty of places in which to make contact. I remember even trying the Bell Telephone Company for a possible job, but was turned down rather brusquely, being told I really had nothing to offer.

Sadly, this was rather true, but my 'free' time with Malcolm was fast running out and I thought I should try anything! I did walk into a commercial TV station and spoke to a woman producer there, but she told me there was no call, at the moment anyway, for my type of voice. After more than three weeks of concentrated searching, I was getting a bit worried. I'd tried just about everything I could think of.

Then one morning, I walked past a commercial radio station which I had not seen before. I decided to try it, went up to reception and spoke to the very attractive young girl at her desk. She listened for a moment as I explained my reason for walking in and she suddenly said: "Hey, for God's sake speak English." (Which actually I was!). Anyway, I thought this was rather a good start and we had a good laugh. She then went on with the encouraging words: "There's a producer upstairs who may be able to help you." She called him up and he came down to see me (I forget his name). But he turned out to be an amazing contact. "I think the man for you to see," he said, "is Rupert Caplan. He's the top radio producer at CBC and does a lot of drama there. Would you like me to put you in touch?"

"Of course," I gave him the obvious answer!

The next day I managed to catch Rupert Caplan on the phone and he said: "Come into the studios on Sunday morning. I'd like to give you an audition." This was exciting news.

A speciality of mine which I'd used for auditions was the passage in 'Oliver Twist' when Oliver asks for more. I thought this might be useful for my audition with Caplan as it contained several 'voices' – Oliver himself, of course, the astonished Beadle, and the 'gentleman in the white waistcoat'.

I presented myself to Rupert Chaplan, who was waiting for me in one of the sound studios. After some friendly introductions, he asked me: "What do you do?" I told him about my reading of the passage in 'Oliver Twist' and he asked me to go into the commentary studio (adjoining his studio). He spoke to me on the talkback and told me to go ahead. He listened intently and when I had finished, he spoke to me again, in his Canadian drawl, and said: "I've a part for you in a play I am doing about the case against modern music. I'd like you to play the conductor who speaks for classical music."

Suddenly, I had a job! There were just two days to go before my free rent time with Malcolm ran out!

Acting with the CBC

A couple of days later I joined a company of actors and actresses in the CBC studios. We rehearsed the play in the morning, then recorded in the afternoon with Caplan stopping us from time to time when he needed us to record a passage again. I put on an older voice and Caplan seemed well pleased. I'm sure I still have the script for that play tucked away in the papers I kept from my time in Canada.

Happily, that was the first of many recordings I did for Rupert Caplan. He produced a number of series, one being *The Bible Story*, which he recorded every Sunday and he asked me to act in this many times. There were some major productions, too, including the famous 'Lorna Doone' story from the book by R.D. Blackmore. He chose a Greek actress for the part of Lorna. She had perfect English, of course, but I thought she might have built up the character more than she did. However, I made friends with her and even took her out to the cinema one evening to see *Around the World in 80 days* with David Niven in the lead; a beautiful film which we both much enjoyed. Even now, when I hear the music from that film I am transported to that cinema in Montreal, and as I write that was some 60 years ago! Memory is a remarkable thing and I return to the mention I made of being reminded of things through sounds or smells from long ago, Mantovani's 'Charmaine' and my mother's Chanel No. 5 scent, for instance.

I forget what part I played in the 'Lorna Doone' production, but I remember finding it most enjoyable.

One of the people I came to know in Montreal was Jo Milner. As mentioned in an earlier chapter, my grandfather, Lord Riverdale, who ran the family steelworks in Sheffield, had journeyed to several countries selling steel and the Balfour speciality of high-speed steel tools. On his travels, my grandfather had set up various agents for Balfours in Australia and New Zealand, I believe, but also in Canada – in Montreal and Vancouver. Balfour's man in Montreal was Jo Milner and he and his wife were most kind to me, inviting me to their home for meals. I was always most grateful, as my fare for lunch was usually cheese and biscuits to save money!

Through my increasing number of contacts, I found myself recommended for a role in William Douglas Home's *The Reluctant Debutante*, an extremely funny play which had enjoyed a long run in London with Wilfred Hyde White as the father. I remember him as being perfect for the part. The 'father' for us was played by Arthur Treacher, who'd come up from New York.

Arthur Treacher was a well-known English actor who had become a 'star' in the States through his TV partnership with the American talk show host, Merv Griffin. He'd become famous by playing the typical English butler, with typical obsequious voice to match. The Americans loved it. He was really good as the father in The Reluctant Debutante and was a big 'draw' for us. For some reason, which I never quite understood, he called me in his deep rich voice 'Mulholland'!

I started in the part of Jane's lover and had to kiss this Jane who was the reluctant debutante. My attempt at this was not well received (well, I had only kissed **my** Jane once!) and in any case, the Jane in the play had very large lips which I did not find particularly attractive. After a couple of rather awkward rehearsals, the producer decided I was not a successful lover and changed me to take the part of the tall 'goofy guardsman'. I found this much more my style and so did the producer.

I was a particularly appropriate choice for the part of the tall guardsman, who came in to propose to Jane carrying his huge bearskin! When we opened with the play in a new theatre called 'The Studio Theatre' it went down well and we attracted good audiences. I enjoyed my part enormously and got plenty of laughs. There was a particular line in which the guardsman was talking about how to get south 'by turning left at Petersfield'.

One night, hoping for a better laugh, with the stupid guardsman not knowing his left from his right, I pointed to my right instead of to my left. I did this, but it was a total change from the words that, night after night, had been etched upon my brain and suddenly I completely 'dried'. In a moment of panic, in the guardsman's really posh voice, I said: "I really don't know what to say." This, quite unexpectedly, brought howls of laughter from the audience and quickly the actress I was on stage with brought everything back on track by reminding me of the words I should have said; and on we went.

The Day I Overslept!

One of the things I found quite difficult to get used to was the fact that our performances at the Studio Theatre ended late, around 11 o'clock. I was therefore never in bed until well after midnight so needed a bit of a 'lie in' next morning.

One day, I slept right through the alarm after a late show on a Saturday night. I awoke after half past nine, the time to rehearse for the recording of another 'Bible Story' in which I had a part. I was appalled and dreadfully worried about being badly late for the recording. I imagined I would be extremely unpopular. I got dressed as speedily as I could, feeling very 'woozy' having had to rush to get up (I always like having plenty of time first thing in the morning). I had to ring for a taxi – more wasted time – and at last the taxi arrived and I was indeed nearly an hour late in the end. But surprisingly, I found my acting colleagues really understanding. I guess there were several who had experienced similar problems. Even Rupert Caplan seemed unconcerned. But having been hauled suddenly out of a deep sleep, it took me some time to feel normal again – but luckily, in time for the recording.

After a fortnight in Montreal, we went on tour with 'The Reluctant Debutante' to Ottawa, working in a building which, having been a cinema, was now converted into a theatre. We played another fortnight there and after the last night, Arthur Treacher presented me with some extremely expensive toiletries and a very pleasant-smelling after-shave. That lasted me a good long time.

I have always been interested in French and when I got back to Montreal I decided to book for a French course at McGill University. The professor I studied with was a Polish Count who spoke beautiful French and equally good English. I found him really delightful to work with, He was quite self-effacing in some ways and displayed perfect manners. I'm not sure that others on the course appreciated him as much as I did.

Being an actor (and a mimic) I was able to give my French-speaking a very realistic French sound and enunciation. In the oral examination at the end of the course I got over 90%. My written exam result was pretty good too. I have always wished I had gone on to do more work on French, but by now I needed money and had little spare time. I was not only performing a number of broadcasts but had also been offered a part in a Coward play *This Happy Breed*. This was going to be performed at the Mountain Playhouse, a theatre on the hill above Montreal town. This was a lot of fun and we had quite good audiences. The only thing that was NOT such fun at the time was the effect of the mosquitoes which came out in force on the hot summer evenings.

One of the actors in the play turned out to be something of a psychic. He 'read' my palm and told me a number of most interesting things. He'd only just met me and knew nothing about my life and background. One of the things he told me was that I would always have plenty of money but would always worry about it. He was right. I have indeed had a lifelong concern about money but, this far anyway, I've always had easily enough. I think it has been the case because I am a saver by nature and this has served me well.

Speaking of money, by October I had saved enough to go by Canadian Pacific Railway, first class, to Vancouver – $1,000 deluxe. To book my ticket, I walked to the station with a thousand dollars cash in my pocket – and walked fast to lessen the possibility of being 'mugged'! It felt terrific to allow myself something of a holiday and I looked forward to it. I packed for the journey and the train set off a couple of days later. We went round the northern shores of the Great Lakes and I sat in the Dome Car towards the rear of the train and could watch the carriages ahead snaking along the lines. The trees were now turning rich reds and browns as the autumn approached and I even spotted the odd moose amongst the trees and fields.

I was pleased I was travelling first class. The food was excellent, served on clean white tablecloths set with silver cutlery. I also had my own personal apartment with a comfortable bunk from which I could watch the passing landscape through the window. I awoke the first morning to see us speeding through the wheat fields, miles and miles of them. I took some movie shots with my 9.5mm camera but was most disappointed later when I got home to find the camera hadn't been working correctly and much of the footage was spoiled as the sprockets hadn't caught properly and the claws had jumped into the frames. A great pity as I had hoped to share pictures of the journey with my parents.

I was on the train for three days and nights and as I looked through the window from my bunk, I saw mile after mile of the golden prairies. On the way, we stopped at Winnipeg, among other places, and I had arranged to meet a Canadian Army officer, Sam (I forget his surname but it was a Scottish one) who had been a friend of my mother's during the War. He had been billeted at the Canadian Army Camp in Petworth Park where a large number of soldiers were awaiting the call for 'D-Day'. Sam was a kind, gentle man who I very much liked. I remembered him turning up at Four-Winds wearing very smart tartan trousers. My mother became very fond of him. I had a really nice chat with Sam, who was waiting for me on the platform at Winnipeg station. Sadly, it was only a brief stop but I was able to report to my mother that I had seen him and passed on her regards. My mother was lonely as it was at a time during the War when my father was away for a year on an extensive camouflage mission which took him to Africa, the Middle East and Far East, India and Ceylon. I recall him telling me about his time at the naval station at Trincomalee in Ceylon.

Earlier, when his ship was sent to Durban, my father happened to meet his brother, Philip Hall, who was also in Durban, with his ship, a corvette of which he was First Lieutenant. I mentioned the story earlier. The two 'boys' had a great time together; a welcome break from the dangers of the war at sea.

The journey through the Rockies was stunning with the mountains standing out in magnificent display. I was entranced and watched our progress from my high position in the Dome Car, the train snaking ahead as it climbed on the track through those famous mountains.

I arrived in Vancouver, where I made contact with the Balfour's agent (I forget his name, I'm afraid) but, as with Jo Milner in Montreal, he and his wife again were most kind and welcoming to me when I got there. I enjoyed a barbecue in their garden and they also took me to the opera to see 'Gianni Schicci' by Puccini, which includes the sublime soprano aria *Oh My Beloved Father*. That's another of the 'triggers' I have mentioned in earlier chapters. Every time I hear a recording of that aria, I am wafted back to that Canadian theatre in Vancouver, again it was some 60 years ago!

Various things happened while I was there. I visited the local radio station to ask whether there might be a newsreader job for me. I was given an audition and was obviously taken quite seriously, but eventually was told my voice was 'just too English!' However, I very much enjoyed my time in Vancouver and even found it possible to visit Vancouver Island and view the Parliament building there on a beautiful sunny day.

The journey back to Montreal was similarly enjoyable and I was able to report back to Malcolm and tell him all about my 'holiday'. During my months in Montreal, Malcolm and I often enjoyed lunch together in restaurants local to the stockbroking firm he was working for, Oswald & Drinkwater (I was always amused by the name!)

By now, it was November and I had decided not to stay for two years as originally planned, however much the Canadians were welcoming and hospitable. Frankly, I was very lonely and wrote to Iona nearly every day. I waited longingly for her letters, which she wrote regularly. It was wonderful to go to the post-box nearby and find another letter from her. She was working as a cook and waitress at the Greystones Hotel, near Budleigh Salterton, in Devon. The hotel was situated high above the cliffs and Iona, when the weather was good, would sit and write to me with a glorious view of the sea ahead.

Meantime, I was still getting radio work and was even booked to narrate a television documentary which I much enjoyed.

In December, I was offered a part in the play *Venus Observed* by Christopher Fry. The producer was the same man who had produced *The Reluctant Debutante* and he was very keen for me to act a part in the play. But I had now decided to return home for Christmas so had to disappoint him, though he tried his best to get me to postpone my departure. But I knew he had quite a coterie of English actors to choose from in Montreal since I had worked with many of them.

I had been told more than once that Montreal was a difficult place for English actors to get work, because of the strong French influence. But once my foot was on the ladder, I had no difficulty finding work. I had chosen Montreal because Malcolm was there, which had given me a good base – except for the mosquitoes which seemed to thrive in Malcolm's apartment and in the summer I got quite badly bitten, especially around the ankles. It always seemed to happen at night when asleep, so one didn't feel them until it was too late! I also knew, of course, that Balfours had an agent in Montreal and Jo Milner had been most helpful in giving me advice about the area.

But now, home beckoned.

I booked a cabin on board a German ship, the last but one to leave Montreal before the St Lawrence Seaway iced up. It was early December so after the Atlantic crossing, I would be home for Christmas. Fine snowflakes were flying in swirls around the open spaces between the carriages as I walked down the train to find a seat on the train to the docks at Quebec. Malcolm had come to see me off. I was so very thankful to him for letting me stay in his apartment. It had given me a good start.

We were lucky with the weather and enjoyed a reasonably smooth Atlantic crossing. It was uneventful, except that there was a bit of a panic one night when a fire was discovered in one of the cabins. I believe it had been started by a cigarette. I awoke to hear a lot of shouting and general racket. But it was all sorted out pretty quickly with German efficiency so I didn't need to reach for my lifebelt!

I heard afterwards that the ship behind us, the last to leave Quebec, had met with a bad storm. I was glad I hadn't been on that ship.

We arrived in the Solent to a thick fog so had to stand off for some time before it cleared enough to go alongside in Southampton Docks. There I was delighted to see my parents who had come to meet the ship. It was wonderful to see them after my many months away. We drove home to Four-Winds with much talk as I related stories of my experiences in Canada.

I was so glad I had changed my mind about the length of my stay in Canada. Two years would definitely have been too long, especially as even during the time I had been away I had experienced a deep loneliness, having left Iona behind. We were, in fact, secretly engaged. In those days it would have shocked and distressed my parents, and Iona's, if she had gone with me. Socially, it just wasn't on. How things have changed in the half century that has passed since. Today, no one would have 'batted an eyelid' if Iona had gone away with me.

But now, I was soon to see her again as we exchanged Christmas presents and I had a most enjoyable rest and the traditional fare of Christmas with the family. It was good to see Clive again, too, as he took a break from his studies at the Royal Academy of Music. It was marvellous to be home…

Chapter 10

BBC, Then Southern TV and a Wedding

We have slipped into another year. It is now 1958 and I've reached the grand old age of 24! How much lies ahead? Yet again, I find myself on the search for contacts and, hopefully, a job. But where to start?

Talking to my father, he mentioned that a very good friend of his, Jack Williams (he had actually courted and married my Sheffield Granny's secretary, Pam) had a brother Lloyd Williams who was in ITV. Lloyd apparently, had a senior post in marketing for the ITV London franchise, Rediffusion. My father suggested that I get in touch with Jack to see if there was any chance of my meeting his brother. Both Jack and Pam had become close friends with my parents and they saw a lot of each other. This was a help. Jack was very pleased to approach his brother to see if there was any possibility of an announcer's job in Rediffusion. It wasn't long, before I'd heard from Lloyd Williams. He asked me up to London to see him in his office. For me, this was an exciting development. Very soon, I was sitting in Lloyd's office and he was quizzing me about what sort of job I was looking for. I told him about my broadcasting experiences in Canada, and that I was now hoping for an announcer's job in London. He told me he'd get in touch with 'Presentation' to get me an audition. "After that," he said, "it was over to me!"

Sure enough, I heard that an audition had been arranged and a day or two later I presented myself to a producer who guided me to a tiny studio with a microphone set up on a small table. Ahead of me was a television monitor with the picture of me on the screen! There were some scripts in front of me containing various news stories. Over the talkback, I was asked to read two or three of them. I felt I could cope with that.

When I'd finished reading, the producer asked me to join him. He then told me that he'd liked what I did, but he was not hopeful that there would be a job for me, as the ITV companies were getting short of money at the time and having to cut down. People were leaving rather than being taken on. This was not good news. But at least I'd been seen and had made some useful contacts.

Of course, no job. So, sadly I just had to move on. Perhaps it would be worth trying Sandy Grandison again, at the BBC? I got in touch, and he said he'd be pleased to see me. Next day I went to Broadcasting House to meet up with him in his office. He welcomed me warmly, particularly when I told him I'd taken his advice, gone abroad and managed to get a considerable amount of broadcasting experience. "Good heavens!" he said with a laugh: "Nobody has ever listened to my advice before!" He then looked thoughtful. "Would you be interested in television?" he went on. I assured him that I most certainly would be interested. "I happen to know," he said: "that Clive Rawes, head of presentation at BBC Television at the Centre, is looking for evening host announcers at the moment. Would you like me to get in touch?" I was not slow in giving an answer! He lifted the phone. He reached Clive Rawes, told him my story, and asked would he give me an audition, then down went the phone and up went my spirits! Sandy said that Clive Rawes would be interested to see me.

The very next day, I took myself to the Television Centre at White City and found Clive Rawes waiting for me. He was most welcoming and explained what he was looking for. He arranged an audition for me then and there. I was suddenly feeling pretty nervous. The result though, was exciting. Clive Rawes said he'd give me a fortnight's trial on the air to see how I got on. I was soon to meet some very famous personalities. Sylvia Peters who was then very much the 'darling' of television announcing, also Alex Mackintosh, who was equally well known and extremely good at the job. This entailed filling in, and promoting future programmes, when the current ones fell short leaving some empty spaces. This was all done in vision in those days with the men wearing black ties. Very smart 'hosts' indeed! I was happy to hear that Clive Rawes liked what I did and asked me to continue for another fortnight.

It was at this time that the 'powers that be', decided to lower the tone of the evening hosts, so from then on, we had to give up the tradition of dinner jackets and wear suits and ties. We all thought this a bad move, of course.

Michael Aspel was just starting as a 'host' having come up from Wales. Michael was great fun and had the wonderful gift of saying just the right thing at the right time, usually most amusingly. We got on really well. After an afternoon shift one day, he took over from me for the evening shift, and as he tied his bow tie for the last time in the mirror of our dressing room, he said: "I don't know, the BBC is going to the dogs!"

By this time, I had taken on an Agent, Peter Crawford, to help me get work. One day, he suddenly rang me saying: "ITV is starting a station in Southampton. They're looking for announcers and news readers, I think you ought to go for an audition."

I was not sure I wanted to go to Southampton. I had heard that Clive was going to offer me a three-month contract. Also, with my fiancée, Iona Gilbert, we had taken a 90-year long lease on a flat in Elvaston Place, near Gloucester Road. It was a really nice flat, and we were looking forward to living there when we had married. We had been engaged for nearly three years but even so, we weren't looking to 'tie the knot' until the following year. We reckoned I'd better have regular money coming in before we finally married. I thought about it for a while, then told Peter I'd be happy to have an audition for 'Southern Television' as it came to be called. So I took myself to the studio in Foley Street, to be met by Roy Rich, the Controller of Southern.

Once again, I was asked to read some scripts at the microphone sitting at a table. Meanwhile I was watched by Roy, standing in the 'gallery' behind the glass dividing us. The studio manager asked me to 'go ahead'. I remember reading some stories about the Isle of Wight, including one about the Duke of Edinburgh sailing in Cowes Week.

The door from the 'gallery' suddenly flew open and Roy Rich came over to me leaning with outstretched arms and his knuckles on the table. "When can you leave 'Auntie BBC'?" he asked. I was taken completely by surprise. Frankly, I'd gone into the audition feeling thoroughly relaxed knowing I had been offered a contract by the BBC. I said, I didn't really know when I could leave the Corporation but said I would find out. "Well," said Roy, "the job's yours if you can be freed." In just a few brief seconds, the outlook on my life had changed dramatically.

I now had to go back to Clive Rawes to explain the situation. He was most understanding, saying: "Of course, you must go."

I gave my new situation a lot of thought, because in many ways my life would be turned upside down. But Peter Crawford was insistent. "It's a great opportunity," he said: "and will give a marvellous chance to learn your craft." I felt this was important advice and explained to Iona what had happened and what

I had decided to take on. She was most supportive, which was a great help to me. But with my move to Southampton we had to release the flat.

At that time there was only one BBC Television channel (it was well before BBC 2 came on the scene) and ITV was in its infancy. Southern Television was being built on the site of an old cinema near Northam Bridge across the River Itchen.

We were now well into June, and I organised a hotel, The St Regulus in Archers Road, where I was to stay until Iona and I were married. My father drove me down to Southampton to deliver me to 'Southern', and I remember negotiating wooden boards across wet concrete in a half-built studio on my way to make my number with Roy Rich, and then Dick Clark, Head of News. Dick had come down from the Daily Telegraph and had as his assistant, Terry Johnston who'd been a reporter on the Brighton Evening Argus. They told me that through July, they would be carrying out 'dummy runs' and I would very much be needed for these. It all sounded pretty exciting.

There were two others joining the News and Presentation Department at the time, Julian Pettifer, who I think had been at University, and Meryl O'Keeffe (remember the name from South Africa?) Meryl had come from news reading and announcing for the BBC's General Overseas Service which I had worked for before departing for Canada. (Most sadly, Meryl died recently. A great loss.)

I spent my first night at the St Regulus, wondering how things were going to turn out. After breakfast the next morning I set off by bus for Southern to be there for 8 o'clock. I remember the conductress explaining to me in detail, much of which I already knew, how the new television station would be built on the site, she said: "Of the old Avenue Cinema. Fancy a new television station for Southampton. I hope they give us good programmes!"

For one of the first dummy runs, Dick Clark had organised an interview with one of the New Forest Agisters. They were the keepers of the Forest and looked after the many ponies which roamed wild amongst the trees and out on the heather covered moorland. I remember Julian Pettifer valiantly trying to keep the handheld microphone in the right place as the Agister's horse got bored and kept shifting around!

Another day, I remember, again in the New Forest, Dick asked me to go and interview the well-known author, Dennis Wheatley, as I remember it, about a new thriller he'd written. He gave me a really good interview and Dick Clark was happy. On another occasion, we were sent to Brighton to interview fishermen on the beach. I don't remember the details, but there was some sort of dispute going on and no fish were being landed. I don't know that we got to the bottom of that story.

There were all sorts of other 'dummy runs', which took us on errands around the south, learning amongst much else how to create features for the news programmes. It was a hot summer and all through that July we three were kept busy.

The Start of Southern Television

Meantime, the day when 'Southern Television' was to go on the air was fast approaching and Julian, Meryl and myself were also having to practise our presentation skills at the microphone crammed into a tiny studio rather like a cupboard! The man who would be putting us on the air, pushing all the necessary buttons on the mixing desk, was none other than Peter Pritchett-Brown whom I'd met at Radio Luxembourg! He was extremely good at his job, running telecine and putting the programmes on the air, at the right time, and in the right order. He seemed to be expert at doing several things at once. Not my expertise, I have to say!

So, in due time, the day came for Southern to go 'live', 30th August, 1958. I was in the studio reading the first news bulletin, ably assisted by Ian Trethowan, who'd come down specially as a well-known personality from ITN. He was, with Robin Day, Reginald Bosenquet and Christopher Chataway (the famous runner), one of the team of newsreaders who were the 'faces' of ITN at the time.

Meryl was on board the Queen Mary in the docks, and I remember the 'line' going down at the critical moment. I don't recall where Julian was reporting from. All went well for me, and I found Ian Trethowan a delightful colleague. He went on, years later, to become the Director General of the BBC and was awarded a Knighthood. In later years at the BBC, I got to know him quite well.

For now though, it was definitely Southern that had to be marketed and I remember, with Julian and Meryl being escorted round various venues for publicity. But, of course, we weren't yet known so people eyed us in a rather puzzled fashion, wondering what it was all about. I remember being driven with a Rotary member to a fete we were asked to open. Unhappily, the poor man hit another car going up the hill from the studios beyond Northam Bridge. His car was rather bent at the front, but no one was hurt, thank goodness, but we were late for the opening we had to perform! I recall having to draw tickets for the

Derby helping to raise funds for a Rotary charity. When we came to the draw, I pulled out my own ticket and had to put it back! Julian, I think did better.

Our main jobs were for the Presentation Department, introducing programmes from the tiny studio next to the control room where Peter Pritchett-Brown sorted the pictures on the several screens ahead of him. He would often tell us what was needed from us next, and usually to carefully measured seconds.

I was also the main newsreader and had to keep abreast of the various stories fed to me by the sub-editors. There were two in particular whom I got to know well, Ron Onions who I believe had come from the Brighton Evening Argus, and Gordon Randall who had been a reporter for one of the Bristol papers. They were both excellent and worked fast. Dick Clark would be in the 'gallery' taking charge of the news bulletins. There was a well-known pop song much broadcast at the time: "Standing on the corner, watching all the girls go by!" and one evening Dick suggested I should sing the song as an introduction to a relevant story. I'm afraid I didn't think that appropriate to a serious news bulletin and didn't oblige. I think Dick considered me a spoilsport! But I was most uncomfortable with the idea. The year 1958 had a pretty hot summer and on one afternoon, Julian came in wearing shorts. Dick suggested he should begin by saying: "Now here's the news in briefs!!" I don't remember Julian obliging with that either. In any case, it would have meant nothing to the viewer as all they saw on the screen was our top half!

And so it went on day by day. Indeed, before long, a new magazine programme was started entitled *Day by Day*.

My Wedding Day

During this time, Iona and I were discussing marriage, and strangely enough, I was beginning to get 'cold feet' about it. I swung from thinking it would be wonderful, to periods of serious doubt. For me, and Iona too, it was going to be a big step. But then I suppose it is for most young couples. However, as time went on, arrangements were made and a date was fixed – Saturday, April 4th, 1959. In those days, you could get tax advantages by marrying before April 5th. We took advantage of that! I'd been at Southern for less than a year.

Pam Williams, accompanied by the famous artist, Adrian Hill, with a top-hatted Jack in the background, on the way to the church for our wedding.

But the day came and we both felt ready for it. We decided to marry at Fernhurst Church which was nearest to Bedham. We had about 150 guests and my mother decorated the church and marquee beautifully with spring flowers.

The day itself was a great gift to us, the sun shone and the daffodils and primroses were in full bloom. Clive was my 'Best Man' and we enjoyed an evening out together in a pub the night before.

The Reverend Jones from Petworth officiated, and I remember his first words 'isn't it a beautiful day!' And so it was. We'd arranged a service with music and singing by the Linden Singers. Clive had written a special anthem for us which the Linden Singers performed beautifully. Iona had two bridesmaids, her sister, Sylvan and a long-standing friend, always known as 'Binnie'; her mother and Iona's mother, Pauline Gilbert, had been to school together.

We had a grand party after the wedding and it was wonderful to be amongst so many family and friends. The champagne flowed and everyone thoroughly enjoyed themselves. We had a photographer, of course who did a great job, and Ted Channel, cameraman from Southern, shot some excellent footage on 16mm film, which we kept afterwards in a tin can. I didn't want old kippers and fruit tins to go clanking on strings behind the car afterwards, so we arranged for a taxi, which took us to our own car parked some way down the road.

A happy greeting from David Richards, by now a senior partner in a smart City accountancy firm – a long way from National Service ordinary seaman!

Julian Pettifer and Meryl O'Keeffe toasting us in Champagne.

Iona with her two bridesmaids. Sister Sylvan on Iona's left, and friend Binnie Black on her right.

With my best man, my brother Clive.

Cutting the cake which was made by Iona's sister, Sylvan.

Leaving the church for the reception.

The happy couple after the ceremony.

Iona with her father, the fine sculptor Donald Gilbert.

All the family; my father and mother with Binnie, Clive and myself to the right of Iona;
Gilberts to the left, including Sylvan, her mother Pauline, father Donald and brother
Robert, then still at Christ's Hospital.

Off to the honeymoon!

We spent a couple of days stay at a family-run private hotel at Singleton, near Chichester, and just managed to see the film of our wedding on Southern TV, but on an ancient television set. The pictures were faded on the screen and quite difficult to see! We spent our two days walking on the Downs and enjoying good food at the hotel.

On the third day we drove to London in a tiny black Austin which my father lent us for the time being. We did not make a good start. As we went through some traffic lights by a large hotel near Hyde Park Corner, I looked in my mirror to see the driver behind us talking to his passenger and looking sideways. At that moment a taxi pulled out from the hotel making the car ahead of us stop suddenly. I just managed to pull up in time, but the fellow behind us, not keeping his eye on the road, rammed us from behind sending us jerking forward into the car ahead. Poor Iona was thrown forward, hitting her leg beneath the dashboard and tearing her beautiful stockings! She was very shocked. We managed to get the car to a garage and were told that there was £200 worth of damage, a lot of money in those days, and no seat belts.

I rang my father who was really good about it, and only too glad we hadn't been hurt, except for Iona's leg, of course. We were booked to go to Positano in Italy for our honeymoon by train the next day, and my father told us not to worry, he'd sort out everything. There was the insurance to deal with too.

Positano.

We made it to Positano, via Rome and booked into a very pleasant hotel where we were most amused to see a tall young fellow coming down the stairs with a hot water bottle. He had clearly just married too, and his young wife obviously wanted to be extra warm!

I'd quickly caught the sun a bit (I'd literally never taken my shirt off to get brown) and walked into the sea for a bathe. Soon after I came out, I began to suffer from heat bumps all over my back which tickled like mad and I found a cold bath was the only way to get relief. I now learnt just how wonderful Iona was at massage (which she later did professionally) and smoothed her hands over me with olive oil. It was marvellously soothing.

Iona's mother, Pauline, had a friend who lived in a large house at Beaulieu in the New Forest. She had a tiny flat at one end of the house which she rented out. Pauline organised for us to stay there. It was a pleasant property with a large garden and a private jetty jutting out into the Beaulieu River. We were really happy there, and our son, Tim, was born in March 1960, at a hospital in Lyndhurst only a mile or two away. Oddly enough, John Boorman, one of Southern's film editors, and his first wife, Chrystal, lived in a flat there. Iona and Chrystal used to walk their prams together. More of John later.

While we were at Beaulieu, I ordered my first boat. It was built in a small boatyard there and cost me, as far as I remember, £150. It was a GP14, a favourite class in those days and a lively craft. Not having done any sailing then, I was careful to take the boat out for a first trial on the Beaulieu River on a quiet day! If the wind had got up, I wouldn't have known how the heck to cope. I still had a lot to learn about sailing!

My first boat.

We left Beaulieu for a flat in large country house near Botley. Then later decided to buy a property with a mortgage. After an extensive search, we discovered a nice house in Titchfield and it became our home for some six years.

Little Crofton Cottage, Titchfield.

My First Car

It was from Beaulieu, then, in the little grey Austin I'd bought, that I left for Southern by 7.30 every morning to be at the studios for 8 o'clock and to another busy day of interviewing, presentation, and news reading.

Interviewing, for Southern Television News, the scientist in charge of life raft research and practise in Portland Harbour, before volunteer sailors jumped in to the sea then clambered on to a nearby experimental life raft. I must say, I thought those sailors were pretty brave!

One of the things I found an awful chore was reading through all the local papers looking for likely stories. Terry Johnston put me on to this. I am not a particularly good reader, certainly not scanning at speed. But Terry was insistent, and I found myself late in the evening trawling through piles of old newspapers, just in case I found something we could follow up.

One story we did follow up (not from my reading of the local papers) was news that the famous racing driver, Mike Hawthorn, would be going in for an important race. Mike owned a garage at Farnham and I was sent with a cameraman to interview him. I found him really charming and he gave me an excellent spontaneous interview. He told me a lot about his life and I felt I'd got to know him pretty well. Dick and Terry were warm in their thanks to me for a good job done.

Another job, sometime later, didn't turn out quite so happily however.

I had been sent to make a feature out of the story about the famous pop singer, Terry Dene, joining up for his National Service. I had to go to the King's Royal Rifles Regiment barracks at Winchester where Terry was joining. I went with a cameraman and soundman to watch Terry, amongst other things, queuing up for his first Army meal. The press, of course, had been in full cry. Terry attracted a huge amount of publicity. We were getting on fine, until I noticed that most of the Press had disappeared.

I had a word with our cameraman who said he had heard that Mike Hawthorn had just been killed on the Guildford bypass. This was a huge shock to me, having interviewed, and got to know him so well, only a short time before.

I was clearly not your 'dyed-in-the-wool' journalist. I just could not distance myself from this dreadful happening, so simply continued capturing the Terry Dene story. When I got back to the studios, however, still feeling stunned by Mike Hawthorn's sudden death, I was met by an apoplectic Dick Clark and an equally furious Terry Johnston, who both went for me in no uncertain terms. It would not be an exaggeration to say they both 'roasted' me! They, as tough journalists, just couldn't understand why I hadn't raced off with the rest of the pack to pick up details of the story and relate it to the camera. "You were there, on the spot," they said. "But for you, we could have been first with the story, a coup for Southern Television News!" I was not popular! I think it took them both quite some time to forgive me. If they ever did!

Interviewing Harry Secombe

But I sometimes came back with some really good stuff, like my interview with Harry Secombe on the Downs above Brighton. He was in a show at the Theatre Royal in Brighton, where I'd performed myself with Cyril Fletcher. It was obviously an opportunity for us to have such a huge 'star' in our news.

Harry was the greatest fun to be with. I made contact with him and he drove me up onto the Downs in his magnificent Rolls. On the way, a dear old man with a stick was crossing the road in front of us. Harry had to slow down, and in his distinctive Secombe voice said: "Ho, ho, we'll get him on the way back!"

The point of the story with Harry was the fact that he was a keen photographer and happened to get much of his equipment from a camera shop in Southampton. He was going on 'safari' to Africa, to 'shoot' elephants and lions, but with his exceedingly expensive cameras!

As I've said, it was a hot summer and the long grasses on the Devil's Dyke above Brighton, were parched and dry, just like in Africa.

So, I got Harry to duck behind a slope and come up to the camera festooned with light metres and his own cameras, parting the grasses as he appeared from behind the brow. He really entered into the whole exercise wonderfully. As he reached our camera, he said, of course: "hallo folks!" with a thumbs-up sign. I collapsed in hopeless mirth and it took me some moments to recover and begin my interview. It was well-nigh impossible to be serious. But the final result was memorable and Dick and Terry were smiling at last!

There was one particular film editor at Southern, who helped me hugely with the skills of interviewing. He was John Boorman who sat up with me into the small hours giving me all manner of hints and taking me through the 'tricks of the trade'. As mentioned earlier he had also been our neighbour in Lyndhurst, a couple of miles from our home in Beaulieu.

I remember him telling me how to manage 'repeat questions', which were vital in giving the editor ways of shortening an interview (they seemed always to be too long!) into useable length. I will never forget John's help, and never feel I have thanked him properly. He has since become an extremely famous film director with some brilliant movies to his name. He had come down to Southern from ITN with another editor, Brian Lewis. They were both expert and were a great credit to the station.

I also made, with Brian Lewis, a most enjoyable documentary about a young, I think Hungarian, violinist who'd come to our area. She played Tchaikovsky's violin concerto superbly and whenever I hear it now, I'm taken back to making that film with Brian Lewis. Extraordinary how certain things stay in the mind.

After about two years, at Southern, the unions started to make things difficult. So boring! At the start, we'd had great freedom just to get on with the job. But in my heart of hearts, I had always wanted to be with the BBC. All of a sudden, a chance presented itself.

I was on the ferry going to the Isle of Wight to cover a story and on board I met a BBC man, Peter Maggs, going across to cover the same story. He told me, confidentially, that the Corporation were about to start an evening news magazine programme based in Southampton. Equally confidentially, I told him I would be most interested to hear more.

The centre of operations for the BBC regionally was in Bristol and the plan, apparently, was to start area programmes based, for the south in Southampton and for the West Region in Plymouth. It wasn't long before I heard that I was being considered as the 'anchor' for the programme in Southampton. This was extremely exciting. I was, of course, already very well known in the south because of my two years plus, with Southern Television, so I suppose was a bit of a 'catch' for the BBC. But it turned out to be a traumatic exercise for me, because the whole thing began to go horribly wrong. Because of this, I think it has been the closest episode in my whole life that could have landed me in a state of deep depression. Would the BBC have me after all?

It took many long and patient months to find out…

Chapter 11

BBC South

To begin with, all seemed to be going well. I was getting encouraging noises from Bristol about the possibility of my joining the new team at Southampton. So I was quite excited! And in due course, a contract arrived from Pat Beech, Assistant Head of West Regional Programmes in Bristol, inviting me to sign and return it if I agreed with its terms.

I looked at it carefully and had doubts about how it would impact on my tax situation. My concern, as a freelance, was to remain on 'Schedule D' for tax, which gave me a lot of flexibility in terms of what could be claimed for business expenses. The BBC contract I had now received, seemed to me to bind me pretty tightly to the Corporation which, for me, allowed little flexibility. I thought I could easily end up as 'Established Staff' – not at all what I had in mind. I decided I should at least obtain legal advice, so went to see my solicitor.

This was my first mistake!

After a while, my solicitor came back with a number of suggested amendments (there was a lot of red pencil!) which would help to secure my best tax position. In my ignorance, I thought the changes looked pretty reasonable and returned the contract to Pat Beech containing all the amendments.

It was just before Easter and I wanted to move things on as quickly as possible. But strangely enough, as I dropped my letter and the contract into the red letterbox (I remember it well, the box was across the road from Southern TV) I had a dreadful intuition that I was being too hasty and doing the wrong thing. I began to wish, deeply, that I'd taken notice of my intuition. The trouble was, though, that it hadn't come to me until the moment my letter, and the amended contract, had dropped into the letterbox!

Pat Beech was going to be away for Easter, so I had an agonising wait for a reply from him. Indeed, the day after I'd posted the contract, I sent a note to his secretary asking her not to open it. But I'd acted too late!

So now, with increasing dread, I had made my second mistake!

It was some time before I at last heard back from Pat Beech, but I had a ghastly shock when I opened his letter and read its contents. I actually felt physically sick; and I'm not exaggerating. Clearly Pat, and his colleagues, were not happy to have a standard BBC contract, which had been the norm for years, greatly questioned. In his letter, he said they were, therefore, advertising for and auditioning a number of candidates and, he said, had found 'at least one journalist who is a promising newscaster'.

The letter continued: *We shall be seeing some thirty senior journalists from all over Britain for new jobs at Southampton… Please, therefore, take this letter as the formal withdrawal of the offer we were discussing.*

I had completely 'blown it'.

There was, though, a 'tiny grain of hope' in his last sentence: 'If we want to proceed we will make a fresh approach'. I thought I should turn to Peter Maggs, the BBC representative in Southampton. He was understanding, but his advice was to 'just wait, have patience. All is not necessarily lost.'

Even so, I became terribly glum and more or less silent

Looking back today, I wonder how I'd allowed myself to get so low. Iona shared with my mother how she had felt. A long time later, Iona told me what she'd said to my mother: "I just don't know what's happened to Martin. He seems to have completely gone away." I'm afraid it was all too true.

At Southern, I put a good face on it and did my best to remain cheerful and keep up the professionalism of the job. But my original passion for Southern Television was eluding me. I remember having to drag my way until late in the evening through the growing pile of local papers. It seemed I seldom spotted a story that would be a good one for us to follow up.

Another thing was beginning to make itself felt. My marriage. I now began to question again. Had I in fact made a ghastly mistake? So concerned was I, indeed, that I went to see my dearest friend Jane in London to share how I was feeling and perhaps to get some idea of direction. She wasn't able to help, of course, but it was good to have someone to talk to. I told her how I was sometimes being really beastly to Iona. Yet Iona was being so patient.

It was certainly a low period in my life. The weeks and months went on. I was still hanging on to the possibility that the BBC might come back to me, while all this time I was feeling frustrated and utterly helpless.

Then, quite suddenly, came a breakthrough. Peter Marshall had now been engaged as the Editor of the new 'South at Six', as it was to be called. Peter was an obvious candidate as he had his own news agency in Portsmouth and was already doing some reporting for the BBC (still based for the South and West in Bristol). He was also very keen and knowledgeable about sport and had done much sports reporting for Bristol.

I'm pretty sure that Peter, together with Peter Maggs, was keen to draw me away from Southern, particularly as I was already a very well known 'face' in the South. As I said earlier, I would be quite a 'catch' as presenter for the new BBC programme in Southampton.

Actually, as I heard later, they took the view that I had been badly advised and that the unfortunate situation that had transpired had not been my fault. Once this thinking took root it changed everything. Now a new draft contract came my way with some very helpful amendments written in by Pat Beech. He began: "Here at last is the draft, in a somewhat rough state. We have had rather a job knocking it into shape as it's a bit unusual…"

There were several helpful explanatory comments which ended with the words: "Clause 13. You will see that I've inserted in ink the word 'worked' here, to make it quite clear that we don't pay if you don't work! I hope this meets all the points we have discussed." This was such a welcome approach and made me realise that the BBC senior staff in Bristol were doing all they possibly could to be helpful and bring things to a conclusion. I signed the final contract when it came and the job was mine. Three hearty cheers!!

I had to tell Roy Rich, of course, and he was generous enough to say they were really sorry I would be leaving, and that I would be much missed.

So it was in late October 1960, that I went to join Peter at the BBC studios, which were being set up in the once smart and pricey hotel, South Western House, in Canute Road, near the Docks in Southampton. There was a railway terminus alongside the hotel where trains had once pulled up carrying passengers destined for one of the 'Queens' leaving for New York the following day. It was at the South Western Hotel that passengers stayed the night. During our evening programme, a train used to grind past, hooting as it went before crossing the main road into the docks. Ron Onions suggested that the driver was telling his wife to "put the kettle on"!

The hotel had also been a large holding place for the troops awaiting 'D-Day', and the stone back stairs were worn down by the passing of hundreds of Army nailed boots!

A Spell in Bristol

Thus, at the end of October 1960, Peter drove me to Bristol to meet Pat Beech and other senior staff including Stuart Wyton, the Regional News Editor, and Laurie Mason, the Assistant News Editor. I remember we drove in sheeting rain, and it often seemed afterwards that it rained whenever I went to Bristol!

I now felt completely different, and it was fantastic at last to have resolved the difficulties which had originally put such a dead stop to negotiations. I chatted away happily to Peter on the way and that was the start of a relationship which lasts to this day. I have to say that I found Peter a wonderful person to work with and for and I had great respect for him as a journalist. He was a good 'decision maker' too and often had to be! I pay tribute to him. I was lucky to be in his team.

As it happened, although I'd now been taken on by the BBC, the Southampton studio centre was still being built and equipped and wasn't quite ready for me, so I was asked by Desmond Hawkins, Head of West Region Programmes, if I could please assist with news reading and presentation duties in Bristol for a month or so. Of course, I was happy to agree to this, and was able to go back home to Iona and the family at weekends. In Bristol I joined Tom Salmon, then famous in the West Country, Ken Duck, a well-known reporter and newsman, together with other sundry characters! But I was glad to be amongst a great team of colleagues.

I actually spent a lot of time early in the evenings at the large studio recording machines, learning how to splice and cut audio tape, using a razor blade and white sticky tape in those days! I greatly enjoyed my time 'helping out' in Bristol and began to feel I was really appreciated.

A particularly memorable character there was Keith Hamilton-Price who looked after assignments to freelancers, and we all looked to him for interesting jobs that meant more fees! On one occasion, he sent me to report on a local football match. This was definitely not my field (if you'll forgive the pun!). But first, I had to go and find out how to use Self-Operated Outside Broadcast Equipment, known for short as a 'SOOBE'. I somehow managed to work my way around the thing and phoned in a reasonably respectable report. Though it would have been done much better by Peter Marshall! But he was now well and truly ensconced in Southampton.

Another of Keith's assignments was for Peter Maggs who had to report from a helicopter on a story that happened at sea. As he worked his way down the ladder from the helicopter to a waiting boat, Peter lost his grip on his portable recording machine (known as an 'Emmy', short I think, for EMI). It was a green box, quite heavy to manage on a ladder, swinging below the helicopter, and it splashed weightily into the sea!

Keith had a huge map of the Region beside him on the wall of his office, and there was a pin marking the spot with a little red flag where Peter had lost his 'Emmy' and Keith had written: *The Maggs Memorial Buoy!* As may be imagined, this created much amusement all round.

Another personality I remember dashing into Keith's office to check some piece of news, was Tony Crabb, who was later sent to Southampton where he wrote the news bulletins for me to read in the 'South at Six' programme.

I am able to write up a lot of the above, particularly my negotiations with Pat Beech, because I happened to keep a file of the BBC letters and contracts of the time. I even found a bill from the hotel I stayed at while I was in Bristol – Brights Hotel, in Clifton. A night's 'b and b' stay, apparently, was twenty-six shillings and sixpence! What would that be today?

One particular meeting at the BBC studios in Whiteladies Road, Bristol, was a call to the office of Frank Gillard (who had become famous for his many eyewitness broadcast despatches from D-Day and the battlefront during the War). He was now Controller of the West Region and he invited me for coffee one morning to welcome me to the BBC and especially to Bristol and Southampton. I was greatly touched by this, as I'd had no such 'welcome' from the Chairman of Southern TV. But to be fair, I think he was based in London.

So my month in Bristol ended at last and off I went to Southampton to be in on the work-up and preparations for the day when 'South at Six' went on the air – the 5th of January, 1961. I can still hear in my head the music that introduced the programme and the fact that another piece of music used to introduce an item was *Portsmouth Point*, by William Walton.

Two of my former colleagues had come over with me from Southern, Gordon Randall and Ron Onions. They had both been sub editors at Southern and I knew them well and recommended them to Peter Marshall. He took me up on the recommendation, particularly Gordon Randall as they had been to school together in Wiltshire and had both gone on to be reporters for local papers in Trowbridge. And as I remember it, Ron had come to Southern from the Brighton Evening Argus. They both joined the newsroom team at South Western House and did a sterling job writing my introductions for me as the presenter of the new BBC programme. Ron somehow always managed to introduce a 'today' element in the words I had to say. He would scour the papers to find something topical.

On the Air with 'South at Six'

I was soon going out with one of our cameramen to work up and film news features. Also, pretty often, I would have to include a live interview in the studio, so I was kept busy! I was now entering a fascinating period which would mean many deadlines as we prepared for a new programme every evening. There was always a great deal to do and we often had little time for any rehearsal.

Reading the News for an edition of South Today.

For me, one of the deadlines I often had to meet came after being out with a cameraman creating a news feature. This was the matter of getting the film back to the studio to give enough time for developing the film (going through the 'soup' as we called it), and for the film editor, Nevil Grist, to edit the story. Many times, this was all done in a considerable rush and while out in the field, I had to keep a careful eye on my watch! In those early days, there was no motorway for a speedy return to the studio, and many of the roads and lanes in the area took a good deal of navigating.

After a few months, the timing of the national BBC News which we followed changed and we could no longer call the programme 'South at Six'. In many ways, we were sad about that. It became 'South Today', and so it has remained and is still going strong today, after over half a century!

Over the years at Southampton, I carried out numerous assignments of various kinds. I cannot by any means remember all the stories I had to follow, but there are some which remain clearly in my memory. Perhaps one of the most memorable and which led to several other stories was standing in Oaklands Park, at Chichester, interviewing Leslie Evershed-Martin about his vision for a new theatre 'in the round'. He had seen such a theatre in Canada, the brain child of the actor, Tyrone Guthrie. Evershed-Martin had to raise the money, of course, but I remember him telling me that he'd negotiated with the Council for a 'peppercorn rent' of one penny a year! In due course, much was to develop from that embryonic beginning.

One major problem for me, and it was a problem, was learning the words of the introductions Ron Onions had written for me. To help to get them into my memory I used to walk up and down speaking them aloud to myself, much to the amusement of everyone! I liked to speak as much as possible direct to camera. We didn't have 'teleprompter' or 'autocue' in those days – the BBC didn't have the money! However, I managed pretty well until one evening I got things wrong and messed up a cue pretty badly.

Of course, this was noticed and Peter Maggs called me into his office next morning for a cup of coffee and a chat. He was clearly worried for my health and family matters. He asked me: "Are you all right? Everything all right at home?" It must have seemed as if I'd had a bad lapse of concentration introducing the programme the night before and I heard later that there'd been a bit of discussion about my suitability for the job. Was I 'losing' it? This put a lot of pressure on me at the time and I took even more care to 'learn my words'. I don't think other presenters were quite so concerned about facing the camera and worked more from the script which meant they had their heads down much of the time.

Richard Dimbleby to the Rescue

However, rescue was at hand. For some reason, I really don't remember why (I think I was on some sort of training course), I had to spend a spell at the BBC studios at Lime Grove in London. It was from here that 'Panorama' went on the air, introduced by Richard Dimbleby. I thought it would be good to make my number with Richard. It so happened he had lived with his family in a fine old farmhouse at Lynchmere, near Haslemere, where we Muncasters had a cottage, with a fantastic view, for 43 years.

Although the Dimblebys had left Lynchmere just before we went there in 1969, Richard, would have watched 'South Today' on occasion anyway and therefore, knew of me. We had a nice chat and I remember asking him if David would be taking over from him. He replied, "I'm not dead yet!"

I didn't know, of course, that he was suffering from cancer. Then I asked him how on earth he remembered all the words of his, often long, introductions to items in the programme. "Oh," he said, "I don't use 'Teleprompters'; they often break down anyway and then you're stuffed. I write up my notes on a piece of A4 and Sellotape them to the cameras." My God, I thought, that's my answer!!

From then on, I introduced 'South Today' using just that technique. My confidence zoomed! I didn't have to learn the words any more. I was a bit short-sighted, so wrote up my notes with a large black felt pen, with various hieroglyphics to save space: 't' was 'the'; 'tt' was 'that'; 'nd' was and; and so on. I also found that the very act of writing down Ron's sentences helped me to know them, so I could give them special inflection and emphasis while always looking straight into the camera, thus making a much better relationship with the audience.

I honestly believe this had something to do with the fact that we were capturing the audience. I heard that Southern were doing some marketing with photographs to find out how many people knew my face and our reporters against those of Southern. I gathered that by a significant margin, more people instantly knew the 'South Today' faces than the personalities on the Southern TV screens. This news went down well with our Southampton team and was also 'transmitted' to the bosses in Bristol!

Another 'face' well recognised was that of Johnny Johnston. He came up to us from Bournemouth and we had the benefit of his wide journalistic contacts in the area. He really was an excellent performer covering a whole range of stories.

It was now felt that we should have a woman reporter in the team and we were later very pleased to have Pat Draper with us. I seem to remember she lived locally and was good when the programme needed the feminine touch.

Also, for a time, Valerie Pitts joined us. She was a most attractive blonde and looked really great on the screen. Her married name was Sargent until her divorce. Then, before very long, 'Val', as we knew her, was 'captured' by the world-famous conductor, Georg Solti. They were married, so Valerie became Lady Solti and went on to do amazing work promoting classical music in many ways, together with her husband's performances on a large number of recordings.

Now, with all the exciting developments, my whole confidence, indeed my life, was dramatically changed and I also gave huge thanks to that consummate professional, Richard Dimbleby, for his invaluable advice. I was enjoying my job so much more. My energy was increased, too. It was a great sadness to me, indeed to the whole broadcasting world and beyond, when Richard Dimbleby died (22nd of December, 1965).

In his book *Here Is the News*, Richard Baker wrote a wonderful tribute to that 'other' Richard. I would like to quote from it here:

"People who make a living with microphones or before cameras understood the sheer hard work that lay behind Richard's unshakable ease, confidence and 'rightness' on the air.

"And then, towards the end, we added to all this the dimension of personal courage and endurance brought about by knowledge of his long illness.

"How poignant, in retrospect, became his commentary on Sir Winston Churchill's funeral. His emotion was apparent as he recited those last valedictory lines *At Bladon.* He must have known he was soon to follow 'the old warrior' to his rest.

"A number of people telephoned or wrote to me, expressing their feelings about Richard Dimbleby. 'His voice,' wrote one lady, 'spoke for us all.'

"Now that voice is silent, and those who knew him personally acutely miss the cheerful, kind, intelligent man to whom it belonged."

I could not possibly have put it better…

There were other occasions which I well remember, particular stories which I was sent to cover. One I recall brought about a huge laugh. Peter Marshall had asked me to go down to the Docks to interview the colonel of the regiment of soldiers returning from the problems of Cyprus. I had washed my hair the night before and in the wind it flew everywhere. I got out my comb and looking into the camera lens as a mirror started to smooth my locks. You may imagine the powerful volume of 'wolf whistles' that rose up from hundreds of 'squaddies' lining the decks and which echoed around the Docks as I battled to tame my hair! Pity the camera wasn't running at that moment to record my embarrassment.

Much earlier, soon after we'd gone on the air in January, I remember struggling up the hill on the road out of Winchester towards Petersfield in heavy snow. At the top, I caught up with a local councillor who was doing his best to organise clearance of this main road, the A272, with the help of a tractor cutting into deep snowdrifts, with the driver working to lift the piles of snow onto the side of the road. I was there to ask why the Council had not foreseen the problem ahead of time, especially after a very clear 'warning' weather forecast. The Council had clearly been badly caught out. Anyway, I remember getting a pretty good interview for the programme, when, of course, snow was a major item in our news coverage at the time.

Over the weeks and months, I interviewed and talked to a number of well-known personalities. One was Lord Mountbatten, in his home, Broadlands, at Romsey. I had, on purpose, put on my naval tie. I knew he'd notice and he said: "Glad to see you're wearing the right tie!" I can't remember the reason for interviewing him, but it may have been to do with the Game Fair which was held at Broadlands one year; and for my first time, I had been recommended by Mountbatten's River Bailiff, Bernard Aldrich, to provide the live commentary on the fishing rod-casting demonstrations. I knew Bernard from my fishing interests and I was commissioned to do this job for the next twelve years. It was a most interesting assignment as the Game Fair visited many of Britain's great country houses, including Harewood House, Blenheim, Longleat and Chatsworth in Derbyshire. It was at Chatsworth that my cousin, Mark Balfour, ran the fishing demonstrations. I'll never forget that one.

Other well-known personalities I interviewed included Evelyn Laye, the famous actress. She gave me an excellent interview about her life and acting roles from the King's Theatre at Southsea where she was appearing. Again, I forget the reason for the story.

The Prime Minister, Sir Alec Douglas-Home (formerly Lord Home) came to the studio for an interview by, I think, our staff reporter, Johnny Johnston, and as he left he turned and looked at me as if to say: "Ah, now I know who you are!" His brother William Douglas-Home, the playwright (who, as I'm sure you will remember, wrote *The Reluctant Debutante* in which I acted with Arthur Treacher in Canada), lived at East Meon in Hampshire and I'm sure after he'd visited various important venues in the south, the PM would have gone on to stay there with his brother.

I also met Harry Secombe again because of his connection with the photography shop in Southampton. This time, it was because he was starting a line of pennies on the pavement outside the shop and publicising the fact that he was building this line of pennies for charity. Being Harry, of course, he attracted a lot of attention.

Interviewing Laurence Olivier

But perhaps the most memorable story for me was the 'topping out' ceremony at the new Chichester Festival Theatre, which was now under construction. Sir Laurence Olivier had been brought in as the Artistic Director for the theatre and he had given the speech to celebrate the 'topping out' ceremony, standing on the platform which was to be the uppermost part of the roof structure. Pints of beer to celebrate were the order of the day. Unfortunately, I was too late for the ceremony itself but was determined to interview Olivier about his connection with this exciting new venture.

I hung around and waited for ages, knowing that Olivier didn't like being interviewed. He was, actually, quite shy. Hoping to be successful in getting an interview, I had organised for our cameraman, Eric Stewart, to set up his camera and gear on the 'topping out' platform. Most of the rest of the press had left and I began wondering if I would, after all, get an interview with Olivier when suddenly, his PA, Virginia Fairweather, came up to me and said confidentially: "If you're ready now, I think he'll do it." Sure enough, I spoke to the great man, and he agreed to go up to the platform where he'd made his speech, although it meant climbing up various ladders to reach the top. All was well until, as I pulled myself up onto the platform, followed by Olivier, I saw Eric Stewart at the other end, shouldering his last item of equipment, his weighty and unwieldy tripod as he lowered himself to the ground. Mercifully, I was able to stop him and explain that we were definitely going to conduct the interview.

It took some time for Eric to gather everything together again from his car and climb back with sundry vital accessories to set up his camera. The sound in this case was also being recorded, via a long cable which went down to one of our engineers, Peter Salkeld, in the BBC recording car to make sure the interview was properly recorded for sound radio. We had also arranged for Peter to be there to capture the interview for Radio Newsreel, in London.

Olivier was awfully good about the delay, while I made conversation with him about very little of import. I even got talking about what it was like to drive a Jaguar, and what was the traffic like from Brighton?

Eventually, when all was set up, we began the interview, and I wanted to know all about his connection with the theatre, what sort of plays he would be wanting to put on and any big acting names he would be likely to engage to perform in them. It all went extremely well in the end. I got the film back to the studio for developing just in time and the interview went out that evening. I was congratulated for achieving such an important and high profile item for the programme. It was also safely broadcast on 'Radio Newsreel' in London.

There was the odd time, however, when my efforts were not so well accepted. A weekly radio programme produced at Broadcasting House, in London, was called *The Eye Witness* and freelances were often used to cover stories for it. I was asked one day to go to interview a lady of a 'certain vintage' who'd had Queen Mary's most beautiful doll's house bequeathed to her. It was thought this would be good material for an interview. The lady in question lived at West Knoyle, a small village in Dorset, which meant a long drive in my car to reach the village and find the right house. I found the lady (unfortunately all this time later, her name eludes me) and she related the story of the doll's house to me and how she'd come to acquire it.

I was really pleased with my efforts. It had all gone well. But unhappily, Peter Marshall wasn't so pleased. When I got back to the studio he called me in to explain that for us in Southampton, *The Eye Witness* was not a priority. As it happened, they had needed to contact me for another story that was developing in an area close to where I was recording my interview. In those days, of course, there were no such things as mobile phones and it was up to reporters to find a phone and stay in contact with the studio. I had not done this. In any case, my experience was that when I did at last find a phone box, it had either been vandalised, or there was a great queue waiting outside. Usually, of course, I was in a hurry!

Peter explained to me in his kind, but firm way, that I needed 'to get my priorities right'. Southampton and 'South Today' were our first concerns, and it was important I remembered that!

There was one other time when I got it badly wrong. There'd been a murder at Yateley, near Farnham, in Surrey, and I was sent to glean whatever facts I could. It was early night when I arrived, having presented 'South Today', and I found the place bristling with Police. There was little information to be had, so I just waited into the night hoping the Police would at least make some sort of statement. The night went on; still nothing. I began to feel I could be of no use and, getting pretty weary, decided to drive home. This was NOT well received and proved to me that I was not the fully versed type of seasoned reporter who would have stayed on without sleep till there were some facts to be gleaned. Next morning, I was called early, I think by Peter Marshall, explaining the team's displeasure at my abandoning the story. My good friend Ron Allison (I shared an office with him at the time), was sent to pick up what he could now that things had 'gone cold'. I don't remember the outcome except for feeling badly ticked off! Ron Allison, by the way, moved on from Southampton to London and became the BBC's Royal Correspondent for a number of years, and a bit later the Queen's Press Secretary.

I was now getting very busy with what had become 'South Today', walking up and down the corridor, as I said earlier, talking to myself, to learn my words, until that memorable day I went to see Richard Dimbleby!

John Arlott Joins the Team

Interesting additions were being made to the programme. Somebody, probably Peter with his love of cricket, had the idea to bring John Arlott into 'South Today'. He lived locally, at what had been an old pub at Alresford, and he was, of course, a hugely well-known and loved personality. His cricket commentaries were legendary and he had a wonderfully poetic way of describing any scene. He was now asked to create a series, which became known as 'John Arlott's A to Z'. He visited interesting villages and towns starting out with names that began with the letter A including Alresford naturally. He then went on to places in the South beginning with the letter B and so on. It was a brilliant idea and, of course, had a very long life! John's descriptions of his chosen places were poetry itself. Another addition was the farmer, David Butler, from Romsey, who simply talked about farming matters with a gentle Hampshire drawl. He always came up with interesting facts and stories and had a knack of filling his given space in the programme, just a few minutes, and finishing to the second.

Another masterstroke, I think it was Peter Marshall's idea, was the addition of Don Osmond to 'South Today'. Don was a brilliant cartoonist who was a regular contributor to the 'Southern Evening Echo'. He was, therefore, already known to our viewers in the Southampton area. He was given a slot at the end of each programme and chatted his way through his live drawing of the cartoon of the day, always something pertaining to that day's news. All the viewers ever saw was Don's right hand, and this soon became his 'secret' that fascinated our audience. Many times, I was asked: "What's Don Osmond really like?" I was always careful, of course, not to give anything away. Don made his slot most amusing too as he always 'took the mickey' out of me. One of his favourite lines was 'Martin Muncaster is so tall he hits his head on the lights!' It was all tremendous fun, and people often told me they watched 'South Today' just to catch Don Osmond's jokes! In fact, we were working in a small studio which had once been a bedroom in the old hotel, and the ceiling was quite low!

I was lucky enough to know the 'complete' Oz!

One of the continuing duties for me, though not every day, was to be in the studio by 6 am to check up and bring up to date, the news scripts that had been left for me overnight and to read the VHF bulletins (Very High Frequency radio was in its infancy) at 7 and 8 am.

To be in the studio by 6am, I had to leave the house at 5.30. It meant an easy drive into Southampton, as there were few cars and lorries that early in the morning and most of the traffic lights were green!

I was always careful to be in the studio some minutes before 6 o'clock. I've always hated being late. One morning, however, somebody must have rung me well before 6 o'clock and I was challenged by Stuart Wyton, no less, in Bristol, asking me why I wasn't in the studio at 6am? I assured him I had been in the studio by 6 o'clock, but I always felt he didn't quite believe me.

I said we were having fun, and so we were, even though we often had to broadcast serious news, as for the instance, stories about how the thalidomide drug had affected families in our area. The effects of the thalidomide drug were dreadful and most distressing and interviewing on the subject could be quite delicate.

On the other hand, there were lighter moments. One of our secretaries, dark haired Penny, was a truly gorgeous girl who always looked stunning. She had a good figure, too. I remember one day we had a story about the beaches in the south, and how in the hot summer they were packed with young girls in bikinis. We created a sandy beach in the studio and, I'm sure it was Ron's idea, to get Penny to be an enticing model lounging in her bikini on our homemade beach! I said we had some fun!

Another trick that caused amusement was the way Tony Crabb would pretend to bowl a cricket ball to me, as I walked up and down the passage learning my words. A silly story, but I still have the picture in my mind of Tony swinging his arm and pretending to let loose a ball in my direction. It didn't do much for my words memorising, of course… but we had a good laugh as I pretended to hit the well-aimed ball with a straight left arm and a suitably timed 'click'.

Next, Stanley Holloway

There were other more serious happenings which caused me, in particular, quite a bit of grief. One of these involved an interview with Stanley Holloway, a big star. He was terrific in *My Fair Lady* as the dustman and singing his song *Get Me to the Church on Time!* He had been playing in the show in New York and returned to Southampton on the Queen Mary. I got Eric Stewart to set up his camera a few yards from the gangway so I could catch Stanley as he came off the ship. He was met by a huge and very shiny chauffeur-driven Rolls. I managed to catch him and ask if he would step out of the Rolls for an interview near our camera. He was delightful and happy to oblige. Actors are usually pleased for the chance to get a bit of 'profile'.

So it all happened perfectly and, of course, he gave me a wonderful, amusing and completely spontaneous interview. I was very happy and walked to Eric to check that all was well. It wasn't! He whispered to me that he'd forgotten to turn on the sound, so my microphone had been 'dead'. This was embarrassing to say the least. I had to explain to Stanley that we'd had some 'technical trouble' and would he mind doing it all again? I could see he was not happy, but fortunately, as a great 'pro', he agreed to re-record the interview. I have to say it wasn't quite as good or as spontaneous as the first 'take', but it was good enough and it appeared in the programme that evening. Others, of course, didn't know the difference between the two interviews as I did!

Another occasion was memorable to me for a very different reason. There was an old chap who cleared the streets in Southampton with a horse and cart. He'd shovel the rubbish into his cart and his friendly horse would just move on to the next pile. The Council in their wisdom had decided to do away with the horse and cart and replace it with an electric truck. Ron thought an interview with the old man would make a nice 'tail piece' for the programme. So I was despatched with Mike Smith, a most experienced and professional cameraman who'd done many jobs for 'South Today', to go to find the old chap with his horse and cart. Mike was quiet and unflappable in any circumstance, and though short in stature, was a tower of strength behind his camera.

After a bit of a search, we caught up with the horse and cart and I invited the old boy to give us an interview. He was fed up with the Council, he said, he'd done the job loyally for many years and was not at all happy about having to abandon his horse which had been his faithful companion for a long time. In his Hampshire dialect he was a wonderful personality to talk to and gave me a memorable interview, ending his diatribe against the Council with the words: "You can talk to a 'orse. You can't talk to an electric truck!" In a way, it was a 'classic', and Ron Onions loved it. Those closing words became a running joke and Ron would greet me with the words: "You can talk to a 'orse!"

Ron was also keen to have a go at news reading and asked me to give him some coaching. After offering him a few tips, I suggested that he might try reading the lunchtime VHF news. This was a 5-minute run-down of a brief selection of news stories of the day. It always ended with about 30 seconds-worth of a weather forecast. Ron did well, until he realised he'd only got 4 seconds left for the forecast. So he finished by saying quickly: "Now the weather – snow on high ground!" He just made it before the 'pips', and that, too, became a running joke! "Snow on high ground!"

There was much, much more, of course, but these are just some of the stories that stay with me. There was one more I think worth mentioning. It occurred to me that it would be an idea on Saturday nights to do a radio programme of music surrounding some of the main stories we'd covered in 'South Today' during the week, giving them a wry and rather different approach. Don Osmond suggested I should call it 'The Late Mr Muncaster', and I even still have the beginnings of a 'pilot' script.

However, this idea got nowhere. Pat Beech thought it had 'no merit'. I didn't agree, but that was the end of it.

It was shortly to become the end of my time with 'South Today', and my move to radio in London. My departure from the programme seemed to begin something of an exodus. Quite soon, several of my colleagues also opted to move on.

A while before, Ron Allison had gone to London to become the BBC's Royal Reporter, then later, as I've said, he went to Buckingham Palace as the Queen's Press Secretary. Ron Onions went on, via the 'Tonight Programme', to the post of the BBC's 'Man in New York'. Gordon Randall, via periods in Bristol & Plymouth, moved on to become News Editor at the BBC's Pebble Mill Studios in Birmingham (as he told me himself much later, 'A very big job indeed!'). Tony Crabb went up to Broadcasting House, then the Television Centre to be instrumental in starting up 'BBC Breakfast Television'.

But apart from Ron Allison, I believe it was Peter Marshall who went first, and he got a job through the most extraordinary set of circumstances, which almost precisely reflected my own.

You'll remember my story of getting into the BBC by failing a Board; well, I discovered later that Peter, like me, had also failed a BBC Board! But the very next day, he was approached by a member of that same appointments Board, John Hartley, the BBC's Home News Editor who had been most impressed by Peter's appearance at the Board the day before, by his journalistic and TV experience and the fact that he'd set up and run a news agency in Portsmouth. Hartley invited Peter to meet him as soon as possible for a confidential meeting. This was arranged for a 'half-way' point, a hotel in Basingstoke. Peter drove to the meeting with no idea of the surprise that lay ahead – just as I had not the slightest idea what was going to come out of the phone call I'd answered from Aiden MacDermot at the BBC.

Over lunch, John Hartley explained to Peter that he'd be moving from BBC TV News, to become Managing Editor of a new television news agency, part-owned by the BBC, which in due time became known as Visnews. John Hartley was in the process of recruiting three Assistant Editors and told Peter he'd like to offer him one of these positions, at a salary even higher than he'd failed to secure at the Appointments Board! As Peter told me later, he was in the mood to give 'a positive response'.

So, that was how the two of us obtained BBC positions by failing our Boards. A quite amazing coincidence.

London Calling

I had certainly become the best-known 'face' in the South of England. Sometimes it got a bit embarrassing, as people would whisper in the streets – 'Isn't that Martin Muncaster?' I even stopped going shopping with Iona. Goodness knows how many stories I covered and how many people I interviewed while I was with 'South Today', but quite suddenly I was put up for a radio job in London. Frank Phillips, one of the famous voices and newsreaders of the War years, was retiring and the Presentation Department at Broadcasting House were looking around for a replacement. It was felt that I had the right kind of voice for the post and I was urged by Peter Maggs, in particular, to accept. It led to much heart searching on my part. I was enjoying 'South Today' hugely and was also doing many stories for radio as well, such as the 'Today' programme in London, Radio Newsreel, and 'Today in the South and West', which went out from Bristol, presented mainly by the excellent broadcaster, Derek Jones. During my years with South Today, being a 'face', I was invited by a whole host of organisations and charities to present or perform readings at all manner of celebratory occasions. Unfortunately, during this period, what with the programme as well, time for home and family was very much at a premium! Although Iona was often invited to be with me at these events. She was a wonderful hostess and for some years was the local Haslemere organiser for the World Wildlife Fund.

In the end I accepted the London offer, at less salary it has to be said, but I took the view that I was going 'national' rather than just remaining regional. So after nearly five years with 'South Today' and two and a half with Southern, I said 'goodbye' to my broadcasting from Southampton. I was also saying 'goodbye' to the many assignments I did, usually for an extra 5-guineas, brought to me by our excellent and much-loved researcher, Anne Bristow. She was marvellous to us freelances and kept a lookout for stories which would not only be fun to do, but which brought us some extra income.

So my choice to leave Southampton was a hard one. But I made it, and the next few years of my professional life must be related in later chapters... But, once again I became embroiled in negotiations about BBC contracts. I could see it was likely to be a long haul! It would be some time before conclusion. I have the memory of having to start at a salary some way less than the seven guineas (i.e. £7.7.0d) a day I was receiving for my 'South Today' contributions. There was a distinct difference of remuneration for 'sound' work than that for television. The daily fee I received for 'South Today', translated to £1,764 for 48 weeks of appearance. Though by the time I left, I remember, my daily fee had been raised to eight guineas (guineas again being the traditional BBC salary nomination at that time!)

In the end, after much discussion to and fro, I managed to get the figure for my annual contributions to BBC Sound Radio raised to £1,950 for two years. But this meant I was exclusively tied to the Corporation. There was no flexibility for doing outside work, so no fees from narration, for instance, for commercial documentaries. Whereas in Southampton, as I've mentioned, there were constant opportunities for fees for various radio programmes. I was also able to agree fees for opening fetes and crowning carnival queens! All good fun and I was actually able to save money in those days. But sadly, as I've said, my many other activities kept me away a lot of the time from the family. That was not popular, but there was still some time to go before I would finally leave 'South Today'.

A day or two before leaving Southampton.

Chapter 12

Going National

After my years with 'South Today', I finally moved to London at the end of October 1964. On my first morning I was asked to join the 'post mortem', as it was called, which the Assistant Editor, Presentation, Andrew Timothy, went through with one or two members of staff. Each morning, the announcers' logs, recording things that had gone wrong with the programmes over the preceding 24 hours of broadcasting, were reviewed. The few things that had gone wrong, were taken very seriously.

On this, my first morning, Andrew introduced me, saying: "This is Martin Muncaster. He's up from the Regions." This was another occasion when I had a sinking feeling in my stomach. Had I got it wrong again? I knew I would certainly miss television having had so much TV experience, but I was sure I just wasn't the material for a national newsroom or top flight programmes, such as 'Tonight' and 'Panorama', and wouldn't have put in for a job in this kind of output, even if there'd been one on offer. So, I simply had to sit with my feelings and get on with the job I was now contracted to do.

I have to say I felt very much the 'new boy', not knowing anything in this completely fresh environment. My mind went back to the time in the GOS studio when I was left alone without knowing where all the phones came from or went to, or indeed how to operate the equipment with which I found myself surrounded. On that occasion, you may remember, I was rescued by the return of Jack de Manio who I was 'trailing'!

I was shortly to find myself in very much the same situation. I spent some time in the Announcers' Green Room looking through various papers, duty schedules and logs, when suddenly a tall, stately looking man came into the room and introduced himself: "Hello, I'm Lidell

, who are you?" The voice, of course, was very well known to me. Indeed, one of the most famous radio voices in Britain and also, as I discovered, a 'stickler' for perfection.

It turned out that Alvar had been deputed to look after me, as I was to 'trail' him during his evening shift. This included the 6 o'clock and 10 o'clock news on the 'Home Service', as it was then, and finally the 11 o'clock bulletin, a full quarter of an hour's read of news for the Third Programme. This, I thought, was quite an honour. I could not have learnt the system from anyone better.

Also included in Alvar's shift was reading the 8 o'clock bulletin for the Light Programme. I don't think Alvar regarded this as quite of the import as the widely respected news bulletins on the Home Service. He then said to me, after he'd read the 6 o'clock: "How about you reading the Light Programme news?" I think he thought I might as well 'go in at the deep end'! So, I spent time in the Newsroom preparing myself for this great event as the scripts gradually came my way from the sub editors. I now realised just how close to the actual moment the writers in the Newsroom released some of the scripts. In particular, this concerned the main story, which was usually long and often had last minute additions. So, there was only a minute or two for me to get to the studio to sit down at the microphone.

The studio manager in the 'gallery' needed a few seconds to check that all the equipment was working properly, and this time I had Alvar sitting alongside to check my performance! Alvar, of course, was the complete professional, very precise and much admired, though I was to learn that he was a bit lacking in the subtle English sense of humour.

Pip, pip, pip, pip, pip – and I began: "This is the BBC Light Programme, here's the news read by..." And I was so nervous, I couldn't say my name properly. I forget what came out, but I do remember the 'Muncaster' bit turned into some sort of mumble, certainly not a clear and precise enunciation of my own name! I think I managed the rest of the bulletin OK, but it wasn't a good beginning.

The Death of Churchill

I now found myself rostered into the announcing schedules, which meant regular shifts news reading, introducing programmes from the Presentation Studio and also reading the weather forecasts.

After a few months I happened to be on duty the day Churchill died, in January 1965. This was a particularly responsible time to be the newsreader. I had the job of reading the tributes that came in from around the world. They included our own Prime Minister, of course, Harold Macmillan, and those of President de Gaulle and President Eisenhower. I had to work through all the bulletins that evening and the following morning.

I include in the Appendix, a copy of a letter of thanks for a particular bulletin from my then boss, Rooney Pelletier.

The following year, my dear brother, Clive, organised and conducted a concert in the Long Library at Blenheim as a tribute to Churchill. With permission and copies of the originals from the BBC, I read again the very bulletins I had read on the Home Service the day Churchill died. Today, we performed to a packed audience, which was a tribute in itself.

Another Churchill Memorial Concert, Clive conducting, me reading.

Presenting 'Today'

After about a year working in Presentation, I had an exciting invitation from Stephen Bonarjee, the Current Affairs Programme Editor. Jack de Manio was already famous as the presenter of the morning 'Today' programme, especially because of the way he often got the time wrong! Jack would introduce the programme for two months, then have a month off, to relieve him of the very early mornings. He was a great character, but sometimes after a 'boozy' evening the night before, he more or less had to be revived to get him into a fit enough state to do his introductions. He certainly had some marvellous producers who loyally stood by him!

189

As you may surmise, Jack could be a bit unpredictable. One story I heard about him concerned a morning when he had to interview in the studio a frightfully important and high-powered government minister. Jack greeted him with the words: "Who are you and why are you here?"

I joined a small group of two or three of us who did stand-in duty for Jack. One was Brian Johnston, the cricket commentator, another was the journalist, John Timpson. This was a great opportunity for me and most enjoyable. I was delighted to receive a copy of a Current Affairs minute, sent round by Stephen Bonarjee, recording: "Thanks to Martin Muncaster for his helpful and encouraging attachment to us as 'Today Presenter'. He proved to be a fully competent 'stand-in' for Jack de Manio and was most co-operative in his relations with all the producers with whom he came in contact."

I found these words most warming, especially as Stephen Bonarjee went on to say: "We should like to give Mr Muncaster a further run in 'Today' during de Manio's absences." All very exciting for me.

There was one particular character I well remember from my stints on 'Today', a young fellow called Richard Stilgoe. He sang some most amusing songs, which I thought very clever. He composed them with a sideways glance at something in the day's news. There was no piano in the studio, so he had to record his songs the night before to be introduced in the programme by Jack de Manio or indeed myself!

Unfortunately, at one of the morning post mortems, which happened after each day's programme, the Editor suddenly said: "I don't really think this Stilgoe chap is adding much to the programme." I didn't agree, as I thought Richard was most amusing and did most certainly add much to the programme's output. The others in the meeting seemed to acquiesce. But I was so new and young that I didn't have the 'bottle' to disagree. So, after that, we no longer had the benefit of my good friend Richard's lively humour. He has, of course, since become extremely famous as a consummate musician, composer and writer of humorous songs. One such, for the Today programme, as he reminded me, was about whether we should join the Common Market, which would be pretty appropriate even today!

Indeed, some years ago he received a knighthood in recognition of his tireless charitable work for which he has received millions of pounds. For years, among much else, he performed a one-man show with Peter Skellern. That was laughs all the way!

During my time with the 'Today' programme, I conducted many interviews, of course, on all manner of subjects. But I particularly remember one story I was sent off to cover. It was about the special publication of Charles Dickens' *A Christmas Carol*.

The man behind this was Dickens' great grandson, Cedric Dickens, and to celebrate he arranged a typical Dickens luncheon at 'The George & Vulture', the famous old pub in the City which, I believe, Dickens used to frequent. We all enjoyed delicious fare and Cedric Dickens explained how he'd decided to bring out this unique and beautifully published edition of the tale of the old miser, Scrooge, who was turned from his 'humbug' view of Christmas to something quite different. *I will honour Christmas in my heart and try to keep it all the year*, the quote which Cedric wrote in the book when he signed it for me. I use it to this day when invited to read from it for charity performances around Christmas.

Actually, everything on Radio 4 normally went along nicely to plan. However, on the odd occasion things could go horribly awry! I remember them well...

One awful mishap happened to me when I was to be the reader of the regular news bulletins one morning from 7 o'clock. It was Sunday and there'd been a change of studio. I had carefully checked, but when I arrived at the studio from the Newsroom, horrors! No table, no chair, no microphone. The studio was empty. I was certain I was in the right place, but was now, with only a couple of minutes to go, in a state of some panic with heart racing. I rushed over to a friendly producer editing a tape for Radio Newsreel in another studio across the corridor, to ask him if he knew what might have happened. He thought for a moment, then said: "Oh, that one is used for drama. There's a commentary cubicle as part of the studio on the next floor."

I tore up the stairs and just made it before the 'pips'. No time to gather my breath, so with heavy breathing, I launched into the introduction and just finished it before I came to a complete halt. Luckily, there was a taped insert after a few seconds of my 'intro', and at last I was able to breathe more easily, gather my wits and complete the bulletin.

Afterwards, my colleague, the excellent Douglas Smith, announcing in the Presentation Studio in the depths of BH, rang to ask me if I was all right. I told him the story and he replied: "My God, I thought you were having a heart attack!" That wasn't such a good day.

Another time, a similar panic happened one morning to Roy Williamson, a newsreader of immense experience. He had been scheduled to read the papers 'slot' prepared by a sub-editor in the Newsroom. One of the announcers always had to read the 5-minute precis within the 'Today' programme at 7 o'clock and again at 8 o'clock.

On this day, it was Roy's turn. He spent a bit of relaxed time in the Announcers' Green Room chatting with a colleague before wandering up to the 'Today' studio on the next floor. He picked up his script and set off, judging the number of minutes needed to reach the studio in good time, then sit down at the microphone.

However, on this day, he'd been just a bit too relaxed. As he reached the 'Today' studio, looking at his script, he suddenly realised with horror that he'd picked up the wrong one. He'd grabbed the 'papers' script prepared for his colleague reading the papers slot on the Light Programme.

Immediate panic! Roy tore back to the Green Room to fetch the right script and ran for all he was worth to get back upstairs to the 'Today' studio in time for his stint at the microphone. But by now, like me, he was completely breathless and quite unable to say a word. John Timpson, who was standing in for Jack de Manio introducing 'Today' that morning, quickly realised Roy's dilemma and took over, allowing Roy time to recover.

On another occasion when I was reading a bulletin, we were running out of time and the editor, standing over me with a hovering pen, started crossing out the lines from the bottom up to shorten the script. I just made it before the next programme began!

Such happenings were all too memorable!

Thinking back to earlier times, I was told a story about Frank Phillips, another highly regarded newsreader, who could be quite naughty. As I've said earlier, we always had to give a voice check for the studio manager in the 'gallery' before reading a bulletin. It was necessary to make sure all the systems were working OK. With a young, brand new female manager, Frank would open his mouth and mime his opening words: "This is the BBC Home Service…" This caused the poor young novice who, having heard no sound from Frank, frantically to check round all the faders and buttons to find out what had happened. Nothing was wrong, of course, and with seconds to go, Frank would finally own up!

There were other stories I think worth relating.

I remember I was scheduled to introduce a series called 'Family Fare', on the Light Programme between 7 and 9 o'clock in the morning. Kenneth Horne used to follow me with 'Housewives' Choice'.

One day, before my shift, I met him in the canteen when he was grabbing some breakfast. I had an idea for introducing him at 9 o'clock. So that day, I began with a poem: "A man, Kenneth Horne, chatting up housewives each morn'…" I wish I could remember the rest, but I do remember that Kenneth Horne followed on from me with: "A man called Muncaster, an established broadcaster…" I really wish I could remember the rest of his poem as well!

And another story, this time about a particular editor in the Newsroom, I remember, who came from Belfast. I can't recall his name, so for the sake of the story, we will call him Denny. He was a delightful fellow, but he always hung on to the bulletin as it developed, keeping it firmly under his elbow as he made final last-moment corrections and additions. I used to find it quite a job to extract the vital pages from him for me to read on air. It often meant a speedy march down the corridor, trying to keep calm, to get to the microphone in time!

One morning, he joined me in the studio as we were expecting a live insert from our reporter in Ireland, W. D. Flackes. Unhappily, at the critical moment, the line went down and we lost contact with Flackes. After a few seconds, Denny breathed heavily into my ear in his thick Irish brogue: "Apologise, Mart'n, and go on to the next story!"

The microphone was 'live', of course, and Denny's instruction certainly added 'colour' to my bulletin that morning!

He also reminded me once that Derry was a County in Northern Ireland and we should, therefore, pronounce Londonderry as two words: London Derry. He said that it was nearly always pronounced, incorrectly, as one word.

Another memorable mishap was occasioned by a broadcast on, I think, the old Light Programme. One morning, the announcer on duty was passed an urgent late story about one of the Beatles (Ringo Starr, I think), who'd had an operation which involved surgically removing his tonsils. This became a classic, because the hapless announcer misread the script and declared with commendable solemnity, that Ringo Starr had had his toenails successfully removed. Not surprisingly, this caused much hilarity in the media and howls of glee from his Corporation colleagues! To 'Aunty' BBC, however, it was quite an embarrassment.

As well as periods on 'Today', there were several different and most enjoyable invitations which came my way for television appearances. There were spells on *Songs of Praise* and *Come Dancing*. I worked on that famous 'dancing' series first with Peter West, then with Terry Wogan. It's since been reinvented as 'Strictly', of course.

On Radio 4, I read many 'Morning Stories', and a wonderful series about a dreadful submarine Chief Stoker's Mate called 'Bootle'. These were written by a brilliant author, by name, Richard Compton-Hall. We'd met in Titchfield and he'd told me about the stories he'd written for radio in Bristol but wasn't happy reading them himself. I offered to read them for him and he jumped at it. Richard was a very special friend and I had a look at some of his early scripts. Having been a submarine Commander himself, he told me his stories were based on "painfully remembered fact!"

I thought they were marvellous, and extremely funny. One of the scripts he sent me included this dreadful character 'Bootle'. I suggested that all Richard's subsequent stories should be titled with words that began with 'B', and so they became, 'Bootle and the Battleship', 'Bootle the Beautiful', 'Bootle at Buckingham Palace', etc., etc.

I put the idea of a series of readings to the Drama Producer, John Cardy. First of all, he told me, he thought, "Who's this announcer fellow putting up ideas?" But he changed his tune completely once I gave him a pilot recording of what the stories would sound like with my giving Bootle a deep-throated Cockney accent. John went on to produce two series to fill the quarter of an hour morning slot which was aired when Parliament was not sitting.

Congratulations – Then a Dilemma

I even received a most congratulatory letter from the then Director General, Sir Ian Trethowan. I wish I'd kept the letter. Subsequently, Radio Solent broadcast no less than 26 'Bootle' stories, exactly right for the local radio station that covered Portsmouth.

In 1975, somebody in the BBC's admin department came to realise that I had been on contract in the Presentation Department for longer than was normally allowed. The rule was, apparently, that the BBC only took on contract announcers for seven years. I had been an announcer and newsreader for ten years. Jim Black, who was then Presentation Editor, called me in one day to explain this to me. "You have a choice," he said. "You can either go freelance or join the established staff."

This was a complete surprise. I'd no idea of the seven-year rule. I knew I didn't want to become 'established staff', losing my important schedule D tax status, yet the idea of being suddenly freelance and without a job was a bit frightening, to say the least! I went home to Iona with this unwelcome news, but she was most supportive. "Of course, you must go freelance," she said. "You always have been that anyway. I know we'll be all right."

I felt better but wasn't really convinced and spent a good deal of time in a state of worry. How could I start as a freelance? Basically, for the second time in my life, I'd been given the sack!!

Jim Black had said: "Come back to me when you've made a decision." The 'safe' way would have been to tell him I'd agree to join the staff. But that still wasn't what I really wanted to do. Then came a surprise option from Jim Black who said he'd give me six months to prepare to go freelance – a huge relief. It would allow me to make contacts with all the producers I knew. Of course, after 10 years at BH, I had got to know the producers of quite a number of the programmes. I talked to several and they were all supportive. What's more they gave me to understand that if I put up ideas they'd be happy to consider them. I soon began to feel very much happier and thanked Jim B for offering me the six-month's grace.

And so I started a new life as a freelance, much supported by Iona. My first plan was to make all the contacts with programme producers that I could. It turned out to be quite a list: 'Today', of course, the producers of 'Morning Story', the religious programmes 'Sunday Half Hour' and 'For all Seasons'. I even spoke to 'Woman's Hour' and offered reading most amusing stories of France and French life written by Richard Compton-Hall. They were hilarious!

One of the duties the announcers were asked to perform (and I was still very much thought of as part of Presentation) were spells at Alexandra Palace reading the bulletins within the 'Town and Around' evening television news magazine (the London version of 'South Today'). This I much enjoyed as it gave me appearances on television again. The programme was introduced by Michael Aspel and it was a great pleasure to have a chance to work with him again. He had by now, of course, become one of the regular readers of the National Television News.

Michael was quite a one for the ladies and he was much taken by a most attractive girl who worked the teleprompter for him. In those days, if I remember rightly, the operator would sit with the handheld device by the monitor, moving up the words of the script in time with the speed of the reader. I suppose Michael was able to see his 'girl' out of the corner of his eye as he read the words moving up the screen. I'm sure I'm right in saying that Michael actually married his teleprompter operator! Michael was a brilliant and most amusing performer, but he had a sad family life in many ways.

For myself, with an 'eye' for television, I even asked the editor of 'Town and Around' – A.C. Fletcher – if there would ever be a need for another presenter. I'd heard tell that there might be, but not so. I still have a letter from him giving the sad news: "So far as 'Town and Around' is concerned, the answer is 'no'. Despite the whispers, the programme will have its full complement of presenters for a long time ahead."

But it was an enjoyable time while it lasted. I was beginning to get work with various other programmes, often when I put up ideas for stories. Iona was a great help with this. Being a good reader, she used to riffle through the local papers looking for possible stories for me to offer producers. She often found really useful ones.

From a contact with a friend, I suddenly had an approach from the COI (the Central Office of Information) to provide radio pieces for a continuing series called 'Punchlines' – short, pithy pieces which gave a 'sideways' look at the news. Iona often found me good contributions for 'Punchlines'. Although the fees were modest, over time they gave me useful income.

Another continuing series of programmes I much enjoyed for Radio 4 was entitled 'An Evening in Old Vienna'. The producer was Peter Chiswell, a South

African who I was sure I'd met when he was a young radio producer in Cape Town – a colleague of Meryl O'Keeffe's. Peter was extremely good at choosing melodic music by Viennese composers, like Franz Lehar and the Strauss family.

Of course, I had to give my introductions using quite a lot of German and one letter I received asked me which part of Germany I came from? So I must have got the pronunciations about right – one in the eye for the Chairman of the Board I'd failed when I said to him I thought I could 'get away' with German pronunciation! If you've read the story in an earlier chapter, you will remember his reply!

For the long-standing 'Countryside' programmes introduced by Wynford Vaughan Thomas, I researched and recorded many features including an historic mail coach journey carrying mails from Bristol to London, which I refer to later. Wynford Vaughan Thomas was another BBC correspondent who famously sent memorable despatches from the battlefront after the Normandy invasions in World War II.

While working on the 'Countryside' programmes, I also met Bob Danvers Walker, the famous Pathé News voice. Another series with which I was much involved was the 'Waterlines' programme, introduced by Cliff Michelmore. That sent me on all manner of stories connected with water, boats and yachting.

Time to Move House

My normal presentation duties meant driving over Portsdown Hill from Titchfield, to catch the train at Havant for Waterloo, then the tube to Oxford Circus and a walk to Broadcasting House. From door to door this meant, allowing time for parking, travelling for two hours plus, and a shift of, perhaps, 4-5 hours. I then had the long trek home!

After nearly four years of all this travel, it became all too clear that we should move to somewhere closer to London. This was a hard choice. We were very happy and well settled in Titchfield, the children were already in schools, and we had made some really good friends, several of them naval, as there were many naval families in an area so close to Portsmouth. We started looking around for a good country cottage with character. After many weeks of fruitless search, we almost gave up until my mother told us she had spotted in the paper the photo of a likely country cottage. "Just right for Iona," she said. Iona had been brought up in an ancient cottage in the woods at Bedham, near Petworth. Shortly after this an estate agent in Haslemere came up with the same property called 'Clouds Hill' at Lynchmere quite near to Haslemere. It was a double cottage in the old Sussex style of stone and brick with hanging tiles above the stone. It sounded very possible and Iona and I decided to view it. We arranged to look over it on a Saturday, on my way to B.H. for one of my overnight shifts.

Clouds Hill. The picture my mother saw in the local paper.

I had to leave plenty of time for my train as we set off for Lynchmere, which neither of us had ever heard of! Fortunately, it was a lovely sunny day. Many of the houses of the village were situated on a high hill. We shortly came alongside a fine country house of considerable size. Standing at the gate was a man who we thought could help us. I asked him if he could direct us to Clouds Hill. "Certainly," he said, "I can tell you precisely. Go down the hill ahead of you and at the bottom the road levels, then take the second drive on your left." We thanked him and passed on. (We had spoken to Geoffrey Oxley, who with his most attractive actress wife, Gillian, later became good friends).

We continued down the hill and reached the second drive, but discovered that a large rope was strung across the entrance. I got out to remove it and as I did so a large Humber car came racing at speed backwards down from the house. The driver jumped out and yelled at us: "What the hell are you doing?" It was Mr Leslie Perkins the owner of Clouds Hill. I explained that we had come to view the cottage, "Oh, I'm so sorry," he said, "I'm fed up with the Hunt which keeps crossing my land and making a frightful mess. Do go up to the house, my wife is waiting for you." It so happened we'd found just the home we were looking for.

Around this time, the early 70s, I was being given a number of weekend overnight duties. As I've said, these duties allowed me to get home in time for lunch on Sundays. I always got to BH early on Saturday afternoons to prepare for my shift, which included reading the various news bulletins, a short while in the Presentation Studio, to give my colleague there a supper break, the late night Third Programme news and Shipping Forecast at midnight. Then across to a Langham bedroom for some sleep. I didn't get much, as I had to get up at 5.00 am to give me time for some breakfast and to read the papers before getting ready to read the Shipping Forecast at 06.30 am. Being a bit of a sailor myself, I always regarded this duty as extremely important. It was there for fishermen and yachtsmen (and women) to give them information about the coming weather systems. I'm afraid this is not always read really well, and with appreciation these days. It needs a special understanding and approach to the way certain information is stressed. For instance, it's important to appreciate the difference between, say, the southeast and southwest. It's necessary for clear meaning to place the stresses in the right place! This would be just one very simple example. But there can be many traps for the unwary in reading the 'Shipping' as we called it.

Another thing that drives me mad is the incorrect stress given to 'the World Service'. Practically everyone, reporters and presenters, including many who should know better, give the stress to the word 'Service'. This is completely wrong. The stress should be on the word 'World'. 'This is the BBC World Service'. The BBC has many services of which the World Service is but one. We know the BBC has many 'Services'. What the listener needs to know, is which of the many is being talked about. I really feel like writing to complain to the D.G. (Director General), but I do wonder if it would make the slightest difference!

After my reading of the 9 o'clock news on Sunday mornings, I was able to get away in good time to catch the 9.50 train from Waterloo to Portsmouth. The fast train always stopped at Haslemere. One morning, however, it didn't get there!

Little did I know that fateful morning what terrifying drama was to befall that train as I climbed sleepily aboard at Waterloo…

Chapter 13

The Surbiton Crash and More

This was in fact one of three occasions when I might well have met a premature end. The first was the Khartoum aircraft lightning strike incident. Then came the second…

Being somewhat short of sleep, I always found myself nodding off after a few minutes on the train. Today I was certainly asleep by Surbiton. It was a lovely July morning, 4th of July 1971, and I was glad to be on my way home to be with the family for a couple of days. I was always given Monday off after a weekend shift.

But suddenly, I was jerked out of my dream state by a terrific explosion and the train started shuddering down the sleepers! At 80 miles an hour, we'd smashed into a ballast wagon which had jumped the tracks. It was one of a long trail of wagons which were now grinding to a halt, with the air thick with dust from the ballast which was flung off the wagon. All at once our train was also grinding to a halt, but with the front coach thrown onto its side and the second coach, in which I was sitting, shunted up on to the end of it. These were terrifying moments as the train tore over the sleepers, juddering its way to a standstill. As we continued to move along, still at some speed (and praying hard!) I placed my feet onto the opposite seat (empty, thank God) to keep my balance as I was thrown around. This undoubtedly saved me from injury. The poor fellow on the other side was jerked all over the place, completely unable to keep his balance. Hospital for him I guessed.

Once we were at a standstill, it was a while before I could gather my wits but realised that I was lucky to be alive! I opened the door by me to jump down onto the track. It was quite a jump as my coach had been thrown up onto the front of the train at a crazy, high angle. I then climbed up onto the end of the front coach lying on its side, wondering what I would find. Helped by a young fellow who joined me (I never really thanked him) we hauled up one of the doors and were amazed by just how heavy it was as we had had to open it upwards.

Once there, we saw an old-ish man who definitely looked the worse for wear, but remarkably wasn't badly hurt. The two of us then clawed our way through wreckage to reach the driver's cab expecting the worst. The driver couldn't possibly have survived such a devastating crash. We were wrong. When we reached him, he was very much alive and not hurt or injured, although somewhat bruised. He had in fact been saved by the fact that the ballast wagon had hit us on the left side. The driver's position was on the right and basically undamaged. A miracle. We pushed open the door above him and he climbed up to get clear. "Thank you, mate," was all he said as he hauled himself into the sunlight.

I got out myself and jumped back down onto the track, noticing small fires burning along the track beside the back carriages which were still standing. Pretty soon, the rescue services were on the scene with ambulances taking shocked passengers and anyone hurt to hospital.

My immediate thought was to ring the BBC newsroom. I found a phone at Surbiton station and it was not long before the TV camera teams arrived and I found myself being interviewed to tell the story, first by the BBC. This interview was followed by one for the ITV team and I had to tell the story all over again and then also to a Radio London reporter. That accident was quite some news for that day, firstly for the Radio 4 lunchtime news.

I remember that when I got back home by taxi, I was able to put Iona's mind at rest, but she had already heard the news. All I had to remind me of the incident was a pretty bad headache! I was glad to have my Monday off to recover from the shock. This had been considerable, but I was quite surprised by how soon I got over it. It was back to normality on Tuesday as I returned to my presentation and news-reading duties.

It was an odd feeling to be passing the crash site again on my way back to Waterloo.

Broadcasting in Colour!

One of the 'extras' I remember from my time back in Southampton was a day at the Royal South Hants Hospital where trials were being held for colour television. I believe it was thought that colour would be helpful to the medical profession and particularly to surgeons carrying out tricky operations. Cliff Michelmore was working as the 'presenter' for the trials and I remember we were both having to cope with the searing heat that came from an array of very bright lights. The early cameras apparently needed these 'hot' lights to provide good colour pictures.

This first experience of colour TV was very much a memory for me in the autumn of 1969 when I was invited to be the presenter of a special concert being given by the Bournemouth Symphony Orchestra to mark the beginning of BBC2. This was to be in colour of course, as BBC2 was broadcasting in colour. I remember being pretty nervous since this was another situation when I had to learn my introductory words. It was to be a major event and the build-up included a packed Friday evening audience in the Bournemouth Winter Gardens.

Standing on the stage, I gave my introductory welcome and description of the first item of the music. I can't recall much about the details of the concert, but I remember the conductor was Constantin Silvestri. He lifted his baton and it all began. I do well remember my feeling that I really could have done the job better. Anyway, it was good enough and we all waited to hear the result of the recording. We waited a long time… and in due course the director, Humphrey Burton, came on stage with a surprise and most unwelcome announcement. "Ladies and gentlemen," he began: "I'm very sorry to have to tell you that we don't have a recording. We had trouble with the recording machine with a hair in the gate, which means we have no pictures at all."

Groans from the audience and orchestra. "I'm afraid," Burton went on: "We will have to ask as many of you who can to come back tomorrow morning when we will have to record the concert again."

Much consternation all round! Would we indeed **have** an audience on a Saturday morning, plus the members of the orchestra and the conductor having to perform the whole thing again? As it happened, we had a Canadian friend who'd come to the concert – in a way to support me. He at least could return with me next day and in fact enough people were able to be there on the Saturday to provide a reasonable audience. For me the whole affair was a blessing. I felt much more relaxed the second time around and my words flowed much more easily. But it was quite difficult to bring the same enthusiasm to a much smaller audience and in a now pretty cold hall. I remember spouting towards a nearly empty balcony. The atmosphere wasn't at all the same as the night before.

However, my performance couldn't have been too bad as the producer, Robin Scott, sent me a very welcome note: "Please forgive me for the delay in writing to thank you for all your efforts in Bournemouth the other day, particularly staying on to redo it the following morning. Needless to say, we are sick to death with post mortems, but I think that the retaken programme should look and sound alright, if not as good as the actual thing. I hope they pay you a respectable staff fee!"

Quite some time before in the early summer of 1969, I had to get permission to appear on my friend Michael Aspel's 'Monday Show'. I was there to present some features for the programme, one I remember being a piece with a farmer in East Sussex who bred collie sheepdogs. He was an interesting character and got one of his dogs to work with sheep on a distant hill. He told me all about the various whistles he used to give the dog instructions. The producer of the programme was delighted with my contribution. It made a good 'telly', he said.

For my features for the 'Monday Show' I was paid the princely sum of 13 guineas (£13.30) but it was all good fun while it lasted!

Looking through my records, I was also interested to turn up an original script for 'Come Dancing' which I presented, as I said earlier, first with Peter West (Terry Wogan later took over from him). This was recorded at the Locarno Ballroom in Portsmouth. Barrie Edgar was the producer and I see we rehearsed with the dancers in the afternoon, had a final run through from 8 pm to 8:45 pm and the recording took place from 9:15 pm to 10 pm. The date was January 1971 and I see from my Locarno Ballroom script that one couple I introduced was a husband and wife team, Brian and Andrea Shrimpton, doing the Boston two-step. She worked for the Army and Brian was an aircraft technician. He was certainly proud of his wife's outfit that night; she was wearing 'a beautiful embroidered apple-green dress, decorated with a multitude of sequins and rhinestones'. This was typical of the sort of descriptions we presenters had to provide for our introductions to the dancers. I was particularly involved when the programme came to locations in the South, as I was recognised by the audiences from my years of television on 'South Today'.

So these were just some of my activities as I worked my way through the years of television and radio.

You'll also remember I said earlier that moving to radio would mean I'd not be able to enjoy the many different assignments and fees that had greatly added to my professional life in Southampton. I thought I'd be more strictly tied to my radio contract at BH. But in fact, as I've said, I was able to add certain 'outside activities', with permission, such as 'Come Dancing', 'The Monday Show', the Bournemouth Concert and the trials for colour television. These came under the terms of 'staff contributions' and extra fees were negotiated and agreed. Any fees that were not allowed came under the term SNF (Staff No Fee). But all the above were permitted BBC additions to my normal work; an important classification.

Looking through my files, I see there were certain other occasions, more commercial, when my requests for what were termed 'outside activities' went through a plethora of considerations. For example, my request to be allowed to 'narrate a film' actually led to much detailed discussion between the Chief of Presentation (Sound) and the Senior Establishment Assistant (Sound), as to whether permission could be given in the first instance for me to 'record a commentary for a documentary geographical film on Britain' for the British Travel Association.

Later, I was asked to narrate an instructional film on 'synthetic ropes' being made by the ICI Film Unit. I rather imagined that somewhere in the system it had become known that I was a sailor and on the subject of 'ropes' would have known what I was talking about. Anyway, I was finally given permission for both these 'outside activities', providing I could assure my 'Masters' that there would be no advertisement, especially on ITV, or any publicity given to my connection with the Corporation. I suppose I must have made a reasonable stab at the ICI commentary, as I was invited several months later to record the narration for another ICI film on 'the making of aluminium'.

When I was tentatively asking for permission to take on these opportunities that were actually outside my Presentation contract, it certainly led to many carefully couched and lengthy type-written memos from 'on high'!

So, freelancing was taking me in many directions.

One set of ideas Iona spotted took me out on the road to create features for a programme entitled 'Jack de Manio Precisely' (echoes of Jack's fame for getting the time wrong!).

One job, I remember, entailed a recording with a ploughman working his team of heavy horses on a farm at Beauworth, near Winchester. It was a classic in its way, as there were very few farms left that still carried on horse ploughing. I fixed up a system of recording the ploughman by giving him a set of earphones (with microphone attached) linked by a cable to my own earphones, so I could hear, and record on my 'Uher' my questions and his answers, while all the time capturing the swish of the plough slicing through the soil, and the clinking of the horses' harness. It really worked, and provided a memorable piece of radio broadcasting, well before there were such things as mobile phones!

I also used this system for an interview with the author, Monica Dickens, who lived at Hindhead. She was a great watcher of badgers and I recorded an interview with her for the 'Countryside' programme. Up a bank in a small valley, on one side of a stream, Monica sat in the darkening evening, by a badger sett feeding the youngsters peanuts and crisps.

I arranged for her to wear headphones with microphone attached (exactly as I had done with the ploughman) and sitting on the bank on the other side of the stream (at a good distance, so as not to frighten the badgers), and connected to her by a long length of cable, I was able to speak with her and hear the crunch of the peanuts and crisps as the badgers greedily munched from Monica's hand. It made for a remarkable interview, as Monica was a natural talker, and the snuffling and crunching of the badgers made for some memorable sound radio.

Another 'Countryside' interview I vividly remember was with the farmer, Tony Reid, in one of his fields at Sheer, near Guildford, as he talked through the birth of a lamb, which had become stuck the wrong way round inside its mother. He had to reach the lamb with the full length of his arm plunged into the birth canal. Tony was another completely natural speaker and gave a fascinating picture of what he was doing as he quietly talked to the microphone. That job meant an early call – half-past four in the morning! It also made 'Pick of the Week'. Very sadly, Tony Reid has recently died.

For twelve years, mostly in the evenings, I also worked as a freelance in the BBC TV Presentation Department at the Television Centre, reading and often recording 'trailers' promoting up and coming programmes. These had to be spoken precisely to the second. One of the series I particularly remember from that time was 'The Onedin line' with Khachaturian's emotive music which spoke so strongly of the sea.

Buying Another Boat

I mentioned earlier how much I enjoyed sailing my first boat on the Beaulieu River when we were living at Beaulieu. I was now interested in obtaining a rather more seaworthy craft. In the late summer of 1961, Iona and I had gone for a holiday in the Isle of Wight, staying at a lodge near Wootton Creek belonging to a cousin of Ursula's (Clive's first wife). Autumn was around the corner and I remember early in the morning picking wonderful mushrooms in a nearby field which we took home for breakfast. Little Tim wasn't yet two and I have this delightful photo of him playing in a puddle on the track by the lodge.

Little Tim investigating a puddle!

With serious interest in the idea of owning a bigger boat, I had already approached a marine agent we knew to ask him to look around. Walking by the harbour at Wootton one morning, the tide was out and I spotted a delightful little yacht sitting on the mud. I could see it was exactly what I was looking for. I asked the Harbourmaster for information about the boat and he told me it belonged to one of the Solent pilots who lived nearby in Ryde. So we went to find his house and luckily found him at home. I forget his name.

We had a chat and he invited us to take a trip in his boat. He told me it was called a 'Westcoaster' and when it was sitting on the mud I saw that it was a bilge keel design. Later in the day, with the tide up, we went out beyond the harbour and I was able to have a good look at the boat and the quality of its construction. It all looked pretty good to me. My pilot friend told me he mostly used his craft for fishing, but that would not be my idea for its use, except perhaps for a bit of mackerel fishing.

I told Iona I thought a 'Westcoaster' would be just the boat for us and once back home at Clouds Hill, I contacted my marine agent friend and asked him to look for a 'Westcoaster'. Within a few days he told us he had found one, second hand and in good condition, at Deacon's Boatyard near the road bridge at Bursledon. He said the price had originally been £1,000, but the owner had lost his partner and had purchased another boat. So he wanted a quick sale and brought the price down to £750. This happened to be the exact amount my 'Sheffield Granny' had left me in her Will. I went to meet the owner, a Mr Foster, and asked for a sail in his 'Westcoaster'. He took me out into the Solent and I very much liked the 'feel' of her. I offered the £750 and the deal was done.

I also went for a test sail in Portsmouth Harbour with the designer, Dennis Rayner, and he asked me if I'd like to 'take her' (the yacht was his demonstration boat). I didn't 'take her' for long, I still hadn't learnt how to sail!

When I finally took over the boat in Deacon's yard, although it was basically in good condition, I could see she needed some cosmetic help. The varnish on the coach roof and for'ard hatch was very much in need of attention, so I bought a scraper from the boatyard chandlery and began to scrape away the varnish, back to the bare wood. At least that was the idea. But I found it hard and a not very effective job. The varnish didn't come away at all easily.

Soon, though, one of the carpenters in the boatyard came to my rescue. He said: "You'll find the old varnish comes away much better if you use Nitromors – it's a liquid paint stripper. Just brush it on and it softens the varnish. You'll find it much easier that way."

I was most grateful to him. I bought a tin of the paint stripper and found the varnish lifted away really easily. That one bit of advice saved me hours of scraping away on old dry varnish. I heard recently that the EU had brought out a directive which removed the very chemical in Nitromors that was effective!

My boat was standing on blocks undercover, but open to the dirt track that ran beside this shed and into the boatyard. The summer was dry and one morning when I had finished the job and was standing back to view my shiny new varnish with pride, a young bloke in a blooming great BMW rushed by raising clouds of dust from the track. What wind there was blew the dust all over my new wet varnish, ruining the effect. I don't swear often but I did that time! The driver never heard me of course – at his speed he was well away by the time I reacted. I learnt a lot in a short time that day!

All too soon, I realised I'd bought the boat of my dreams, but with practically no knowledge of sailing. I'd spent a morning in a 'whaler' when I was in the Navy, you may remember. I had enjoyed a very little time sailing with Clive in a delightful 18-foot craft he called 'Puffin', but I was in no way ready to skipper a boat myself. My first 'sortie' happened to be with Clive (a much better sailor than myself anyway) on a trip across the Solent to Cowes. I thought that would give me some early experience.

Out we went from the Hamble and into the Solent. It was a fresh, sunny day and all looked well. Quite soon, however, the wind freshened considerably from the West and it was clear that we would have to shorten sail. I went to loosen the main halyard from its cleat on the mast and started to haul down the mainsail, only to find that the halyard had jammed in the sheeve at the top of the mast. I could neither haul it up nor down. Help! Now what?

Clive was at the helm so wasn't able to help. My RNSA burgee was flying happily at the masthead and it occurred to me that I could loosen its halyard and jiggle the stick under the main halyard and endeavour to lift it free of the sheeve. No luck, however much jiggling I tried! Clive then sensibly suggested that I bring the main along the boom and wrap it to the mast. Grand idea! This I did, but we were then left with only the jib up for'ard to navigate the boat. But to reach Cowes, we needed to go to windward and the jib wouldn't be much help for that!

So we resorted to the engine and met the waves, now building in a stiff breeze, head on. It was certainly a wet and bumpy ride. We made Cowes at last and I saw ahead to starboard two piles without any craft moored between them. The tide, now coming in strongly, helped us along nicely as I aimed for the second pile, confident we could easily tie up to it and ease the boat astern to the pile behind us.

This was a moment when my lack of knowledge of the effects of wind and tide made itself rapidly felt! Of course, with the tide behind us it rammed the bow of the boat with a hefty thump against the second pile bending my anchor fairlead! Clive valiantly and with extreme difficulty managed to wrap a rope around the pile so we were at least secured at that end. But, of course, the flooding tide now swung the boat round so that we were quickly facing the second pile down tide and quite unable against the tide to get a rope back to the first pile yards away. This ungainly sequence of events is really quite difficult clearly to describe, but it was certainly an unhappy picture.

Next, my dear, helpful brother took to the dinghy with a coil of rope with the idea of rowing back to the first pile, thereby to secure the boat fore and aft. But the more he energetically pulled on the dinghy oars, letting out the rope, the heavier in the water it became such that he was rowing to a standstill! Clive found this uproariously funny and laughed his head off. Goodness knows how, but with a bit of help from the engine, we finally got secured between the two piles. My RNSA burgee was safely down in the cockpit out of sight! I turned, hoping not to have been spotted, but saw with horror there was a smartly dressed officer in blazer and white cap standing on the platform of the Royal Yacht Squadron with a telescope to his eye. He had witnessed the whole ghastly scenario!

Apart from my brief trip with Mr Foster, this had been my first real 'voyage' in my newly acquired craft. I fervently hoped all my sailing adventures henceforward would not have any similar conclusions!

I was now taking the trouble to find out more about my little yacht, and at 20 ft. she was certainly little against the larger, classy yachts that sailed the Solent and well beyond. My 'Westcoaster' had been designed as a sturdy wooden family boat by the ex-corvette RN Commander, Dennis Rayner who I had met earlier. She was built of double-skinned marine ply so was strong in construction. There were four berths below, a neat little galley area for a paraffin cooker on the port side and a useful table and drawers to starboard. It was light inside as there were several windows down the sides and a larger window below the for'ard hatch. There was also space there for a 'loo'.

I had bought the boat with some useful extras, including a very good compass, sundry tools and a rubber dinghy – the one Clive had used doing sterling work that day against the tide – an event I wasn't too keen to relate to sailing friends. It was best forgotten!

Richard Baker Aboard

Another occasion I have definitely not forgotten involved a sail with my good friend Richard Baker, the famous television newsreader and presenter of many other programmes, particularly those involving music. It was not Cowes this time but Wootton Creek; we'd had a wonderful sail across the Solent and decided to moor at Wootton Creek for the night.

In the morning, we both felt in need of a shave and a good wash. Ashore there was a facility, mainly perhaps for the ferry passengers, but we saw no reason why we couldn't use the loo there and the basins to freshen up. I was half-way through shaving when an officious little fellow came in and spoke to me. "You're from a boat, aren't you? I saw you come across. This place is exclusively for ferry passengers. I will have to ask you to leave."

"Well," I said, "I hope you will allow me to finish shaving."

His tone suddenly changed. He'd recognised me and the voice. "Aren't you on the telly? You're Martin Muncaster?"

"Well, yes."

"Oh I'm delighted to meet you," said the man. "You just carry on, no problem. Please leave it as you found it." And off he went smiling broadly.

Meantime, Richard had disappeared in to one of the lavatory cubicles. When he opened the door and came out, he said to me, "I thought I'd leave that one to you!"

But another incident, much more serious, a long time later, led to my arrest (see chapter 17).

An Invitation to Scotland

Soon after we moved to Clouds Hill, I heard from John Rickman, the ITV racing correspondent. With his wife Peggy and family, John lived at Lynchmere high up on the hill above nearby Shottermill. They had heard of our move and to welcome us to the village they invited us to dinner. As we talked, John mentioned that some while back he'd bought an old Trinity House lighthouse station on the Isle of Jura, off the west coast of Scotland. He wondered if we would like to holiday there. "It's awfully basic," he said. "No electricity, no phone and drinking water comes from a spring running out of a rock." Standing as it did on a promontory at one side of the wide Lowlandman's Bay, it enjoyed a stunning view of the 'Paps of Jura' in the distance. The main village was Craighouse, with a hotel and the single shop on the island.

John explained that the only way to get to the old house – 'a gaunt building and not very beautiful' – was by boat. If we would like to go there for a holiday it meant two ferries, one from Kennacraig on the mainland, across the Sound of Jura to Port Askaig on the island of Islay, then across the stretch of sea between the two islands to Jura. We both thought it sounded idyllic and since Iona had been brought up in the woods at Bedham, near Petworth, in a very tumbledown old cottage, she was used to basic living!

Ollie was only five and John warned us that there wasn't much for children on Jura. But we knew the eldest, Tim, would love fishing off the rocks and our collie dog, Patsie, would need lots of exercise. She was already rushing round the house, trying to catch up with the children as round and round they went doing their best to outrun her!

We made it clear to John that we would love to go to Jura. I'd drive up with our second-hand Ford, which I'd recently bought – and take the first major part of the journey by 'Motorail' from King's Cross to Stirling. John gave us all manner of instructions to help us enjoy what he called 'Jura living' and at the end of July, 1969, we were ready to set off on a brand new adventure.

A most important instruction from John was details of how to contact the local boatman, 'Dougie'. He would take me and the children in the boat, while Iona drove round to the tiny hamlet of Ardfernal where she was to leave the car and scramble down to the edge of the Bay where 'Dougie' would, as John said: "Pluck her off the rocks and into his boat." He would then take us over to the little pier below a grass track leading up to the house, helping us with our luggage. It was important to remember to give 'Dougie', as well as his fee for the boat, a 'dram' of whiskey as a 'thankyou' for all his help. So we were sure to put a bottle of whiskey in the car!

I would take ten days off from my 'freelance' broadcasting at the end of July and the beginning of August. Actually, it was the worst time for midges – but John didn't warn us about that!

We were all very excited...

Chapter 14

Jura Living

So it was that on a morning in late July 1969, we prepared ourselves for a holiday in Scotland, ten days away from the mad rush of everything in the South. I had booked us sleepers on the Motorail from King's Cross and after I pushed the last welly boot into the last bit of space in the back of the hatchback, we set off with the three children in the back and our collie Patsie at Iona's feet in the front.

Peggy had mentioned to Iona to take plenty of extra food stores as there weren't always plentiful supplies in the shop. Somehow, Iona had managed to pack in a load of tins, some extra bread and other necessities. Every space in the car was utilised, leaving a hole in the middle at the back so that I could see traffic to the rear. Miranda sat in the middle with Tim and Ollie on each side. We arrived at King's Cross in good time and, having taken what we needed for the night, I drove the car up on to the Motorail wagon where it was strapped down.

Our first test was to get Patsie into our compartment without being seen by the guard. Correctly, she should have been tied up in the guard's van. But, by instinct, she must have known and as soon as we were into our compartment, she dived under the bed and disappeared from sight! The children found the Motorail good fun and, even sharing a compartment next to ours, managed to get some sleep. Iona and I dropped off soon after the train had started; then woke up again at Crewe. I remember loud clangings and shuntings that went on as a new engine was attached. As I looked out of the window, I saw the night staff moving about the platform. I still have a memory of the sounds that assailed us at Crewe in the middle of the night.

We arrived at our destination, Stirling, at about 5:30 a.m. on a nice sunny morning. We then had the long drive across Scotland to the low end of Loch Lomond, then on via Arrochar and up the long steep glen past the top of Loch Fyne to Inverary. John had suggested we push on to a hotel he recommended at

Lochgair, where we could take a break and spend the night. The children were exhausted by now and I was getting pretty sleepy myself after the early start. We were glad of a night's rest before moving on after breakfast the next morning to the ferry at Kennacraig. Even that drive meant another 30 miles or so in the car. In those early days, the car was swung over onto the ferry deck by derrick; an interesting operation. I don't remember the exact timings, but that the ferry took us down Loch West Tarbert and across the Sound of Jura to the pier at Craighouse.

There to greet us was Dougie; John had alerted him. I was indeed glad to see him. He helped us hump the luggage and all our extras into his boat by the Craighouse pier, then explained to Iona where to leave the car, via the single road that runs up the island and to turn off at the small hamlet called Ardfernal, on a hill high above Lowlandman's Bay. From there she was to scramble down 'to be plucked off the rocks', to use John's instruction, and climb aboard the boat. As Iona drove away in the car, the rest of us jumped aboard and we set off to collect her. All a great adventure for the children.

Fortunately, it was a lovely sunny day, for which we were extremely grateful. True to John's promise, having given us the key, Dougie helped us with the luggage up the grassy slope to the house. John's description was right: it was a large, gaunt place which had originally housed the families of the lighthouse keepers who took turns, a fortnight at a time, to tend the lighthouse on a large rock out in 'The Sound of Jura'. In years gone by, before they had a motor launch, the keepers had to row out to the rock to relieve their companions, doubtless in pretty well all weathers.

Having given Dougie his 'dram', which he was most happy to receive, he left us to our own devices as we watched his boat motor away into the distance. We now had to explore the house, taking it all in. There was a kitchen with a Rayburn stove, a sitting room with candles and a paraffin lamp for evenings, and a bathroom. John had somehow managed to get a bath across from Craighouse. This was the most welcome addition with the water heated by the Rayburn. In the corridor, hard by the kitchen, there was a cupboard in which John kept all his tools. He had also left a notebook full of nuggets of valuable advice for facile Jura living.

Stuck on the door of the cupboard there was an admonishment, writ large:
"For domestic bliss, put it back!"

There were, in fact, four flats for the four lighthouse families, two upstairs and two down. The upstairs flats were reached via a flight of stone steps to an outside door. It was all very basic and meant we were virtually camping but under the roof of a house! The loo upstairs was simply an Elsan, which I had to empty every couple of days, chucking the contents into a small quarry open to the sea and well away from the house. I noticed the nettles grew very strongly there!

So began our holiday. Having chosen which bedrooms to use, we all slept well and for our first breakfast Iona served up some delicious egg bread. I had fired up the Rayburn in the evening with kindling left by John, and some coal which we 'mined' from a large coal bunker behind the house. There was a good pile of coal left behind by the keepers. There used to be a little 'puffer' which delivered coal to the lighthouse each year. We hoped the supply of coal would last a long time as we had already decided this old place would be good for holidays in future years. The children loved it, and were even now giving Patsie lots of exercise, rushing around the building and over the rocks on a rise of land behind the house.

Truly Memorable

Little did we know it then, but we were to spend holidays at the lighthouses (as they were called by the locals) for a dozen years.

Looking back now, I can relate all manner of stories and happenings which made our stays on Jura truly memorable. So here goes:

On this first visit, we had to get used to John's dinghy with an outboard which often had to be coaxed into life. We used the dinghy on engine to take us across the Bay to an inlet amongst the rocks where we could haul the boat up above the tide, then climb the hill to Ardfernal above to reach the car where Iona had parked it. We then all piled in and drove down what the children called the Jura motorway, in fact basically a single-track road with passing places that ran the length of the island, to the shop in Craighouse. This was where Iona would sort out any extra supplies we would need before our next visit to Craighouse. We had to judge the weather, too. A strong wind from the Sou'west straight into the Bay could work up a pretty rough sea and I wasn't keen to brave it unless absolutely necessary.

Once back to the house, we judged it a good idea to make our number with Morag and her sister at the farm, more or less a mile's steady trudge away across the moorland. This was a wide stretch of ground, called a 'raised beach' I seem to remember, with the open sea of the Jura Sound on one side, and Lowlandman's Bay on the other. The family at the farm were most welcoming. John had already told them of our arrival. Morag had one cow she milked every day and she strained the milk through a stocking filter into a bucket. We were glad she used the filter, as there were always a lot of flies about which could easily end up on the milk's surface. Morag gave us a little can to carry the milk back to the house where, for safety, Iona always boiled it before we used it. This was comforting.

Morag also had lots of hens which ranged freely around the farm, so we had plenty of fresh eggs. These gave us some fine breakfasts. There was a very long, rough track to the farm from the main road, but it was not suitable for cars so we didn't try it during our first visit, but used the boat for our travels to Craighouse and the shop each time pulling the boat up into the rocky inlet to a safe level above the tide.

What a time we had, and I wrote a poem after our first visit, putting to words the scene which surrounded us in Lowlandman's Bay. I gave it a title:

The Poetry of Peace

An Isle full of noises,
And voices…
Where the sound of the seals and the sea mingle with the mists,
Where the heather hues tell the tale of the rains and the fleeting sun,
Where the brown burns bubble, pell-mell
Down the braes, to meet the ebb and flow of the tide
Where the great shadowy 'Paps' stand sentinel,
To guide the winds and guard this store of peace.
Oh! for the peace
Of this sceptred, sweet scented Isle,
Set by the Jura Sound.
Oh! for the gentle quiet that holds the happy hours in check; where time takes rest
From the headlong world, and Nature alone
Brings company.
Listen! For there pipes the oystercatcher
Across the bay, and the rocks reply.
There the gull wheels to the wind

And the slipslop of the sea reminds us of our puddling and paddling.
Here is Truth, here Beauty – in her million melting shades
God made
To tired hearts and longing minds a gift, a glory
That journeys away with the soul's memory…
Till another time
Another time, by and by;
On this Isle –
Full of noises, and voices…

One of the things I learned very soon on our first holiday, was the fact that at Ardlussa, near the top of the island, there was an expansive salmon loch. I went up one morning to try it out, casting a wet fly, but caught nothing. However, as I stood casting on a promontory where there was a hut, and beside which a river ran out of the loch, a man walked from the other side carrying two large salmon! This, of course, gave me much encouragement. The 'salmon carrier' turned out to be Mr Fletcher, the owner of the large house further up the road at Ardlussa. He told me there had recently been a lot of rain which had created a spate in the river bringing salmon up from the sea. This meant there were rising fish which could take a fly.

When the time or weather were wrong, one could cast for hours from the bank with no action from the fish at all. There was also a boat which I could take out, row to the other side, and drift down on the wind, casting as I went. Over the years, I went many times for a day's fishing and came home with an empty bag.

After our first visit to Jura, which had been so memorable, I can remember feeling sad, and almost in a way 'homesick' for Jura as, on our way home, I awoke and looked out of the window as the Motorail rattled into the outskirts of London. It felt, somehow, as if we were returning to the 'unreal' world, which was taking us away from the marvellous peace of the magical island of Jura. But, at least, I knew we would return the next year.

Indeed, on a later visit, my fishing luck changed. There had certainly been a lot of rain and I judged it worth a try on the loch.

Up I went in the car, parked it on the side of the track near the loch, walked to the hut, and set up my rod (given to me, incidentally, as a present by Bill Rowsell, my 80 year old friend, who'd taught me fishing years before.) All of a sudden, as I cast, I saw this slight hump of a rising fish and cast my fly over it, but felt my fly hit stones on the bottom and it jammed. I thought: "Blast! How typical, you have one chance and ruin it."

Catching My Salmon

I tugged and tugged at the rod to see if I could free the fly from the bottom; then suddenly I saw a flash of silver. I was into a salmon! It had to be a big one as it felt heavy to the rod and shot away from me, the reel screeching as I let out more line. This was hugely exciting! I knew I had to be careful as I was using my trout rod, not man enough for hauling in a heavy salmon. This one had to be several pounds. Not getting too excited and tightening the rod gently, it took me about half an hour gradually to tire the salmon and pull it towards me. I only had a net, so would have to be extremely careful, inching the salmon over it. At this point a walker happened to come by, saw what I was doing and offered to hold the net while I worked with the rod to coax the salmon to the bank. As I got it close, my helper reached forward with the net, but just caught the tail of the salmon and it shot away again. I could so easily have lost my precious catch! Luckily, the hook held, and after about 40 minutes I had my salmon on the bank. Huge relief. It was a beautiful specimen, eleven pounds, and I thanked the fish for allowing me to catch it.

As I sorted everything out and looked at the water again, I saw the enticing hump of another salmon on the move. I cast to it, and sure enough had it on. It held for a few short minutes, then the line went slack. This time, the fish was obviously only lightly hooked. Every fisherman knows that feeling of disappointment when a fish you are sure you've got for the bag, suddenly leaps out of the water, shaking away the hook, and escapes. No good casting again in that area. After losing my second salmon, I did, however, catch a shining sea trout, more than a pound, so I reckoned I'd had a pretty good morning. I put my salmon into the boot of a car and made for home.

Only a sea trout this time, but it was over a pound.

The great salmon and the rather smaller sea trout!

This year, the family at the farm had spent money on the track, so I was able to drive slowly to the farm. As I left the Ardlussa loch and reached the road by a bridge over the river, round the corner came Charlie, driver of the island bus, which he used to take children to and from school. He leaped out of the driving seat saying: "I hear you've got a salmon." God knows how he knew, but there is a 'bush telegraph' on the island and the locals know about a piece of news almost before it's happened. "Can I have a wee look," said Charlie, and I proudly lifted open the boot. "Ochh! That's a beauty," said Charlie, and after carefully inspecting my prize, he set off down the road in his bus, smiling happily. When I got back to the farm of course they knew all about it, and I had to display it again.

On this occasion, I had gone to Jura only with Iona. The children weren't with us. So naughtily, I hung the fish on a stick over my shoulder so that it was hidden down my back. I returned to the house with a tired gait to find Iona standing outside to welcome me. She said: "How did you get on?"

"Disappointing today I'm afraid, darling," I replied. "Nothing showing." Then I turned around to reveal the fish hanging down my back. Iona literally shrieked. She was taken completely by surprise and we had a jolly good laugh. I cut a large piece of the tail and gave some to Morag at the farm.

Each year on our trips to Jura, we'd usually driven up and stayed with Iona's sister, Sylvan and her husband, Michael, on the way. They lived in a very nice house at Newcastle-under-Lyme, and we stayed with them overnight, leaving at around 03:45 in the morning, so as to beat the early Glasgow traffic, then stop for breakfast at a Little Chef.

This time, we gave Michael and Sylvan a generous portion of the tail of the salmon on our way home. We had the idea to share that whole salmon with John and Peggy for dinner back at Lynchmere. There is nothing to beat a fresh natural salmon. Farmed salmon are just not the same; the flavour is quite different.

For our trips to Jura, we always went at the end of July, and arrived in time for the sports day held every year in the grounds of the big house up at Ardlussa; always good fun. Miranda used to join in for the running races and always won. She was a very fast runner. The egg and spoon and potato races created much shouting and laughter.

The spoon and potato race!

John told us he used to cheat by holding his potato on the spoon surreptitiously with his thumb. One year it deluged with rain and the Minister who ran the show valiantly did his very best to get people to join in the fun. "Come along noo," he would call out. "It's only a wee drop o' rain!" That day, the sandwiches, which were served through a downstairs window hatch of the house, became pretty damp and soggy. But it didn't dampen the Scots who were well used to drenching rain.

The Boat Race

Another time, we went in for the boat race around Craighouse Harbour. A wonderful character called Jack Paton was the race officer and he called out the time to go before starting the race. He seemed to give the impression that there was plenty of time for the entries to prepare their boats, so no one hurried. Then suddenly in his loud Scots accent he would yell out into his megaphone '30 seconds!!' That led immediately to much grabbing of tillers and setting of sails until Jack actually started the race. We were delighted to come in third. But then, there were actually only three boats in the race!

It was always a challenge to get back to our dinghy, tucked in among the rocks, haul it back into the water, heave away at the starter of the engine, usually a number of times, and set off across the Bay. This was always an enjoyable ride and I was careful to show the children which knot (a bowline) to use to make the boat fast to a big stake on the other side near the pier.

Then we went up the track to the house, past the big iron water butt filled by the spring which ran out of the rock. The tank was really there for the cattle, but we put a bucket under the spring which quickly filled and gave us our drinking water. Getting the bucket filled was a daily task, as was the long walk to the farm for our milk and eggs and any letters which the postman, who trudged down the track from the road every day, had left for us. The post meant a lot to me, as it often contained cheques from the BBC for work I had done for various programmes in the weeks before our Jura holidays.

One of the great joys of our holidays on Jura for the boys and obviously for me, was the fishing. Tim did spend time fishing for pollock off the rocks and he would go out into the bay with the dinghy and several times brought back some fine mackerel. One day, however, he caught several on the line at once. They then tugged on the line so strongly that they pulled Tim's rod and reel over the stern of the boat and into the water, never to be seen again. Poor Tim returned to the house looking really disconsolate. We were sorry for the mackerel stuck on the line. However, there were other possibilities.

Up on the hill above the farm and across the road, we used to wend our way together to a beautiful loch. It was hidden from view until we got quite near. It contained lots of fish and the boys with a worm, and me with a wet fly, used to take home some lovely trout which, coming from such clean water, made especially tasty eating. On one afternoon, however, Tim and Ollie went off alone. An hour or so later, Iona spotted them coming back, obviously unhappy. There was certainly a problem, as Ollie had caught Tim's hook with some trailing cast, in his cheek. Mercifully, Tim's casting hadn't hit Ollie in the eye. When they got back, I wondered how on earth to get the hook out of his cheek? I then had a brainwave. I thought Iona's nail scissors might just be strong enough to cut the barb off the shank of the hook. So I quickly pushed the hook right through the skin. Poor Ollie certainly shrieked as I cut the barb off the shank. I could then quickly push it back and out of Ollie's cheek and my first, and hopefully last, act as a surgeon was over and done. The little mark on Ollie's cheek soon healed.

During the years we were on Jura, John renovated the old boatman's cottage down by the pier. He did a grand job with this and made it most habitable and comfortable. He and Peggy stayed there when visiting the island themselves.

One year we found our kettle had a leak and we sent an emergency message to Peggy. We all waited for the arrival of the ferry from Port Askaig on Islay, to see John and Peggy coming to Jura for their stay. We well remember the wonderful sight of Peggy stepping ashore, proudly brandishing a brand-new kettle. Such things were major happenings on Jura.

John and Peggy Rickman with all we Muncasters (including Patsie), on the track as we make for the 'lighthouses' by 'Hafflinger'.

Actually, each time we were there, we spent a day on Islay, paying visits to interesting places, such as the whisky factory, and seeing great vats of the spirit in various stages of manufacture. One year we discovered a field leading to a beautiful bay and picked loads of delicious mushrooms.

Stalking a Stag

One morning at the house, Tim spotted a fine stag grazing amongst the rocks on the rise of land behind the house. He decided to stalk it. I went with him, taking my Super-8 camera, and amazingly, managed to get some nice cine shots. But however slowly and carefully we crept forward, the deer would sense us and move away a few yards. In the end, we drove it right to the edge of the water and were amazed to see it leap in and start swimming. In fact, it swam all the way across the mouth of the Bay, and I was able to get a shot, though rather distant, as the animal, showing a fine pair of antlers, made its way through the water. It was a very special moment. I had no idea a stag could swim. With his stills camera Tim got a beautiful shot of the stag on the ridge against the sky. He entered his photo into a World Wildlife Fund competition and won first prize. Helped no doubt by the fact that Iona had kept his surname off the entry form as she was a leading light with the WWF in those days and also part of the judging panel! Tim's photo can be seen at the end of the book.

Towards the end of our summer days on Jura, we were beginning to run out of coal. We needed it for the Rayburn. So we went to Islay's coal merchant to stock up. We heaved several bags into the back of the car, but driving slowly down the rough track to the farm, the bumping was just too much with all that weight for the old Ford hatchback and there were soon ominous creakings from the springs. I think we got home all right but not without concern for the car. The repairs turned out to be pretty expensive!

In July 1994, Ollie planned some solo walking and camping. He went all the way to the deserted north end of the island, sat on some rocks, and took this self-portrait pointing to the famous Paps of Jura in the far distance. Later he actually climbed one of the Paps.

Ollie pointing to the Paps.

On one of our early visits, the children had an idea. They helped me film the title 'The Jura Story', along with a 'Thanks to John and Peggy', which we scratched in the sand on the beach near Craighouse. I believe Ollie has it in mind to edit all the shots together to combine old and new. That would bring back some great memories.

But I do believe the most memorable memory, if I may put it that way, happened as a result of small features of about three minutes each which I recorded for a night-time music series on Radio 2. I was one of two or three of us who recorded 'newsie' little features to be broadcast in amongst the music. I recorded several for a series I entitled 'Jura Living' and of course, they included all manner of amusing things that happened to us on our yearly visits to the island, many of which I have related here.

One particular feature, however, got me into terrible trouble. And there's quite a tale to it…

The Minister on the island had his own stretch of beach below the Manse where he and his wife lived. The Minister was pretty handy with a gun, and one cold February morning he had shot a shell duck swimming along his bit of beach. He then waded into the water to retrieve his prize. Unhappily, the wind and tide had drifted the duck away from the beach into deeper water and the Minister was hard put to it to reach out and grab the duck. He at last lifted the dripping bird and as he started back to the shore he spotted Dougie sitting watching in his car.

The Minister approached him with a cheery: "Good morning, Dougie." But Dougie who'd espied everything, replied accusingly in a low Scottish voice: "A poacher never likes an audience."

The Minister had actually related this story to me himself, and I found it extremely funny. Rashly, I thought this would make a wonderful piece for my contributions to Radio 2. Indeed, it was given a second hearing on 'Pick of the Week'. Big problem. The poor Minister was hauled in for a serious dressing down. In fact, he was in dire danger of being undressed, or should I say, defrocked. For him the whole affair was most embarrassing and on a Sunday morning when John and Peggy were there, we joined them for the morning service. Afterwards, the Minister collared me whispering ominously: "I need a word with you," and steered me round to the back of the church, away from prying ears.

He was very, very cross and related to me the whole sorry tale of the dreadful time he'd had being accused by the Elders. He honestly thought I had done it on purpose to get at him. The thought hadn't entered my head of course, but it took him a long time over copious cups of tea with his wife in the Manse before I felt forgiven. I'm not sure he ever believed me that it had simply been a jolly good story for my Radio 2 series.

Actually, nothing might have happened at all, until the Minister's seniors heard the repeat of the programme. My mistake was mentioning that it had happened on Jura. Unfortunately, that had revealed the actual Minister involved.

A big mistake, indeed, and a bad misjudgement by me. I was extremely sorry for the poor minister who was a delightful fellow.

Chapter 15

More Freelancing and a Range of Work

Many times, I've lost count, I've been asked how long I was a broadcaster. The answer is some 40 years, starting in 1956 with Radio Luxembourg and the General Overseas Service of the BBC, and ending with a series for BBC South in the mid-90s. These last episodes were delightful features, not necessarily newsy, entitled 'Southern Ways'. They reflected interesting things that were going on in the South, mostly in the countryside. One of the stories was based around Lynchmere church, which was a thousand years old, and I had compered a pageant which told its story.

A person who was very much involved in writing up the pageant and who indeed did a huge amount to give Lynchmere a 'profile', including running the annual pantomime, was Michael Tibbs, whose father had been Vicar of Lynchmere. Having started with shots in my own garden, I interviewed Michael by the church with the graveyard ablaze with white daisies in full flower. Michael gave us some most interesting history about Lynchmere and the church.

For another of these 'Southern Ways' films we told the story of the Hindhead Highwayman and the gibbet which stands on a high point above the famed 'Devil's Punch Bowl'. It was all a lot of fun, and I enjoyed filming the series immensely. I may also add that when the Dimbleby family lived at Lynchmere, the boys, David and Jonathan, used to take part in Michael's pantomime. There is a plaque in memory of their father, Richard, in the wall by the church.

A quite different area of professional endeavour came with my being commissioned to introduce many videos for the Holiday Property Bond. This took me to France and Portugal, Scotland and many venues around Britain. In the appendices I have included a copy of one of the HPB brochures.

A couple of years or so after the book on my father was published I was approached by a man called Arthur Hooker, who was one of the select list of people who had ordered the leather-bound edition of the book which, as I mentioned, included a dozen fine Claude Muncaster etchings.

Arthur Hooker was a senior director of the impressive, international engineering company W.S. Atkins, based at Epsom. There had apparently been talk amongst the directors about the idea of publishing a book about the company's 50-year history. It was certainly interesting. William Atkins had previously run a moderately small contracting business, one of the many companies helping to construct sections of the famous Mulberry Harbour that assisted the D-Day landings.

After the War, he heard about the plan to build a massive steelworks, the Abbey Works, at Port Talbot in Wales. By some adroit and skilful salesmanship, Atkins had obtained the contract to design and build the works, even though he had nothing like enough staff for the job! Being a natural entrepreneur, and not taking 'no' for an answer, he had sat stolidly outside the office of Freddy Cartwright, the man who was in charge of the job, until he agreed to talk to this bothersome young fellow. Knowing that he hadn't anything like enough engineers for such a huge task, he still managed to persuade the chief that he, Atkins, was the man for the job. Having been contracted for it, he then started to employ young engineers for all the different aspects of the work. Many of the staff he needed he found in men being demobbed from the Army after the War. He quickly gathered a team of enthusiastic engineers who were excited by the prospect of being involved in such a major project. Thus, Atkins became equipped to take on the design and construction of the huge new Abbey Works. With his new team he was able to include many fresh ideas into the job.

When Arthur Hooker had read his leather-bound copy of my book, *The Wind in the Oak*, it occurred to him that I might be someone who could write up the history of W.S. Atkins, by this time, of course, a company which had developed considerably and now had civil, mechanical and electrical departments.

Atkins had also been involved in the early development of computers. It was a great story to tell, and Arthur persuaded Sir William, (he had recently been knighted) to talk with me about the possibility of my writing up the history of the company.

Meantime, while all this was going on, I was still managing to fit in a bit of sailing and took Richard Baker on another trip. We were doing fine until over Portsmouth I saw the skies turning an ominous black. Peter Urmston, our doctor's father and an expert yachtsman, had explained to me what a 'line squall' looked like, and I was sure we were in for just that. I knew I had to shorten sail, but wasn't quick enough, and there were suddenly huge drops of rain, then a mighty wind. With too much sail up, the boat heeled right over. It seemed we might shortly get extremely wet. Richard went white! I'm sure he thought we would end up in the water. But luckily, 'Cottontail', though small, was a sturdy craft and soon came up into wind, though with the sails shaking alarmingly and making much noise. It took me some time to reduce the main and get everything sorted out. Actually, we had been hit by a line squall, but it blew through fairly quickly, and very little water had come over the coaming and into the cockpit. Anyway, we decided to go back to the peace and quiet of the harbour and picked up a mooring at Bosham.

While I was pottering about the boat squaring things off and tidying up, Richard sat in the cockpit working on some proofs of a book he was writing for the publishers, David and Charles, a music Quiz Book. He looked up at one stage and said to me: "You ought to do this Martin, how about writing a yachtsman's quiz book?"

I thought this a good idea and later got agreement from David and Charles to publish my book. It took a lot of work. But I managed to include many elements which would be of interest to sailors. It was great fun to write but certainly took a lot of research. It included chapters on seamanship, sea personalities, maritime music, racing, navigation, sea mysteries, creatures at sea, submarines, and a whole lot more. It took many, many months to prepare and the quiz included some excellent hand-drawn illustrations.

I wish I could say it sold well, but it went the way of so many books that are interesting and well-written in themselves, but just don't take off in the market. Today, I am sad to say, we are in 'celebrity' mode. It is the big names that capture the public interest, a lot of it of course, as a result of expensive marketing and the 'telly'.

I was by now getting on with the history of the Atkins book and was given an office, and often working well into the evenings, was left an excellent supper by the company cook! I was paid well for my work, and felt really rather spoilt, especially by Sir William's excellent secretary, Pauline Packer, who actually typed out my manuscript for *The Yachtsmen's Quiz Book*. I got a lot of assistance from various sailing experts including John Williams who was a marvellous help with the questions for the navigation chapter.

When published, the book looked really quite good. My only sadness was that David and Charles did practically nothing to help in marketing the book. I actually had to go around myself offering my book to chandleries and yacht clubs around the South coast. I hadn't bargained to have to do that!

The Atkins book took a great deal of steady work, but turned out to be very interesting and including quite a bit of travel. My idea was to go around and speak to all the original directors who had created Atkins' early team. I wanted to get their memories of the early days and record the interviews I had with them. There were many, and I found their various stories most absorbing. Pauline Packer was stalwart, transcribing all my recorded interviews so that I had paper scripts to work on. My plan was to write, I hoped, a good readable narrative with much illustration of some of the main Atkins projects, and to have these captioned by the engineers involved. I knew it would be best for engineers to write up the captions so that all details would be correct. That would be a considerable job in itself.

I was taken around several of the major Atkins works in Britain including the massive Drax power station, major motorways and bridges, and the mining complex at Selby, Yorkshire. I was even taken down a deep mineshaft there. I also went abroad to Algiers where Atkins were working with the Russians on building the huge El Hadjir Steelworks.

All my involvement in work on the book for Atkins kept me very busy for a couple of years. But in the end, I found myself working by 'committee'. Everyone had their own ideas about how the book should be written and it was impossible to please everybody. The book was finally put together by the engineers and it was published by Atkins Holdings Ltd. in 1988 under the title *Partners – 50 years of WS & P*.

This is not the place for me to go into detail of the huge range of Atkins activities described in the book. Anyone interested could do no better than contact the Atkins Company direct to obtain a copy of the book; it's quite a tome.

A 'Face' and Now a 'Voice'

At one time, being the best-known 'face' in the South, it could be said that I had enjoyed a certain celebrity status myself. But television is a fickle medium and in those terms, I was pretty soon forgotten! However, on moving to national radio, I actually became one of the best-known 'voices' in Britain. That was to last for quite some time. Even now, many people say: "Oh, I remember **that voice!**"

In fact, my voice now being so well known, led to an invitation to join the 'voices' on Melody Radio, in London. This was a new feature in the radio calendar. It was the brainchild of Lord Hanson who had seen radio stations in the States which were run and presented virtually by one broadcaster. Hanson saw that there was a 'hole' in BBC broadcasting. He thought there was room for a station offering more melody – the big bands playing the great tunes, songs from the forties, fifties and sixties, sung by the likes of Frank Sinatra and many other famous singers. Radio 2 didn't quite do it, and certainly not Radio 3. So 'Melody' started broadcasting and was picking up good audiences in and around London. Hanson had a considerable collection of vinyl recordings which he donated to Melody Radio, together with a large number of CD's. These were used by all the announcers who had good, strong voices and spoke in clear, what is known as 'received English'. Thus 'Melody' had its own particular sound. There were several ex-BBC producers working at Melody Radio and I believe it was through them that I was approached. It was a completely new way of broadcasting as far as I was concerned. The announcer was pretty well alone, with a list of music which was played in order with spoken links in between. He also had to read the regular news bulletins. It was all very different from my work with the BBC when one had a producer who was with you in the control room and an engineer who ran the tapes and checked the levels.

On 2nd February 1991, I wrote in my diary: *I am feeling terrified inside about my coming duties with 'Melody'*. In fact, I had a heck of a job getting used to the 'Melody' way of putting music on the air and very nearly got sacked because I made so many mistakes in the beginning. But fortunately, the Head of Presentation, Peter Black, was most patient with me. I had exactly the right voice for the station, after all, and was pretty famous vocally as well! Luckily, it wasn't long before I began to get used to announcing and putting on the records and discs and got on really well with my announcing colleagues. Our shifts were four to five hours and I soon built up some confidence.

I organised my own way of working, getting the playlists the night before my shift and working up the timings on the way home in the train. Maths, as you may remember, was not my strong point! Even with this care and preparation, one morning I spun a disc at the wrong speed and had to apologise and extricate myself as smoothly as possible to put things right. A few moments later the phone rang and a voice said: "You got out of that very well." It was Lord Hanson!

Some Memorable Meetings

When I was sorting out CDs one morning for my next Melody shift, one of the secretaries, sitting at her desk reading a book, suddenly let out a wild shriek. As it happened, she was reading Alan Clark's Diaries and had come across my name! Sometime before, in July 1983, I had been working at a summer musical evening at Saltwood Castle, Clark's home in Kent. The concert was staged in aid of the Historic Houses Association. The musicians were the two Dolmetsch twins, Jeanne and Marguerite, playing I'm sure on recorders and viols. I was there to recite and perform readings which included the exchange of letters between Henry VIII and Anne Boleyn. Alan Clark had kindly decided to attend the evening and he had been most moved by the letters. He said the twins played 'most pleasingly', and mentioned Martin Muncaster as narrator. It was suddenly coming across my name in the diaries which caused our young secretary to come out with such a screech! I particularly remember that concert, it all happened on my birthday, July 17th.

I broadcast with 'Melody Radio' for three years and much enjoyed my time there. However, after that period there were staff changes, people came in with different ideas and the station soon became just another pop station which I thought a great pity. I was told I wasn't needed anymore! Not long after, Lord Hanson retired and 'Melody' was closed down. I was sorry it went that way. Until the changes, it had been doing a pretty good job.

Another name that has cropped up in my life 'doing a pretty good job' is that of Jenni Murray. After me, she spent some time with South Today, but has since, of course, become extremely famous for her work as a regular mainstay of Woman's Hour on Radio 4. She does a terrific job for that programme along with Jane Garvey. I often listen and they bring help and understanding to men, too.

Discovering Self-Transformation

I had now become involved in a fascinating and totally different type of project, a big surprise for me which, in a way, came out of the blue. One day in the Spring of 1985 Iona and I had been invited to lunch by a great friend of ours Loveday Gabriel, wife of our solicitor, Noel Gabriel. Loveday had invited us as she had just been most impressed by a workshop she'd signed up for called

231

'Being a Woman'. The workshop was run by an organisation called 'Self Transformation', and Loveday had found she had learnt a lot about herself, at a deep level, which was changing her life. We listened, fascinated, to what Loveday had to tell us, and she urged us to sign up for one of these 'self-transformation' workshops. We began to know it as ST for short. The organisation had been put together by an American, Walter Bellin and his Australian wife, Gita, using Western spiritual psychology with Eastern understandings. Apart from the actual workshops, they also ran introductory evenings, which anyone interested could go to in order to learn more about the organisation and what was meant by 'Self Transformation'.

At that time, working through my radio duties in London, I had begun to feel stuck and rather depressed, wondering after about a decade of doing virtually the same thing day after day, how I could move forward. Iona, usually bright and happy herself, had obviously noticed a change in me.

Apparently, she had said to a friend: "I just don't know how I can hold up Martin anymore?" Indeed, I was feeling my confidence was taking a plunge. It seemed to me that everything I tried just turned to dust. None of the ideas I was putting up to producers were being accepted. It was certainly depressing. Nothing exciting was happening in my life.

Now, Iona greatly encouraged me to go to one of the ST introductory evenings. These were run simply to give people information. There was no pressure to join up. So Iona got to know that some of these introductory evenings were being run in London. One they heard about was taking place at a hotel near Paddington station. Reluctantly, I agreed to go. In due course, I was extremely glad I did!

There was a young man there who was running an ST course for a group of people in Bristol. He began to tell us all about the ST course and how people were finding it was changing their lives. I was totally fascinated by what he was explaining to the group of us who joined the introductory evening that day. I realised I was hearing exactly what I needed, and with Iona came away with a leaflet detailing just how 'Self-Transformation' was helping people with an understanding of what was actually driving their lives.

So I joined up for a London course in April 1985. It would take six weeks of several evening lectures and two intensive weekend workshops. It was in fact quite scary as I couldn't be sure exactly what I would be letting myself in for, but I did learn a lot from it. However, we were particularly asked not to evangelise, so I must leave it at that.

Chapter 16

The Final Exhibition

Tragically, though not surprisingly, my father was never the same again after his accident in South Africa, though he did slowly improve and began to move around reasonably well. But for an artist, worse was to come. He started to realise that he was losing his sight. The development of cataracts made it impossible for him to paint and he decided to give up what had been a vital and creative part of his whole professional life.

This was a very great sadness to him. But back in 1968, he did decide to arrange one final exhibition. This took place at a gallery in Arundel and attracted huge interest, particularly as he'd spoken about the exhibition one evening on South Today television. He entitled it '50 Years a Painter'.

I can remember going to the Gallery and seeing a queue of people waiting outside to get in; I'd never seen that before! Father was selling so many paintings that he had to go back to the studio to bring back piles of sketches, unmounted and unframed. The exhibition was particularly interesting too, as it covered four generations of the family; there was a work by my grandfather, Oliver Hall; and in addition to all the Claude Muncasters, there was also my own modest painting I'd done in South Africa and a little drawing by Clive's eldest son, Maximilian. It was all most exciting.

I don't remember the figures, but I know that for once, my father did really well financially. But sadly, this was scant good fortune. The doctor advised us that in order to at least improve his sight, he should undergo a cataract operation. It was arranged for him to go to the top eye hospital, Moorfields, in London. But now, another problem was beginning to show up. He was diagnosed with a weak heart and this could possibly be troublesome when it came to an operation and a full anaesthetic. However, with the help of drugs, the medics believed that the operation for cataract would not be a concern.

But there was drama to come. In the middle of the operation, his heart stopped and there was panic all round! By a happy chance, however, the heart team was visiting the hospital that very day and with frantic urgency, they were called into the theatre. Another godsend for my father. With great professionalism, the team got my father's heart beating again and it was decided to complete the operation.

I had gone to see my father that day to give him some comfort and support. I waited outside his room until I was told he was awake and able to be visited. It was not a happy time for me. As he came out of the anaesthetic, I heard him being dreadfully sick, a sound I had learned to hate, as he was so often ill when at home and had retired to bed with a migraine. These used to hit him badly and leave him for 48 hours with a ghastly headache. I think these migraines often happened when he'd been through a period of considerable stress. Fulfilling a large commission to a deadline always meant stress for him, particularly when he had to deliver several black and white detailed pen and ink drawings for a magazine like *The Sphere*.

The 'Athlone Castle' of the Union Castle mail fleet in the King George V dry-dock at Southampton. One of my father's amazingly detailed pen and ink drawings for the Sphere magazine.

Today, of course, a cataract operation is almost routine and incredibly effective, as I well know myself having had to go through the operation. In many ways, it has truly changed my life and much to the better.

For my father, however, the problems and difficulties with his eyes continued. He was prescribed spectacles with three different lenses, which he found really hard to manage. He would reach for something on the dining room table, for instance, and miss the article he was aiming for, or knock one over! I have to say he was incredibly good about it all and often made a joke of it.

At about this time, I suggested to the producers in the BBC Radio Religious Department that he would be an excellent presenter of 'Thought for the Day'. This idea was accepted and my father broadcast a number of the programmes, attracting hundreds of letters. His talks always began with an excerpt from Mozart's 'Flute Concerto'.

In one of the series, I read a short poem of his choice to introduce his 'Thought' – or perhaps 'thoughts' would be more accurate. He always spoke on themes that came from the heart of an artist, so it was refreshing to hear something that wasn't 'churchy'.

While I was at the BBC and involved with "Thought for the Day" broadcasts, I was fortunate enough to meet some extremely famous performers. 'Household' names, indeed.

One such was the actor, Kenneth More.

After he had presented his week of 'thoughts', I was able to have a good chat with him. A few days later, quite by chance, I met him walking down a street in Soho. I think we'd both been recording and narrating commercials, and we talked again. Such a delightful chap. I told him I remembered seeing the premiere of that marvellous film, "Genevieve", in which he starred, among others, with that beautiful actress, Dinah Sheridan.

I met her at a friend's luncheon party one day and she told me hilarious stories about things that had gone wrong in making that film about the old vintage car. Kenneth More, apparently, had been particularly funny!

Another 'name' was that of Anna Neagle. Like Kenneth, she had broadcast a week of her 'thoughts', and again I was able to have a chat with her.

A day or two later, I visited Anna's London home and had enjoyed a most interesting conversation about her experiences in films. Whilst there, I also met her husband, Herbert Wilcox, the celebrated film director. His enormously popular films, starring Anna Neagle, included: "Piccadilly Incident", "Spring in

Park Lane", "Maytime in Mayfair" and "Odette". Terrific movies. There were many others, too.

Another time, I was delighted to introduce Vera Lynn for a radio programme about her life. I found her such a lovely person, so completely natural.

I'm afraid by now my father was becoming very poorly and I had to take my recorder to 'Whitelocks' for him to speak into the microphone at home. Travelling to London would now take too much out of him. The doctors were doing their best to keep him going; he actually told me that he was counting out seventeen different pills a day – some to counteract the side effects of others!

The scenario was not good and we all became increasingly worried. I found his voice was becoming weaker too when I recorded for him. He had lost a lot of the timbre and vocal power which had been so much of his personality. Indeed, my mother once told me she'd married my father for his voice. I've earlier alluded to that, too, as she thought he sounded so much like Paul Robeson.

So time went on and I kept up my duties at the BBC. Meanwhile, my father was becoming weaker and spending most of his time upstairs in bed. My mother, knowing time was getting short, arranged for Clive to come home from the States and he was there just in time.

The End Comes for My Father

One morning a little later when I was at home, my mother rang me clearly concerned. "I think you had better come, Martin," she said. There was something in her voice which made me realise I had to be quick. I rushed out to the car, only to find that it had a puncture. Horrors! I now had to change the wheel as quickly as I could, then tore off to Sutton, breaking a few speed restrictions, I'm afraid.

My father was sitting up in bed with his eyes closed. I sat on the bed with him, holding his hand. I was amazed to discover how soft it was. We were all in the room, my mother, Clive and myself, while I explained to him that I'd found the car had a puncture and I'd had to change a wheel in double-quick time. He certainly heard what I said as he chuckled with quiet laughter.

Moments later, he sat a little forward and said clearly: "It's wonderful to see that beautiful face again." I felt it was probably his mother, whom he adored, and who had come to 'help him over the stile'. He then slowly pursed his lips and was gone. His body fell a little to one side and I tried to straighten him up. But I felt the whole weight of his body and was unable to move him. Meanwhile, my mother and Clive rushed out of the room, quite unable to take the tragedy of the

237

moment. But I stayed with him for quite a while, praying that he was now at peace and returned to his spiritual home.

It so happened that father's very special friend, Jack Williams, came in to see us at that very time and I told him that father had just died, minutes earlier. Jack suddenly started up the stairs saying: "I must see the body!" But I stopped him, possibly wrongly, but I was certain that my father would not have wanted to be hovered over. He hated any fuss. Actually, earlier that evening, my mother's next door neighbour, Robert Minnitt, called in to comfort her. They became close and very special friends and, in fact, later married.

Some special arrangements were made for my father's funeral. He'd left a wish that he be drawn up to the church on a traditional farm wagon, pulled by a carthorse. And so it was on a cool early December day that the coffin, covered in flowers, made its way up the hill. It was a fine sight as the wagon was drawn along by a great Shire horse. All the family, Iona, myself, and my children together with their cousins, some of Clive's boys, and Clive himself, of course, all made a wonderful family group walking up the hill together to St John's Church at Sutton. Trotting along with us was our collie dog, Patsie.

Times like this can bring back memories. Seeing our collie, wagging her tail happily, brought a clear memory of my father's collie dog, Meg, which he had bought from a farmer in the Lake District when we were on holiday at Newby Bridge. My father adored that dog. She shadowed him wherever he went and used to sit in an old chair next to his desk in the studio. He always took Meg with him when he walked down the lane to the post box. In his desk, he had a small drawer in which he kept his stamps. When he'd finished writing his letters, he'd open the drawer to get out the necessary stamps. Opening the drawer hardly made a sound, but as soon as he pulled it out, Meg would jump from the chair and go straight to the door! It was the signal for a walk. These collies are incredibly intelligent.

So many thoughts ran through my mind as we all walked up to the Church, with my mother waiting for us at the top. A photographer had positioned himself at the bottom of the hill and I'd asked my mother if she was happy for the colourful scene to be photographed. She was not at all happy with the idea, so I had to ask the photographer to refrain from taking shots. Just for once, I later wished I had gone against my mother's wishes. It meant we had no record of a unique and memorable family occasion. I was sure my father would have wished us to have a record.

The service in the Church was most moving, with some of Clive's music and a CD of a beautiful aria from Mendelssohn's 'Elijah'. My father was then buried quite near to his mother's grave in the same churchyard.

Next day, I was working in the kitchen, doing some tidying and washing up. I put on the 'Elijah' CD and was suddenly filled with grief, bursting into floods of tears. I realised I hadn't yet fully grieved for my father's passing. I was so deeply grateful to him for all he had done for me through the years of my life, especially towards the end. We had been very close…

'Clouds Hill' and an Invitation to Poros

Now I want to shift the scene a bit and go back to our early days at Clouds Hill. It was our family home, in fact, for forty-three years. It was a typical, beamed Sussex cottage – two cottages together actually – but still small for a growing family. We had four bedrooms, a tiny bathroom and a study upstairs for me in one of the bedrooms; there was a good-sized kitchen, a small dining room and a comfortable sitting room with an inglenook fireplace. With its historic old oak beams, it was a place of great character and had a history which went back to the 16th century. It also enjoyed a fantastic view over a large meadow and away to a beautiful hill called Green Hill, this side of Fernhurst. The only playroom for the children was a lean-to, shed-like room, small but good for the children before they grew too big for it. But they had marvellous space outside across wide lawns and, as I've said, had great fun chasing round the house with the dog trying to catch them! Tim was the leader and he was usually the one who made up all sorts of games.

We'd only been at Clouds Hill for a few months when a man came up the drive on his horse and introduced himself as David Bawtree. He told us he lived with his family in a cottage across the lane. He'd come to welcome us to the village, but also to issue an invitation. He told us he had a fine old 40ft yacht, 'Genesta', which he kept on the island of Poros in Greece. He chartered the yacht in the summer, but in the spring he always organised what he called a 'shake-down cruise'. Would we like to join him next time to help him crew the yacht for a few days?

This sounded like an enticing invitation and we agreed to take it up. We would be going in early April, about six weeks ahead. It seemed to work out all right, the boys would be at school and Miranda at the Convent in Midhurst. Iona asked her mother, Pauline, to help out as necessary with the children for the time we'd be away. However, I was concerned that we'd return at the date arranged as I was involved with a concert, for which I had to get back.

When the time came, we had to get to a travel office in London to catch a bus with David (I think his son Robin was there too) to take us to Luton. We'd be taking off in the middle of the night for a flight to Athens. From there, we had to take a boat to Piraeus and thence by ferry to Poros. By the time we were there, we were pretty sleepy!

Sailing with David Bawtree turned out to be quite an adventure. On the first day, he was keen to try out his new BMW engine on the yacht. We went off to sea in the early afternoon to give the engine a good run. However, I noticed an alarming amount of smoke issuing from the engine as we motored along. I was worried by this and mentioned it to David. He didn't seem to have noticed. "Oh, nothing to worry about," he said. "It always takes a new engine time to settle down!" But being a bit of a sailor myself, I was damned sure that all was not well with the engine and was concerned that if the situation was allowed to continue, we might soon be dealing with a fire!

At last, I got David to agree to go back into harbour and there we found out what the problem had been. The oil cap on top of the engine hadn't been properly wound home and oil was spitting out onto a very hot surface. No wonder there were clouds of smoke! A good thing it wasn't petrol, which would have burst into flame! On examination, we weren't surprised to find that the drip tray below the engine was full of oil.

David decided he must get his friendly engineer, Kostos, to come and check the engine and clear the oil from the tray. It was diesel, so had a strong smell. Kostos duly arrived and, head down, set about the task of clearing out the oil and began by opening the tap in the corner of the drip tray. Well, that was the idea. He worked for some time with a special spanner to loosen the tap. At last, with a shout of Greek victory, he held up the tap in his oily fingers.

Unhappily, with little command of English, he'd misunderstood which tap he was supposed to loosen. The actual tap he was holding up was the one needed to drain the sump oil from the engine. With horror, we watched as the sump oil gurgled away into the bilges!! David, as it happened, was pretty laid back. With a sorry look on his face, all he said, with feeling, was: "Oh!"

We were now faced with the awful job of cleaning out the bilges. However, by good chance there was a young American student, keen for a sail in a classic 40-ft yacht, and he offered to take on the job. He really got on with it enthusiastically, using copious amounts of Fairy Liquid and many cloths. It took him a couple of hours and when he'd finished, David asked us if we would like a sail. We set off along the coast, but without the kind American student, who didn't get his sail. We thought this rather hard of David, but he didn't even mention it.

As we sailed, David got out his toolbox to check his selection. Quite a mixture. I must admit that I reckoned those tools had seen better days. I was also concerned that the sails were not well set, but again, our skipper didn't seem to notice. It wasn't my boat so I kept quiet!

The next day, David decided he'd take a trip over to the little island of Kythnos, some miles to the east. We had a grand sail in good weather, taking with us his son Robin and a young French girl who'd come for the ride. There was another girl from New Zealand with us, too, but I don't remember her name.

We arrived in the late afternoon and the girls then got together to make some supper. But we needed victuals. So we all walked up the island to a small village, seeing an old lady at her spinning wheel in the sun. There was a bakery in the village and a shop to buy eggs. Iona found it difficult to get across the need for eggs; the shopkeeper had no English at all. Then Iona had an idea. She put her hand behind her, making a clucking noise as if she'd just laid an egg and the shopkeeper got the idea at once!

The island was pretty hot and seemed volcanic as the soil was hard and dry. But even so, there were small flowers showing in those dusty surroundings. It was almost biblical. We stayed a couple of days, moored alongside a pontoon in the little harbour. Then David wanted to get back to Poros, but there was suddenly a problem. A strong wind had got up and as David sailed the boat away from the island, we met a very rough sea. David was not happy to punch his way, probably for hours, through the rising rollers and decided to turn back to the safety of the harbour. It was a good decision. We heard that there'd been an earthquake in Turkey, followed by a huge storm, the effect of which we were now getting the benefit. So we were stormbound!

For me, this was suddenly a problem. I had to get back home by a certain date for the concert I was to be involved in and couldn't wait for David to decide to leave Kythnos. Luckily there was a phone in the little island post office, but I had to use my shaky French to make myself understood by the postmaster. I had to arrange new flights for Iona and myself, being unable to take the planned flight back with David. I managed to get through to British Airways and had to pay, of course, to make it home in time for the concert. It happened to be important as, I seem to remember, Princess Alexandra was the Royal guest!

We found that there was a daily ferry to Athens which came into Kythnos, hooting loudly and not staying long. After lunch that afternoon, we heard it coming and had to get our things together in a great rush. David had acquired a dinghy and we were rowed out to the ferry at speed. Once aboard we then had a very bumpy passage to Athens. It was extremely rough. Both Iona and I were thrown about all over the place! Luckily, by now we were used to the movement at sea.

I don't remember much about the rest of the journey. I think we stayed at a hotel overnight before collecting our tickets from the British Airways office. But we made it home in time for the concert – though we were sad to leave 'Genesta' and the chance of a good sail back to Athens with David and his crew.

This was another occasion, which I could have worked into a nice recorded feature for radio with plenty of interviews and lively 'atmosphere'. But unhappily, I hadn't thought ahead. I didn't have my Uher with me so missed a grand opportunity!

Historical note:

In writing this book, I am relying to a large degree on memory. On the whole, having checked where possible, my memories have served me well and are pretty accurate. However, there may be some cases where dates, for instance, don't quite match, but the stories themselves are totally true. As described at the end of this chapter, I know for certain that I had to get home by a particular date and had to leave 'Genesta' early; but without a diary record, I have written that the reason for my urgent return was probably the requirement to present an important concert. My memory is not quite clear on the detail of that. But I had done much 'presenting' in my life and knew I was definitely needed.

Chapter 17

Fishy Tails

I will now back track awhile to some family matters, which I would like to include in the narrative.

Tim had left Cranleigh, it was now 1973, and he was looking around for a job. He'd been for a short course at Sparsholt College, near Winchester. He definitely didn't want to get involved with pigs or forestry, but he was drawn to Fish Farming. Meantime, we had the idea, Tim having left school rather early, of his taking a course in further education. Chichester seemed the obvious choice and he went to the College there.

Poor Tim lasted just one term. He flatly refused to go back there again. I was hoping that some further education might help him find a job. But he was insistent. He had, in fact, loathed being at the College, not to put too fine a point on it! I therefore suggested that it would be a good idea if he looked around for some work.

He had actually heard of a local fish farm at Hammer, near Haslemere, and went to see the owner, Chris Moller. He must have made an impression, as Chris took him on to assist his partner, Paul Swann. Tim quickly got on well with Paul, and very soon had learnt a lot about the business of running a fish farm.

It wasn't long before Tim had thoughts of creating his own fish farm, albeit in a small way. At the bottom of our meadow there was a stream which ran out of the pinewoods on Cowdray land. Tim was certain that by using this stream, which according to neighbours had never dried out, he could dig at least two good ponds for trout. So he got together with a friend who had a 'Hymac', and they set about creating the ponds with the stream running through them. Chris Moller was most kind, giving Tim various bits of useful kit, and also his first fish. It was a great enterprise for Tim and he began to make a success of his idea, even finding people who wanted some stocking. I believe he also bought in some fish, both brown and rainbow trout.

But disaster was on the horizon…

One night there was a violent storm with lashing rain. The stream flooded and in the morning Tim found most of his precious fish lying half dead on the surface. Flowing through the pinewoods and over the pine needles the water had become quite acid, the worst thing for trout. The best water for trout flowed in chalk streams which were alkaline. So, Tim was presented with a real problem. How to get over it?

Someone, probably Chris Moller, suggested that if he could alter the 'pH' of the water and make it more alkaline, he might solve the problem. So Tim, being ingenious, acquired a huge water tank, set it up at the top of one of the ponds, then filled it with many buckets of water. He then bought bags of lime and tossed a lot of it in to the bottom of the tank. Next, he fitted up a small pipe, which led into the first tank. By convection, he started the water flowing gently from the tank and in to the top pond. There was a pipe in the end of the top pond to allow water to flow into the second pond and out of the bottom of that back into the stream. So both ponds, got the benefit of the limed water.

This addition of limed water from the tank worked like magic. Tim found that as soon as the lime was flowing into the trout ponds, the fish survived! The only concern was making sure the water tank was kept filled and the lime flowing. We all helped by filling buckets from the stream and tipping the water in to the tank. The movement of the water in the tank also helped to mix in the lime.

Tim now realised he had a business, so decided to get his 'Hymac' friend to build him a third tank so he could grow more fish. He really was making a success of his enterprise and was making a bit of money, albeit with the help he had from Chris Moller. So he thought he should do a bit of marketing and asked Brother Ollie to take some pictures. Oliver is a natural with a camera and has an 'eye' for a shot, rather as my father had an 'eye' for a subject.

Especially for Tim, Oliver was even climbing trees to get high shots and I remember being most impressed at the time. I told him he ought to consider making a profession with his camera, and Iona acquired a BBC Appointments application form for Oliver to sign. I believe Iona even filled it in for him, but when it came to it, Oliver told me (years later) that he just didn't have enough confidence to sign the form. That was a shame, it might have started him on the route to becoming a BBC cameraman.

However, he went on with his filming and with a group of friends in Haslemere, made a little comedy/thriller he called 'Rubbish'. It was based on a couple having had a heated argument and one of the couple had 'bumped' off their partner. The 'murderer' then paid the local dustmen to carry off the body in a bin. The film crew didn't have any props, so they used gardening gloves and wellies to stick out from under the lid of the dustbin as the dustmen carried off the bin down our drive! I can remember having a jolly good laugh when Ollie showed me the film. He even put sound and FX on the film.

I don't remember what Tim did with the photos Oliver had taken of the three trout ponds, but Tim was soon beginning to realise that his three ponds weren't giving him enough profit so he started researching around for a larger site. I went with him to take a look at one site he'd found near Treyford, not far from Elsted. It was a small stream and Tim became concerned that it might dry up in the summer. In any case, he would have to get permission from the farmer, or farmers, who owned the land the stream ran through. So that was really a non-starter.

Searching through Ordnance Survey maps, Tim spotted what looked a good chalk river, the Ashford stream, which ran out of the hills above Steep and ran on to join the Rother which skirted Petersfield. There was a perfect site in a valley near a farmhouse owned by Sir Bernard Burrows, who I believe had been our Ambassador in Turkey. Tim went to see him, and Sir Bernard told him that in times gone by there had been carp ponds in the valley below his farm. Tim looked at the site, was impressed and offered to purchase the site to create, he hoped, a profitable fish farm. I lent him the money, £14,000 I seem to remember, and Tim had a project.

It was all very exciting, and Tim did a terrific job getting several ponds dug ready for the trout. Each pond had an inlet direct from the river. Hatches at the bottom of the ponds made it possible for the water levels to be managed to maintain the best levels for keeping the fish healthy. Tim had bins of food pellets which he threw on to the surface of the ponds at particular times, and the fish would rush greedily for the pellets, making the water 'boil'!

He started to do really well and began to build up many customers who needed their ponds and rivers stocked with brown and rainbow trout. He bought a Toyota truck and a trailer which held tanks for the fish he needed to deliver for stocking.

The fish farm was most professional and he kept the grass mown between all the ponds. But after some time, he was beginning to find that keeping enough fish to make a profit meant there were too many in each tank. The fish became too crowded and to keep them free of disease, he had to introduce certain chemicals into the water. This worked well for a while, but it was proving difficult to maintain a balance between the numbers of fish in the pond and the need to serve all the customers. It was hard work and particularly stressful, especially when carting the ordered fish with his Toyota and trailer on hot summer days when it was necessary to keep water in the tanks cool for the journey, sometimes many miles. An electric pump, worked from the car battery, helped to pump air into the tanks, but it was often a worry to know if the fish had survived when Tim arrived at the customer's lake or river.

It all worked well for quite a time, until Tim found he just wasn't making a profit and had to give up the enterprise. He eventually sold to a builder who had bought Sir Bernard's property and Tim paid me back every penny of the £14,000 I'd lent him.

Meantime, I was enjoying fishing the Upper Hamble with various friends. There were only ever four of us in our little syndicate and we each only had to pay £30 to fund the fees to the farmers. One of them, Peter Bignall, who allowed us to fish along the banks of his fields – was happy with £60, and George Hodgkinson on the other side of the river was also paid £60. So for £120 we all had really cheap fishing for each season. In the Spring, we got together to clear the banks of overhanging branches and heave out any unwanted logs or broken branches that lay in the water. It was all most enjoyable and worked well for years. Indeed, personally, I have now fished that delightful stream for nearly 60 years!

Hunting for trout on the Upper Hamble.

One beautiful sunny day, Iona and I had a wonderful sail from Chichester Harbour (where I kept the boat) to the submarine base, HMS Dolphin, in Portsmouth Harbour. I had the idea of visiting my friend Richard Compton-Hall who was now Director of the Submarine Museum at Gosport. I think I had arranged to see him about another 'Bootle' story.

I was delighted with the way 'Cottontail' had sailed into the entrance to Portsmouth Harbour. The wind was not too strong and we tacked happily, taking up the wind on each side of the sail as we made steady progress. I then realised I hadn't checked astern for a while, turned to look aft and suddenly saw the massive bow of one of Her Majesty's frigates bearing down on us with the 'Ship's Company' ranged smartly at attention around the fo'c's'le. Help! This was not good.

But fortune was with us and I was able to tack swiftly out of the way. I turned the corner towards HMS Dolphin, dropped the main and gently sailed under the jib alongside the pontoon, stepping ashore holding the fore and aft warps, tied up and felt it had been a job well done.

Then Iona said: "Look, there's a black launch coming towards us. It looks like the Police. I'll go below and make the soup." I was hailed from the black launch: "Cottontail, I'm coming aboard."

Actually, he didn't have to. I was already standing on the pontoon watching the launch come alongside. It was indeed the Police – the Harbour Police – and the officer who stepped ashore began to explain: "With the Queen's Harbourmaster's compliments, sir, I have to tell you that you embarrassed the movements of the Captain of the frigate and you have to accompany me to the Police Office." This was not welcome news! I'd been arrested!

As we walked, the officer suddenly stopped in his tracks and stared at me – hard. "Aren't you…" he began. "Aren't you on the telly? Martin Mumblecaster, isn't it?" I'm sure he didn't actually **say** that, but it sounded very much like it, he was so taken off his guard finding himself walking along with a 'celebrity'. I replied that I was indeed Martin Muncaster, saying I was extremely sorry that I had embarrassed the captain of the frigate and very much wanted to apologise to him personally. "We'll have to wait until they get a line ashore," said the officer.

We were by now in the Police Office and we had to wait a while. Then, after a check, the officer handed me the phone. "We've got through to the captain," he said. I took the phone and spoke: "Captain, sir?"

"Yes," came the reply. I said I wanted to apologise profusely for getting in his way as he entered Harbour, accepting that it was entirely my fault. "I felt for you," he said. "Been in similar circumstances myself. Trouble is, if I bend one of Her Majesty's vessels it comes a bit expensive!" He was most understanding and we parted on the best of terms. I thanked the officer from the Harbour Police for his kind assistance and went back for a welcome cup of soup.

I'd learnt a whole lot that day!

Actually, it need never have happened. As I've mentioned, I was a Signalman in the Navy during my National Service and flying on the flagstaff at the entrance to the harbour, there was a signal in flags, basically saying: "Keep clear! HM ships operating in the harbour." I had missed it! I was so concerned about navigating my boat safely in the entrance channel that my eye was taken elsewhere. No excuse. If I'd seen the signal I would have kept well clear of the entrance. I could say I ended up as embarrassed as the Captain of the Frigate. It was a lesson well learned.

On another occasion, the result could have been extremely dangerous. Again, I was having a delightful sail with Iona in the Solent off the Isle of Wight, keeping clear of the deep-water channel used by the big cruise ships – or so I thought. Looking away to the east we saw the 'France' coming steadily up the channel towards us. Big ship, we thought! We were near a large buoy marking the

Bramble Bank. This is a shallow spit of sand, so shallow indeed, I heard that at low spring tides in the summer, people even played cricket on the sand when it dried out.

Iona helming 'Cottontail' with the new varnish gleaming!

Trying to discern the 'Bembridge Gap'.

The 'France' was now getting uncomfortably near and it was coming much faster than I'd realised. A 'cable' or so from the buoy, I thought we were safe. Not so. As the massive black bow of the ship began to tower over us I panicked and grabbed the starter to fire up the engine. Iona then said with remarkable calm: "Why don't we move away on the other tack?" Of course, that was the thing to do. I immediately put the boat about and we sailed quickly away. What I hadn't realised was that the big ships used the Bramble Bank buoy to turn into Southampton Water and on into the docks. The feeling of relief was considerable as we sailed away clear from the 'France'. Very frightening had been the five loud hoots warning us to keep clear. It was a close shave!

This Time – Safety First

There is one other incident I well remember. I had taken Miranda for a sail and we went to Bembridge. We tied up alongside the quay at the end of the harbour and climbed up onto the quay and were able to look down on the boat from above. I was delighted to see what a beautiful shape she actually was, with the varnish on the coach roof, for'ard hatch and the seats in the cockpit shining in the sun. We then went off to a local café for some lunch.

When we returned to the boat to sail back to Chichester the wind had freshened considerably. We prepared to leave and as we sailed out of the entrance I realised the sea had got pretty rough from increasingly strong winds from the nor'west. The skies were black and I could see we would find it hard to push the boat against a rising sea. What was more, apart from my young Miranda I was on my own. If we had any sort of crisis – Miranda overboard for instance, heaven forbid! – I might not be able to cope. I decided that the safest option was to return to harbour. So I brought the boat around and with the wind astern had a super sail back to safety.

As we ran in, a fisherman in his large, sturdy sea boat passed us leaving harbour. He called out to me: "Sensible decision!" So we decided to leave 'Cottontail' in the care of the Harbourmaster until I could return to collect her. It was actually a week before I was able to do this, but as we headed for home by bus and ferry, I was happy with the decision I'd made.

Other memorable occasions which gave us great delight were making programmes using 'Cottontail' and arranged by John Frost, an excellent and most creative producer working in Southampton with 'South Today'. The basic idea was to make documentaries about a sailing family. In the first one, I remember sailing the boat up and down in Chichester Harbour for John and the cameraman to get really beautiful shots of 'Cottontail' under sail. It was great to be broadcasting again.

I decided to name my new boat 'Cottontail'. Here, positioning the boat for the TV cameras.

... And the sails well set.

By then, I had done quite a lot to improve the boat's sailing characteristics. These included (for sailing enthusiasts) a mainsheet horse which enabled a much more equal haul down on the mainsheet. When I bought the boat, there was only a double sheet rove through a block on one side so on the other tack there was only a single sheet which meant the sails couldn't be hauled down so strongly and thereby set so well. I had also made a bowsprit out of an old ash oar which gave me another sail for'ard. This certainly helped the balance of the boat and in good weather I could keep just a finger on the helm. A lovely feeling. I think this addition gave another quarter of a knot.

John had some splendid ideas for shots. We even suggested he'd get a nice sequence filming our collie dog, Patsie, digging into the dunes at East Head. She'd found a bunny hole and was working her way into it with huge energy, great clods of sand flying out behind her. Great pictures! Ollie also reminded me of another sequence with Patsie tearing after and catching a 'Frisbee' in the air. It was all a lot of fun, with sailing sequences and picnicking on the beach, all part of the family outing. It made a very watchable documentary.

Another film John wanted to make with us was more a series of two programmes. He had the idea of sailing the boat round the Island. I thought it wise to have a professional on board with us so I invited my good friend John Williams to join us. John was a man of huge experience; he wasn't just a master mariner, he was an 'extra master'! I had been to his navigation classes which he ran at the Navigation School in Warsash and he'd sailed with me several times including a cracking good sail we had to Poole. We stayed overnight and enjoyed a speedy downwind sail back to Lymington and New Town Creek. We stayed in the creek for the night, watched by some very inquisitive swans.

So I reckoned that if we had John with us for the filming he could navigate the boat, getting 'Cottontail' into all the angles John Frost wanted, leaving me free to concentrate on the shooting and any presentations I had to do to camera.

It all worked well and I think John F was happy with the sequences, including various runs ashore to visit interesting places on the island, specially a beach known for its fossils. We even sailed around the Needles and the Needles Lighthouse. One thing let us down for fine sailing however, the weather! It was absolutely beautiful with hot sun, but with a big high pressure over us there was next to no wind. But the sunny weather gave us some super shots of the boat anyway.

I didn't always sail in 'Cottontail'. I had one or two other enjoyable sailing offers in other people's boats. I've mentioned our adventures in Greece and a particular invitation which took me to Sweden and back across the North Sea.

A very good friend of ours, John Worlidge, Chairman of Wiggins Teape, the paper company, had a fine 34-ft 'Sweden yacht', built at Hellsingborg, in Sweden. He'd had to return it to the builders for repairs to the teak decking which had been coming adrift. After the necessary work, he didn't have time, unfortunately, to sail the boat back to the UK himself, so asked an ex-Navy Commander friend, Sandy McCarthy, to do the job for him. Sandy lived locally in Haslemere and got together what he called 'a scratch crew' of three friends. He kindly included me, knowing I had spent time in the Navy. Not that I could have helped much with the navigation!!

Sandy was a splendid and very experienced skipper. He gave us a fine time and a lot of fun. His droll sense of humour, in all conditions, even panics (!), stayed with him and he gave us many laughs. Indeed, I was so amused that each time he came out with something funny, I dived into the fo'c's'le up for'ard and wrote down his 'sayings'. At the end of the trip, we had printed a little booklet of 'Sandy's Salty Sayings' and presented this to him with much ceremony at a special celebration party.

For the record, below are some of the quotes from the book of 'Salty Sayings':

A McCarthy maxim: "During your time at sea, you will learn much from seeing things done well; you will learn far, far more from seeing them done badly!"

Skipper's Terminology:	Meanings:
Absolutely no rush:	Do it now!
I'm situating the appreciation:	I am in full command of the present eventuality
A right fundungulus:	A mariner's phrase used to describe a minor mishap (usually applied to another yacht's evolution; e.g. as she dismantles the jetty coming alongside!)

"Air!" (spoken roundly):	This command can be defined only by the Skipper in person
A message of encouragement:	This ship is run on the principle that if the crew is seen to be enjoying themselves it must be stopped!
"This is the best cup of Bovril ever":	From the cook below, "What 'e doesn't know is that it's Marmite"
The culinary delights of 'Cuppa Soup'	This tastes precisely the same as the last packet!
Don't do anything rash:	Try not to jump over the side
When saluting, lead with the elbow:	By the way it is at least five minutes since you last saluted me!
etc. etc. etc.	etc. etc. etc.

Actually, these 'sayings' had been occasioned by all manner of experiences along the way, as we sailed from Hellsingborg, down through the Danish islands, then through the Kiel Canal with fishermen hopefully dangling their 'lures' along the banks. Then on into the Dutch canals, at one point going aground and being completely stuck, tricky in a canal with no tide! From the Skipper: "This really doesn't look very promising!"

We were journeying in the Spring and the landscape around the canals was most beautiful. We went north to Heligoland, the island held by the Germans during the War, I believe. We stayed overnight, and I well remember our supper of the most delicious fresh fish I've ever tasted! Then back to Holland, taking a brief break at Den Helder, a harbour at a gap in the coast. From there we set sail for our crossing of the North Sea. Fortunately, we enjoyed pretty good weather. However, sailing through the night with precious little sleep, I remember a moment as we approached Harwich when Sandy asked me to check our position on the chart. I went below to return to Sandy with the news that all seemed well. Not quite well with me, however.

The lack of sleep had caught up with me and as I got back to the cockpit, I literally fell asleep standing up and collapsed in a crumpled heap with Sandy saying: "You really must take more water with it, Martin!"

We made Harwich safely, where I left the boat, leaving Sandy with help from the others, to return John's boat to the Hamble. It had all been a marvellous and most unusual experience.

'Cottontail' Goes Home for the Winter

In the autumn, I always trailed the boat home to sit in our drive for the winter to allow me to do any necessary work on it. In fact, this amounted to a great deal of work. A wooden boat needs a lot of maintenance. I used to take off the hatches and the slatted seats in the cockpit for revarnishing. The footholds along the sides of the deck also had to be revarnished. I worked in the small lean-to room (once the children's playroom) off the dining room to thoroughly rub down with 'wet and dry' sandpaper, then varnish, the items I had removed. I kept the room warm, even in the winter, so the varnish would run easily.

The mast and rigging had to be unshipped and stored in the garage. In the Spring, the mast had to be rubbed down and revarnished and all the rigging greased. Doing all this maintenance, I could be sure that everything was seaworthy, especially that the rigging wires were in good order. When at sea, it's a good feeling that all the rigging is safe and strong, especially when it gets a bit rough!

One year, with the boat sitting undercover in the drive, with a specially shaped hammer, I chipped off all the old anti-fouling on the iron bilge keels – a long and tiring job, but necessary to keep the bottom clean for better sailing. Another year, I repainted the whole inside of the cabin. It freshened it up nicely.

We waited for a nice warm Spring day to paint the hull (Iona was a wonderful help) with the boat's deep blue enamel, and also all the white enamel on the back of the cabin in the cockpit. This was actually a very tricky job. Too much paint on the brush and it would drip down in 'curtains'. Not enough on the brush and the paint didn't cover properly. But we both got quite good at it with practise, and 'Cottontail' looked like a new boat in the Spring, usually about May, and before the tourists arrived, we took a few days sailing in Chichester Harbour, or over to the Isle of Wight. This was always a special time we had together. But I soon had to get back to my freelance work and more broadcasting.

Chapter 18

Miranda's Wedding – and NEWAYS

Moving on, 1984, turned out to be an interesting and full year.

First, after having my boat for 22 years, I had to say 'goodbye' to her. I was finding that after all my painstaking work through the winter, I was only sailing in her on the odd occasion. I was now getting very busy professionally and time was at a premium. In any case, I needed the money! I got a good price for 'Cottontail', around £4,000, a lot more than I'd paid for the boat. Nevertheless, it was a great sadness to me as I watched my precious craft being trailed away down our drive. Tears were rather near. I had sold her to a man who lived at Christchurch, in Hampshire. I very much hoped he'd look after her well.

Around three years later, in August 1987, we had to prepare for Miranda's wedding. She married a most charming young Army officer, Gareth Thompson. He was on short-term commission.

A wedding day is a most special and memorable occasion for any family and Miranda's certainly came up trumps. As it happened, Miranda's marriage had taken place before the 'great storm' of October that year. I remember waking up in the night of October the 16th with Iona beside me in bed, to the sound of that violent storm. It was extremely noisy. Getting up and looking out of the window we saw flashing blue lights at the electricity sub-station in the valley. It was all pretty scary. Michael Fish, the BBC weatherman at the time, hadn't forecast the storm hitting the south and had told us not to worry. It would miss us. But it didn't! He's never heard the end of it, poor chap! The nearby electricity pole had been pushed over and the wire had pulled bricks and tiles out of our roof. We lost electricity for several days and the telephone for a month. Even our taps were dry for a while. We were thankful that we had spring water from the pond!

The wedding itself was very beautiful and went without a hitch in the local St Peter's Church at Lynchmere. Members of the Haslemere Choir, with whom I'd sung for many years, sang Clive's *Wedding Anthem*, which he had composed in 1959 for my wedding to Iona at Fittleworth Church. I also read, feeling deeply moved, the passage on Marriage from the famous book, *The Prophet*, by Kahlil Gibran.

After the service, my uncle Robin in his smart classic Talbot, drove the happy couple back to Clouds Hill for the reception. The flowers in the marquee were a picture and the champagne flowed. It was so hot that we men had to take off our jackets, revealing in some cases a display of very colourful braces! Gareth spoke really well with much humour.

All in all, a grand day, with Miranda going away in a smart dark blue outfit with hat to match. I must say, I breathed a sigh of relief that, with no wind, the marquee was still standing!

'Going away' Miranda in her dark blue outfit with hat to match.

Off to Iona

After the wedding, when most people had left, our dear friend, Caroline Weatherby, spoke to me and invited us to join a group of friends for a spiritual (not religious) 'retreat' on the Isle of Iona in a few days' time. We readily agreed. Iona had been named after the island, as it was where her parents had spent their honeymoon.

The journey was quite a trek. Again, we stayed the night with Iona's sister Sylvan and her husband Michael in their house near Newcastle-under-Lyme. Again, we left at 3.45 next morning to miss the early traffic in Glasgow. Once past Glasgow, we stopped for a much-needed breakfast in a 'Little Chef', then drove on to Oban to catch the ferry to Mull. Once at the terminal, we met up with several friends who were also catching the ferry. Then it was across Mull, nearly an hour's drive, to the village of Fionnphort, leaving the car at the top of the hill, to take the next ferry across the Sound of Iona to the Island itself.

Arriving at a large concrete ramp where the ferry ground to a halt, we were at last at our final destination. We all walked up the hill to the Columba Hotel where we were to stay. It was good to be there.

We sorted out our room, then went down to supper. We were at once introduced to Amanda Salmon, one of the Cadbury family. She became a good friend, as did her cousin, Dr Martin Walker, who with his wife, Jemma, ran the retreat.

It was an absorbing time, with Jemma giving talks on spiritual lines in the mornings, and, most interestingly, asking if anyone had had any dreams. Many had, of course, and it was fascinating to hear about people's dream experiences, and how Jemma endeavoured to interpret them. Some interesting things came out. I don't remember any of my dreams, but I do recall that something I dreamed about had connections in my life later on.

On the Wednesday, we all walked over to the bay where St Columba is reputed to have landed when he came to Iona from Ireland. This was a beautiful bay enclosed by lichen-covered rocks and we collected coloured stones from the pebbly beach. The sun shone for us on that day and it made what Jemma termed our 'pilgrimage' even more enjoyable.

On another day, we climbed aboard a local fisherman's motor boat and visited the Island of Staffa, some walking into 'Fingal's Cave' with memories of Mendelssohn's beguiling Hebridean music. One afternoon, Martin took me to the old marble quarry. Historic, rusting machinery lay abandoned, the famous Iona marble having been worked out. I did, however, find a large, smooth marble stone, glinting wet at the tide line. I carried it home and have it to this day.

All in all, over the few days, we had a wonderful time with our group of dear friends. Our 'silent breakfasts' were something different, actually most enjoyable, though the quiet meant the clatter of plates, cups and saucers became much more noticeable and Amanda told me how on one occasion she and Martin got the giggles and just couldn't stop. Apparently, there were a few glowering faces that morning from those who didn't appreciate the joke!

We spent some time visiting the Abbey before we left the island. Years earlier, I had been to the island to record a feature for the BBC's Religious Department. I remember the Abbey then needing some restoration. But by the time we were there for our 'retreats', it had been repaired and much improved.

After my time at BH and years of freelancing, I was clearly still kept extremely busy. Looking through my diaries completely at random, I am reminded that over time I was often asked to present on special occasions for charity and I found that 1991, in particular, was another very full year indeed. In February, it was the year I joined Melody Radio, so was kept busily broadcasting on a regular basis.

Memorable, was the day I joined prominent figures from the worlds of broadcasting and politics who gathered at St Martin-in-the-Fields, London, for a Service of Thanksgiving for the life of Sir Ian Trethowan, who I have spoken of warmly in other chapters.

On the 5th September, I see I took part in the last 'South Today' from the old South Western House studios. It was from there that we had started the original 'South at Six'. On this day, BBC South moved into new purpose-built headquarters opposite the Civic Centre in Southampton.

Later, on Saturday 14th December, in aid of a West Sussex Macmillan Appeal for Cancer Relief, I introduced a Christmas programme of words and music with the world-famous singer Mary O'Hara. It took place at the famous and historic Parham Park, near Storrington in Sussex.

It was also the year I fitted in another visit with friends to the Isle of Iona. In fact, I visited the Isle of Iona a couple more times over the years. On the second occasion, I took my tape recorder and came away with the hypnotic sound of the waves breaking and curling up the beach at the north end of the island. A magical island indeed; just the material for a feature on the Radio 4 'Countryside' programme.

One of the most unusual and historic stories which I covered for the 'Countryside' on Radio 4 was about an original mail coach run from Bristol to London. The old coach in smart and polished 'livery', belonged to the insurance company, Norwich Union, which was brought out for special charity events or great ceremonial occasions. This was most definitely a ceremonial one!

The coach was driven by the then famous expert coachman, John Parker, who loved his horses. For this particular event, he was commissioned to drive the old mail coach from Bristol to London. It was the first time there'd been such a mail coach run for 200 years.

I joined the coach with other 'selected' passengers at the point known as *'The Nail', in Bristol. John Parker was going to drive his team of horses all the way from there to the City of London. It was a memorable spectacle, redolent of a Dickens scene, with us all dressed up in traditional greatcoats and sporting colourful scarves and top hats. Luckily, the weather was with us.

They're away! The coach and four leave Bristol.

Crowds all the way

THOUSANDS lined the route of the record-breaking journey to London as the first-ever Mail Coach run from Bristol 200 years ago was re-created. Crowds cheered at every stop — past Bath Abbey and through Chippenham's rush-hour traffic.

There was hardly room to change the horses in Marlborough as the crowd surged forward. It was the same story at Newbury in the early hours of the morning and even just before sunrise at Slough there were still knots of well-wishers.

The fastest team change of the journey at Chiswick beat the 96-year-old record and then it was down the Mall, past Buckingham Palace and on to Post Office H.Q. in London's Edward St. It was a shattered but triumphant John Parker who got down from the box.

The coach and four leaves Bristol

I managed to acquire this photo from the Norwich Union Archive. That's me in the top hat, behind John Parker and to his left.

The plan was to take the coach through the night, changing the horses en route at an ancient coaching inn at Marlborough and other places along the way. We had with us the 'Postilion', standing proudly on the step at the back of the coach, blowing his long brass post horn from time to time, as he greeted the long lines of spectators in fields by the road waving and cheering as we clattered along the highway.

It was indeed a unique journey and I got some good spontaneous interviews with some of the 'passengers' and with John Parker himself as he held the reins, talking to his horses. I also recorded the shouts of encouragement from the onlookers and the sound of the hooves of the horses and their jingling harnesses. Wonderful radio.

As we drove into London past Buckingham Palace, down The Mall and on to the Post Office HQ in Edward Street, we all cheered heartily as we arrived in the early dawn next morning, hearing that our 'mails' were delivered before those of the Post Office!

That historic 'run' was certainly most enjoyable and thoroughly worthwhile. It made for quite a highlight in the current edition of the 'Countryside' programme.

History note: *'The Nail'

This was simply a post upon which dealers, striking a bargain, would agree to the contract by placing their money 'on the nail', i.e. on the aforementioned 'post'. Hence the origination of the term 'on the nail' when a purchase is paid for immediately in cash.

By now, Iona had become fascinated by a therapy called 'Touch for Health' which she had heard about from a friend who lived locally. In time, she became really expert, and started by using me as a 'guinea pig', lying on a blanket stretched out on our dining room table, which was big enough for my long body!

Iona also became interested in massage and joined a course up in Blackpool. Why it took place there, I can't recall, but I used to drive her up to Hindhead to catch a 'National' bus which took her all the way to Blackpool. With this therapy, too, Iona became really expert and in due course attracted many patients. I had no idea who they were, except sometimes I caught sight of one as she, or he, passed the dining room window before I was banished to the kitchen!

The years jogged on, with Tim still at the fish farm at Steep and Miranda starting a Montessori School in Dulwich after passing through a course at Prince's Gate, in London (she and Gareth now had a flat at East Dulwich). She started her own school in September 1989 with just a few children, but built it up to over 70 and had to take on staff to help her.

Meantime, Tim had heard that a businessman called Piers Whitley had bought the farm at Steep. He was keen to keep the fish farm going and asked Tim to be his Manager. This was terrific news for Tim. As he said himself, he could build up the farm with somebody else's money! He threw himself into the job with renewed energy and thoroughly enjoyed working for Piers. He was given a flat in a converted farm building and was really comfortable. He actually found that Piers was very careful with his money and when Tim needed particular new tools he had to do quite a bit of persuading to get Piers to agree the expense! As I remember it, Tim got rid of his old Toyota truck and exchanged it for a smart new one which gave him huge pleasure. He used to grade the fish from the ponds depending on the sizes ordered by his customers, and then drive the fish in tanks on his trailer to the customer's venue. It was hard work, but Tim was young and very strong and was dedicated to the farm. He was actually making some money. He also had a lovely border collie he called Ben.

Tim took great pride in arriving at the various venues, ponds, lakes and rivers, for his customers, smack on time. He hated being late (took after his father in that!) and said it was bad for business to keep people waiting.

Meanwhile, my own professional life continued and Iona was doing well with her therapies, massage and 'Touch for Health'. I was much impressed by the speed at which she practised them, needing a check on an array of Bach Remedy bottles to find out the relevant one for a particular patient.

Discovering 'NEWAYS'

Iona, her usual bright and happy self.

Now, in August 1996, came an extraordinary change in our lives. Iona had been to a seminar on health supplements with a friend, who gave her a tape to listen to. It was a recording of an American doctor's talk about the health problems caused by a lack of minerals in the body. Iona listened in the car on the way home. She was impressed by what she heard and bought a bottle of minerals which her friend had acquired from an American Company called NEWAYS. When she'd finished the bottle, she wanted to order some more. But her friend said: "I can't keep posting you bottles, why don't you sign up with NEWAYS as I have, and you'll get the supplements you want wholesale, direct from the company." Iona did just that, and so began a trail of events which brought incredible financial returns, but, sadly in the end, most distressing tragedy…

At the time, Tim was getting a bit bored with continually having to grade fish into the tanks and then driving miles, often in summer heat, to serve his customers. Iona quite soon had a whole lot of information about NEWAYS, which was doing particularly well in Australia. The brochures and paperwork came to Iona from Australia and she put them all on to the dining room table intending to read them later. Tim spotted the papers and asked Iona if he could read them. Naturally, she was happy for Tim to look through them.

Tim then studied them in great detail and asked Iona how he could become involved. He saw the opportunity of starting a new business. He said: "I think this Company will be great in Britain." Iona told him that all he had to do was join with her in the business of NEWAYS, and so, under her, she signed up Tim as a distributor. Tim then realised that he, in turn, would have to encourage lots of other people to join him in the network marketing business of NEWAYS. He had been most impressed by the doctor's talk on the tape about the serious effects of lack of minerals. So he copied the tape and started sending it out to people he thought would be interested. One of these, not surprisingly, was Piers Whitley and taking his courage in his hands, Tim presented himself wearing a business suit and carrying a smart briefcase, at Piers Whitley's door.

A whole new story of Tim's life was about to open up. When Piers heard what Tim had to tell him about NEWAYS and his new business, Piers honestly thought (as he told me later) "that Tim had lost his marbles!" However, Tim obviously had powers of persuasion as he successfully got Piers to buy a bottle of Maximol (as the mineral supplements were then called), together with a pot of Revenol, which was a supplement of various vitamins needed for bodily health.

As it happened, Piers found these supplements worked well for him and Tim persuaded Piers to join him in NEWAYS. This was a masterstroke. Tim had already signed up his brother Oliver and discovered that Piers had an excellent list of therapists likely to be interested in what NEWAYS had to offer – actually a catalogue of many products, including a cosmetic range. They split the list of names between the three of them, ninety names each, and sent out huge numbers of the tape Tim had copied. Soon, they were getting call after call, particularly from therapists wanting to try the supplements and sell them on. Tim proved to be a great salesman over the phone. He didn't have to meet complete strangers face to face. Oliver, too, was getting an exciting reaction from the tape. I can remember the two boys eating supper with us and having to keep jumping up to answer the phone. Things were really moving and money from sales was coming in abundantly. One special thing was finding this picture of Tim and 'Sumi', the love of his life. She had been a model. They were together for a long time. I am delighted to be able to include this photo of them standing by the lake at Clouds Hill.

Tim and 'Sumi' by the Clouds Hill lake which Tim had designed.

I didn't join myself. I reckoned it was the boys' business and I didn't want to 'muscle in'. The personality behind NEWAYS was an American called Tom Mower who was a chemist by trade and had put together a range of ingredients which people found most effective. Tom had an amazing charisma and a magnetism that drew people towards him. He generated a huge attraction when he spoke from the stage at large NEWAYS meetings and was able to expound at length about his various products. He certainly had a way of getting across to his audience. Thus, Tim and Ollie were building a thriving business, particularly with Piers and others signing up hundreds of people. Piers was 'specially good at 'closing a sale' and always getting people to buy a bottle of Maximol, together with a pot of Revenol, before the enquirers were off the phone! He argued that the two supplements worked well in tandem. More and more people were joining NEWAYS, attracted by the supplements which worked for them.

The money started to roll in as huge numbers were signed up with NEWAYS. It soon began to grow from hundreds to thousands and Tim and Ollie were sending out many hundreds of tapes. One evening, sitting around the supper table, the boys mentioned that I really should join Iona in her NEWAYS business. All I had to do was buy £75-worth of supplements to qualify for a commission. The boys urged me to take notice.

Thank goodness I did!

The following month, a cheque for £3,500 came through the post, much more than I'd received from a month's work for the BBC! Of course, I was hooked, and began to approach people myself to build my own business. I brought people into it in a small way and made some good friends, but what I achieved was miles away from the business Tim and Ollie were creating.

I was benefiting because, as husband and wife, we were a partnership and much of Tim's success moved up the line financially to Iona and me. We all had to remember that it had been Iona's forward thinking that was giving us such a new life. Iona had, in fact, studied nutrition anyway and was wonderful in the way she could help people with advice on which NEWAYS supplements to take and for what problems. I can hear her even now, speaking on the phone most helpfully to anyone who enquired about their health difficulties and how to use NEWAYS products. We worked together, Iona with her knowledge of the supplements, while I concentrated on the marketing and signing up people into our business. It was working well and was most exciting. It was certainly a busy time.

But it was not to last…

The Muncaster's had actually headed the largest NEWAYS group, with many hundreds of distributors in the line. The other main NEWAYS business was headed up by one Larry Brooks – a man of boundless energy with an enviable, and most successful, sales technique. Enjoying a certain congenial public face, Larry surrounded himself with endless contacts.

One such was the famous cricketer, Geoffrey Boycott, with his distinctive Yorkshire twang and, on one occasion, Larry organised a meeting with 'Geoff' for several of our top people over a lunch at Lord's Cricket Ground. Afterwards, we repaired to the bar, and who should I see with a glinting glass in his hand but none other than Stephen Fry!

Never one for missing contacts myself, I thought I should 'engineer' an introduction, and I must (I hope with benevolent approach), have mentioned my name. He turned to me in great surprise saying in those unmistakable Fry modulations: "Martin Muncaster? Good heavens, I was brought up with your voice on Radio 4! It really is good to see you." For my part, I was delighted actually to meet this inimitable 'star' of stage and screen who I have always greatly admired.

Not unnaturally, I felt much complimented, and we were able to enjoy a bit of a chat about this and that. Interestingly, there was something about his warm and welcoming manner that reminded me of my father.

It was certainly a memorable day for me and possibly even for him.

Incidentally, he was generous enough to mention my name in his book *The Fry Chronicles*, along with a string of other Radio 4 household names. Spending so much of my time at BH, I was well acquainted with nearly all of them.

Not surprisingly, among many theatrical names in his book, Fry makes much mention of his very special and long-standing friend, Hugh Laurie, another actor I, personally, greatly admire. He, like me, is a member of the Garrick Club.

Sadly, there came a time when NEWAYS was beginning to collapse. The Mower family were in deep trouble financially, especially in terms of tax.

The leaders were even called to a special meeting in Paris to find out how the top distributors (Diamonds), were thinking about the way things were going. However, another American company, Modere, finally bought NEWAYS (at a price it must be said!).

So, after huge success, for NEWAYS, it all ended in tears.

My last NEWAYS experience took the Diamonds to a momentous meeting in Germany, where we were treated by a senior director to an enthusiastic and somewhat excitable lecture about Modere, the new company that was about to swallow up our hard earned supplements business at a stroke…

Chapter 19

Hospital and More Hospital

Before long, I was beginning to notice that Iona was getting slower. I remember seeing her walking slowly up the meadow to the house, much slower than before. But I dismissed it, thinking to myself: "Well, she is over 60 now, she's bound to be slower."

But then, I noticed something else more worrying. I was concerned that she seemed to be laughing, rather hysterically, at things I didn't find funny at all. Also, our secretary at the time, Iris Graham, who in her younger days had been a nurse and midwife working at the famous Middlesex hospital in London, warned me that she thought Iona was getting unwell. Again, I was so busy that I didn't take enough notice and hoped she was wrong. I most certainly **should** have taken notice.

One morning I had taken a cup of tea to Iona as she sat up in bed, and the phone rang. Nothing strange about that, it was ringing a lot these days. But there was now something **very strange** about Iona. She grabbed my arm in a vice-like grip and yelled at me: "Don't answer it!" and then went on loudly saying: "listen, listen, listen!!" Then, frankly, she just went mad, making weird gestures with her fingers and hands. It was frightening and I'd no idea what to do.

I suddenly thought of Iris, I'd better ring Iris. She got the message immediately, dropped everything and was with me within about 25 minutes from her flat in Petersfield. By now, Iona was up and throwing things about! Oliver, thank goodness, was back with us having been away for a time. He had, literally, to shout at Iona to try to calm her down. I was most concerned that she might lock herself into the bathroom, in which case we might very well have had to call the Police to release her. They would have had to knock down the door!

Calling the Doctor

My next move was to call our doctor, John Sedgwick, in Liss. He was working with patients in the surgery. But he must have heard something urgent in my voice, dropped everything and (like Iris) was at the door hardly 20 minutes later. He sat with me in the sitting room and said briefly: "Martin, I want you to tell me the whole story."

I know it now, but of course didn't know then, that we were in for some thirteen years of sickness and tragedy... Iona was seriously ill.

It all happened on the May 5th, 2000, as I write almost exactly seventeen years ago. So much has occurred in those seventeen years.

I have decided to include the following details in this account of my life, as they had a huge effect on me for a considerable time. It actually became quite a challenge to keep going with my broadcasting profession.

I think it is fair to say that we tend only to hear about the positive times of those who become famous. Yet they have so often had many setbacks and lifetime struggles along the way. Now, on this sad day in May 2000 I sat with Dr Sedgwick, a dear friend as well as our GP, to explain to him what had happened to Iona.

He listened intently. When I'd finished, he said: "I must go up and see Iona." I now waited for him to talk with Iona and make his diagnosis. He was upstairs with Iona for quite some time, and when he at last came down he told me that he had tried and tried to get Iona to agree to take something to help her calm down. But she absolutely refused to take any medication. Hardly surprising, perhaps, given the alternative therapies she practised.

We had a long discussion and John Sedgwick ended by saying: "Given the circumstances, I'm very sorry to say I will have to 'section' her." He had clearly done his very best to avoid this and finally, he said: "Can I use the phone?"

I handed him the phone I had in the dining room as I used the table as a bit of an office. I could spread out more there than on my narrow desk upstairs. John pulled up a chair and sat down, saying: "Martin, this will probably take me five hours!" He had a list of numbers he now had to call. He had to find an 'on call' consultant psychiatrist and also a social worker who would have to come to Clouds Hill to interview Iona in order to confirm that she needed to be 'sectioned'. The social worker then had to find a bed for her. In this case, it was to be at the specialist Graylingwell Psychiatric Hospital in Chichester, the hospital for patients with psychiatric problems like Iona's. John Sedgwick told me that the social worker who attended Iona would have to accompany her in the ambulance to ensure that she was properly admitted. With all the calls and research he had to make, I could see that our dear doctor was in for the long haul!

Sure enough, it was late afternoon before he'd finished. Now, we had to wait for the social worker to arrive and interview Iona before official permission could be given for her to be 'sectioned'. It was all most distressing.

Having got the permission he needed and contacted the necessary medical professionals, John called an ambulance to take Iona to hospital. When we got her to the front door and she saw the ambulance, she was so furious she clouted poor John in the face! "Don't worry," he said, "I'm used to it!" Then, with the social worker on board, we watched as the ambulance bumped off down our drive.

It had certainly been a stressful time and I opened a bottle of wine to sit with John and review the day. I said: "What do we do now?"

He replied: "One of three things. You can choose ECT, a drug regime, or do nothing." I told him I hated the idea of ECT, but he said: "Well, it works. We don't really know why, but it does work."

I asked: "But for how long?" remembering it had lasted for some twenty years with my mother.

"Well, that depends," he replied, "people are different, but in many cases the results are almost magical. We'll have to see how it helps Iona, if you want to give permission for that route."

So, I was now faced with a pretty major decision.

My Mother's Problem – and Family Reactions

But I must turn back a couple of years to the problems I had with my mother. We had reached an extremely difficult time with her, and Robert Minnitt himself was now in a rest home, Barlavington Manor residential care home, near Sutton. But my mother had been there before him and had created huge difficulties as it was not a secure home and sometimes she would escape and walk out into the road. This seemed all too familiar! I was given an urgent ultimatum from the home. I was told to remove her immediately, because if my mother had created an accident, the homeowners would have lost their licence! Robert, thank goodness, was giving no such trouble.

Happier times. Robert and Mama in the garden at "Whitelocks", needless to say, in front of their stunning magnolia.

We found a home, 'Rosemary Park' at Marley Heights, near Haslemere, which looked pretty good and they were happy to accept my mother as a resident. With all the troubles I'd had, I just couldn't bring myself to take my mother to the home, and my darling Iona, perfectly well at that time, offered to take my mother for a drive, but then took her to the home.

My poor mother was absolutely furious and made her feelings very clear to me when I went to visit her. She was also angry that we'd had to sell the house at Sutton. I had not wanted to tell her, but apparently, Robert had 'let the cat out of the bag!'

Clive, all three thousand miles away, was really upset that mother had been put into a home. But, of course, I did agree with him that it was awful for her. She had had a privileged life before marrying my father who came from more humble circumstances. His father, Oliver Hall, as I mentioned earlier, a fine artist and an RA, suffered from having a well-to-do father who had gambled away all the family money. The Halls were, therefore, quite poor. This was all the harder as Oliver, a brilliant etcher, had been doing well, until the bottom 'fell out of the market', leaving him stretched for funds. My own father remembers how Oliver was frugal with everything, even down to making sure that the boys only took a teaspoon each when there was cream on the table. "Don't take more than your share!" he would say. He had quite strict religious views and, according to my father, would read a passage from the Bible at breakfast over their cooling porridge! My father had many stories like that.

Without my mother's money, we would have had an equally frugal life. My father was a master painter (one of the best half dozen watercolour painters of his time, it was said), but he was hopeless with money. He'd make good commissions but the fees he earned were quickly gone!

Despite their different backgrounds my parents were very much in love and my mother kept up a remarkably 'up market' lifestyle for the family. So now, it was terrible for her to find herself brought down to the low-grade life of what could only be termed a home for the mentally disabled. It was a horrid decision we had to take, but with Robert now very frail and unable to cope with running a home by himself and having a deeply depressed wife, we, very sadly, had no option. For me, it was a matter of just keeping things going, and trying to live as normal a life as possible, visiting mother as much as I could. But it was dreadfully depressing seeing her going downhill.

So we reached the turn of the century and the year 2000. At this point I had my mother in a home, Robert in another home, and Iona languishing in Graylingwell. It was, indeed, a sorry situation.

The Haslemere home, having had her with them for several months, were now concerned that my mother had suffered a stroke and she had been transferred to the Royal Surrey Hospital at Guildford. I managed to visit her, but she seemed very low. Then, at 3am on June 15th, the next day in fact, the phone rang and the matron looking after my mother said to me, very kindly: "I have to tell you that your mother has just passed away, would you like to see her?" Of course, my answer was in the affirmative. I quickly dressed, got in to the car and drove to Guildford on a beautiful June morning as the sun was rising. All the lights were green on the way to Guildford and I was able to be with my mother for a while, feeling her forehead, which was still warm. I can only say I felt pleased and relieved for her that she was now at peace after years of difficulty and distress. I felt she could now re-join my father which, for me anyway, was a comfort.

Iona Was Recovering

My thoughts and concerns now had to turn to Iona. But another considerable difficulty was, before long, to present itself. In fact, having had some ECT treatment, Iona was recovering well. By mid-July, she was more or less back to herself and I remember walking with her around the wide lawns near the Graylingwell Hospital and talking with her quite normally.

It wasn't long before she was allowed home and things were looking pretty good. I took her to see John Sedgwick in his surgery and he was clearly pleased with her improvement. He then asked her if she was taking the medication – an antidepressant. At first, she said she was taking it. But John pressed her. He obviously detected something in her voice which worried him: "Are you really taking the medication, Iona?" he asked again.

A pause, and then she answered: "Well, no, I'm not taking it actually, John, I don't need it."

At this point, our doctor became quite angry. "Iona, you must take the medication, or you'll find yourself ill again." John Sedgwick clearly showed his concern. He knew full well what was likely to be the result of his patient not taking the necessary precautions.

Iona seemed to take it all as a bit of a joke. She was sure she was right. In fact, she told me later that she was taking the pills, pretending to swallow them then going to the bathroom and spitting them out. I was to learn that people with depression could be extremely devious.

John was so concerned that he wrote me a letter, saying he could no longer take responsibility for Iona's health if she refused the doctor's professional advice. And indeed, it wasn't long before she began to show the first signs that she was going downhill again. I hoped I was imagining it. Sadly, I wasn't. Before Christmas I found myself visiting her in Graylingwell again! Dr Wilkinson, the psychiatrist John Sedgwick had engaged, had admitted Iona.

It was a sad, sad story. I remember taking her the family presents on Christmas Day and sitting on her bed helping her to open them, but she hardly knew what they were or who they were from. There was only a slow and muted reaction from her. I could hardly bear it.

Some Reflections

Any person or any family who have had to deal with the sad and protracted decline of a dearly loved one into dementia, will know all too well what that experience is like.

In our family case, it was a wife and mother who sank slowly into desperate illness, a decline which extended over some 13 years. It was a case of hospital and more hospital, doses of ECT and periods of near-death bronchial pneumonia, which gradually became worse and took a toll of increasing strain for me as a husband, as well as our family and the carers.

There must be many millions who will relate closely to such a story and it is therefore superfluous for me to tell our particular tale in detail. Suffice to say we received continuing and loving support from many quarters until the inevitable came.

Iona – A Mystery

As John Sedgwick had reflected some time earlier, Iona was certainly presenting as 'a mystery'! It was so difficult to know what to do. It became a huge problem for me with a serious cough turning to pneumonia. So, I had to ask myself, 'What next?'

Fortunately, the problem was finally taken out of my hands. One morning after Jill and Demara, two of my carers, had got Iona up and dressed, they took me into the kitchen, shut the door and spoke to me, Jill first. She said: "Martin, it is now taking two of us to deal with Iona."

Demara followed saying: "It is just an awful struggle getting Iona up and about now. It's heavy work and needs two of us. She really needs 24-hour care."

This conversation, quite an 'ultimatum', made me realise just how serious the situation had become. There was urgent need for a completely new approach. Much as I hated the idea, it was now going to be necessary to admit Iona to a home. But which one and where?

So began yet another chapter and after much research, Iona was admitted to a care home in Haslemere. It was here after two years, in the end, having to use a wheelchair, that she finally passed away on the 27th of February 2013.

After a private family funeral, we wanted to organise a memorial to Iona. Once arranged, it was held in Lynchmere Church on June 1st. It was a beautiful and most moving occasion with my dear granddaughter doing a special reading. I brought together members of the Froxfield Choir, much helped by Sara with her lovely soprano voice. Earlier, as I said, she had brought me into this choir. They sang Clive's 'Wedding Anthem' most beautifully. I was reminded again that this had been sung at my wedding to Iona on April 4th, 1959 in Fittleworth Church.

So, on this lovely summer day, with the church full to capacity, we paid tribute to Iona and gave thanks for her life. Some friends had come from far and wide to be there for this unique and memorable occasion. To seal it all with wonderful music, my dear friend, William Godfree, gave us a resounding performance of Widor's magnificent organ Toccata. I have to say, I had a quiet cry…

My wife, Iona, had been a wonderful, caring and home-loving mother to our three children, and a special and deeply loved companion to myself over a marriage that lasted 52 years. The whole long-lasting experience, it has to be said, was deeply painful, but I feel there is no need to plunge my readers into a sadness which is now history and has to be let go.

As I have so often heard it said: "Life just has to go on." Fortunately for me, it is doing just that and I am eternally grateful that I still have my many interests and projects that sustain me as I live my own continuing life, in good health, thank goodness, apart from a recent fall, which set me back a bit, but I'm recovering well.

After all the traumas, I was fortunate enough to find solace with a very dear friend, Sara Flint, who had in fact, for some time with others, been Iona's professional carer

with a partner, Aphra Peard, in a business they called 'Friends Indeed'. I was grateful that in time Sara became a very special 'friend indeed' to me. She was, of course, having been closely in touch with the problems, fully aware of what I had been going through. Indeed, appreciating my exhaustion, she took a photo of me in her garden fast asleep in a reclining chair!

We eventually came to share each other's houses and even took brief holidays together. It is not too much to infer that towards the end, as things got steadily worse, Sara had more or less saved my sanity! She became a wonderfully understanding and loving companion.

Unhappily, however, there were some desperate and shattering challenges yet to come.

Another Busy Year

But for now, there was nothing for it, but to just carry on with life; and I could see 2005, for example, was going to be another very busy year.

As my diary records: *In January, a group of our friends, distributors in our NEWAYS business, went to Brussels to attend a court hearing at the European Court of Justice. It was all about an EU Food Supplements Directive which we hotly disputed. We had engaged an excellent lawyer who made a good case for us. But we weren't sure we got very far with our case against the bureaucracy and red tape of the massive 'Brussels machine'.*

On a quite different course, I had joined BNI (Business Network International), which meant breakfast meetings once a week in Haslemere, starting at 7 am. I hoped to make some good business contacts. Going round the room after breakfast, we were all given one minute to explain our business and why we wanted referrals. Some people made good contacts. I talked about NEWAYS, but without the reaction I'd hoped for.

I also went to Holland for NEWAYS meetings set up by my friend Jon Turner who kept up contact with our distributors there. Jon gave me some wonderful support. As it happened, I had also been to Holland a number of times to record narrations for various documentaries. I usually went to Amsterdam for companies that needed an English voice. One documentary was fascinating, all about flight and the different aircraft used for all manner of reasons and different geographical locations. There were recordings at home, too, for jobs fixed up by my agents, Rhubarb.

At the end of June, I went to my cousin, John Prodger's, funeral. I had been fishing with him a number of times. John's mother, Rhona Prodger was there, too. Rhona, now 102, was my father's direct cousin. Audrey Hope came as well. She and Richard, my cousin, had been really kind to Rhona. She lived near to them at Berkhamsted.

My time was filled in many different ways.

On the 2nd of December, for my dear artist and writer friend, Pat Harvey, working as an Adult Education Tutor for West Sussex County Council, I opened an Exhibition of Marine Paintings in Watercolour she was holding in Littlehampton for her students. Through the year, as in many years, my diary had certainly been full.

Among special friends who had visited my brother Clive and his wife, Dulcie, on a number of occasions at their home in Princeton, New Jersey, were Peter and Rita Marshall. Peter was the first Editor of 'South Today' as I've

mentioned earlier, and who is still a very good friend half a century later! Indeed, he has most generously offered to edit my book. Who better?

Soon after starting work on my autobiography, I heard that John Tanton had died. I was most sad to have this news as John was a very good friend from broadcasting days and had been most kind to Iona and me. We met him in New York on one of our earlier visits to Clive and Dulcie. Many times, he was invited by them to spend Christmas Day at their home in Princeton. He was also a special friend of Peter and Rita Marshall, so he will be greatly missed by us all.

Not All 'Downs'

I feel I have come to a point in this book at which I really mustn't allow the impression that I've had a sad and difficult life. There have been some 'down' times and I've written about them. But I've been looking through my diaries and am reminded that I've really had a great life. The pages of my diaries were packed with incidents. I've been most fortunate to have had work that I have much enjoyed and, as I write, still am enjoying when work turns up from my agent in London. It has been a life full of interest and all manner of different happenings. I've had absorbing hobbies; my cinema to start with, which was such a passion in the early days, then golf at Cowdray with Clive and my father, and trout fishing which has taken me to wonderful places and meetings with most interesting people. The day I caught that magnificent salmon on Jura was indeed a highlight!

In 1970, just after our move to Lynchmere, I was invited to perform the words for 'Peter and the Wolf' for the Haslemere Musical Society. John Power, a jolly good cellist, was the Chairman then and after the Society's performance of 'Peter and the Wolf', John suggested I should join the choir, which I did and was a bass member for some forty years. I was also invited to act as presenter of several works for the society that need a narrator, such as reading the words for 'King David'. I must have made some impression as there were several ladies with damp eyes afterwards.

I have performed numbers of presentations, including for some fifteen years narrating elements of the Dolmetch Festivals at Haslemere. I was President of the Chichester Area Talking News for the Blind for quite some time, and have been a member of the Keats luncheon club in Chichester, having given them, years ago, the benefit of my 'Silly Sussex' stories in the West Sussex dialect, taught to me by my father. I've worked with my good friend, William Godfree, telling my stories and singing Flanders and Swann and Richard Stilgoe songs. These occasions have been huge fun and created howls of laughter. William is a brilliant pianist and singer and our audiences love him! We gave the Keats Club the benefit of a performance one year on the Club's Ladies' Day.

Looking back a bit, years ago I was invited by a naval Captain friend to join what was then The Navy League and he also asked me to be a Vice President. Since then, the organisation through various evolutions, became 'The British Maritime Foundation' with the mission to bring to the public's attention a better understanding of our need for the sea. An island nation, some 95% of our trade comes and goes by sea, and to encourage people to get involved, the Foundation gives out awards to authors, journalists and TV and film producers to put forward their products for consideration. There is also an award for the HM ship that has made a significant contribution in the year to the Foundation's mission.

Ex-ITN producer, the brilliant Rob White, the first winner of the Media Award, produces a short film, which I have several times presented, to introduce the year's contributions to the audience (much gold braid on these occasions!) at the Awards Dinner, held in the imposing dining hall at the Institute of Directors in Pall Mall. The Awards are introduced by the Chairman of the Foundation, Julian Parker, and handed out by a Royal personage or the First Sea Lord.

As a matter of interest, the roots of the Maritime Foundation go back quite a long way. The beginnings of the Foundation lie in the revival of the Navy League, which was discarded in 1967 as a result of the first aircraft carrier cancellation and the decision in 1980 by Mr John Nott to put the RN's surface fleet up for sale. This resulted in the formation of the British Maritime League and the British Maritime Charitable Foundation, which were subsumed in a single charity in 1991 and now known simply as the Maritime Foundation.

The Foundation Awards are regarded as most significant and important, and the occasions of the annual dinners, which include a number of high-profile guests, attract widespread interest.

And Now into Films!

Together with all my many commercial recordings for film narrations and adverts, I've had the greatest fun having a role in two films. The first was

'Cleanskin', a thriller about a Government agent (Sean Bean) trying to track down a young terrorist, blowing up buildings in London. During the film, an election had been going on and I ended up as the new Home Secretary. I was placed at a spot on the South Bank with the House of Commons in the background across the river, promising the public that the new Government would track down 'these dreadful terrorists'. A small part, but I thoroughly enjoyed the exercise.

I was, of course, delighted to be in the movie and arranged for a special showing of 'Cleanskin' at the Haslemere Hall. Unhappily, this didn't go down well with the 'blue-rinsed' ladies of Haslemere and some walked out! In trying to raise an audience, I'd told the choir about the showing and apparently people were upset by the violence in the film. My fault was not to warn the audience that there was violence in the film and it seemed I'd lost quite a few of my friends in the choir that night. I felt it incumbent upon me to apologise for not mentioning the violence and, luckily, I was forgiven!

Actually, Hadi Hajaig, who'd written, directed and produced the film, was ahead of his time. The violence in the film was largely *implied*; we didn't, for instance, see pictures of a beheading; but very soon, most dreadful beheadings were actually happening around the world and to completely innocent people! The character in our film who lost his head, got his 'comeuppance'. He had been responsible for dreadful tortures and beatings in Iraq, but escaped to try to hide in England. Our 'Cleanskin' agent, Sean Bean, had tracked him down keeping horses on a remote farm. This led to a huge fight. It was, actually, a really good film, but the agent who took it on did the absolute minimum to market it. So people didn't know about it.

The other film I'm in is a romantic, comedy thriller, 'Blue Iguana'. It is being edited as I write and is about a dodgy diamond collector. It has a superb cast, including the top American 'star', Sam Rockwell who was recently awarded an Oscar for his supporting role in the famous 'Three Billboards' film. Simon Callow is another big star with whom I worked in a couple of scenes. Again, huge fun and in this case, very funny!

I also spent some years with an ex-actress, Susie Tarver, teaching senior business executives, including the chairmen and secretaries of large companies, how to deal with the media. For many of our 'clients', it could be daunting to find themselves facing a camera and having to explain, for instance, why they'd allowed their factory to go up in flames! It was all good fun, but sometimes quite testing for us!

More recently, at the time of the Armistice Weekend in November 2018, marking the end of the First World War 100 years before, I gave several performances at concerts including poetry, prose and music that amazingly had emanated from that horrific war. One major concert I presented to a large audience with a professional cast, was termed 'The War to End all Wars'. But, of course, it was really only the prelude to the Second World War, when it was 'to happen all over again!'

You will remember that it was being a bit of a mimic that got me into the Guildhall. At the Armistice concerts, I gave an impersonation of a Churchill speech using his actual words with lisp and all!

After these performances, I received many very kind comments. One person said when she closed her eyes Churchill was in the room. I must have got it about right!

Chapter 20

Two Moves and a Long Wait

Now, it was a matter of facing a new life. Everything was changing on all fronts.

With Iona gone, it was necessary, rather urgently, to organise the sale of Clouds Hill, where we had lived as a family for 43 years. The annuity I had years before arranged for Iona's care suddenly became a serious concern. Stupidly I had not realised the ongoing effects of having borrowed money on the house. My financial man had most kindly fixed the loan for the best reduction of Inheritance Tax; but, of course, once the clock started ticking, the interest on the loan became a major factor in the state of our finances. What had passed me by was the fact that there was interest building up on the interest, such that there would in due course be a huge bill to pay to clear what was owed to the mortgage company. I checked up on this and found that I now owed half a million pounds!! This was scary to say the least!

I spoke to a longstanding friend, George Tremlett, whom I knew had for many years been an estate agent. He now advised me to approach Strutt and Parker in Haslemere to get them to value Clouds Hill and organise the sale. George brought over a senior Director, William Wellington, who came up with a figure of £1.2million. "Don't go over the top," he said, "It puts people off." If we achieved his advised price I would still have something over, having paid off the mortgage company their £500,000, with which to buy myself another home. I would clearly have to 'lower my sights', as C.H. was a double cottage with seven or eight acres of land, an orchard and recently the addition of the very fine trout lake. 'Willie', as he was always known, also advised me to have professional photographs taken for the brochure they would publish. It was now June so the house and garden were looking good.

The photographer soon arrived on a sunny day and walked around taking his pictures. I was most interested to see that for some high shots, he fixed a camera on a very long pole which gave him some unusual angles. When the brochure finally came out, I thought it made the property look really enticing.

'Willie' also advised me to wait until September before Strutt and Parker announced the sale. He said, by September, people were home from holiday, the children were back at school, and parents who wanted to, or had to move house, were free to look around.

In no time, it seemed September was upon us and Strutt and Parker announced the sale, including information on their website. Almost immediately potential purchasers arrived. There was an interesting offer from the Hadfield family. Nigel Hadfield was a housemaster at the Charterhouse Public School at Godalming. I was keen to let them have a look around as I thought it would be good to have another family at Clouds Hill. Nigel told me they had once lived nearby at Woolbeding and loved the area. I also had a considerably larger offer from a developer. But I was worried he'd come in and knock the place down.

Nigel and Lucy had three children, two boys and a girl like us. I seem to remember they tried offering a price lower than the 'Guide Price', but 'Willie' pushed them to the full price, arguing that they were offering for a unique property.

Now began some very tricky and protracted negotiations. Apparently, the Hadfield's solicitor had spotted that a small patch of rough land, partly wooded, at the east end of the lake, didn't appear on the Deeds. Also, it was argued that it wasn't fenced and therefore had no marked boundary. Further, it didn't appear on the Land Registry records. It was part of a parcel of land through which ran a stream and I had bought this from Geoffrey Oxley, thinking I might one day create a lake down there. Geoffrey no longer needed or wanted the land which was quite separate from his family's house at the top of the hill. Originally, the properties there had their water pumped up from the stream by a ram and the area of land had been owned by the owners of the 'big house'. This became redundant, of course, with the coming of mains water.

Clearly, the small patch of land now in question had been missed in the original sale. Thus, instead of moving ahead in a basically straightforward manner, the whole matter became extremely complicated with a great deal of to-ing and fro-ing between solicitors, building up my costs! I even went to my next-door neighbour to check her boundary against mine and her map fitted neatly alongside mine.

Now, there was more delay involved, as the Land Registry had to check the measurement of the land and its supposed boundary. We had to engage a professional agent to come and carry out the measurements. Stephen, our devoted gardener, came up with an idea – to fence the area with wire and poles to properly mark the boundary. There was talk, too, of taking out an insurance against any future dispute that might arise over ownership of the land. It was all incredibly messy and time consuming.

A Brainwave!

However, we at last arranged a visit from a Land Registry officer to come and investigate. He was a nice fellow, and I hoped he would look favourably upon our problem.

Then I had a brainwave. I suddenly remembered that there was a piece of rusty old fence that ran across the stream at the head of the piece of land in question. What was more, it joined up with the bank that ran all down our property and along the edge of the lake. I pointed this out to the officer (he having plied me with questions), and he suddenly said: "That's fine. That's just what I wanted to hear." He investigated the bit of old fence and was happy. "I'll send an instruction to the office," he went on: "and you should have agreement by Friday." – (it was now Tuesday). Friday came and went and so did a lot more days. We eventually heard that the Registry had to advertise to ensure there was nobody in the wings waiting to dispute our ownership.

So, another six weeks of agonising wait. At one point, on the phone, Nigel had said: "I think we're having second thoughts." What? But eventually, it all came together and we had 'completion' in March 2014. So Stephen's idea of poles and wire luckily wasn't needed. I had already moved into a flat in Petersfield the November before (of which more later). Relief at last!

About now, Stephen, knowing I was going to have to sell, announced that he wanted to retire, but kindly said he'd stay for the time being looking after the C.H. lawns, the meadow path down to the lake and all the mowing around the lake itself. In any case, I wanted it to look good for any potential purchasers. So I knew Stephen would stay until I left, having sold. He had been stalwart and utterly reliable for nearly twenty years and now was a huge help getting rid of the mass of stuff we had acquired over the decades and stored on shelves in the big storeroom at the back of the barn. It all had to be gone through and sorted into piles along the wall of the garage. There were six huge 'mountains' which Stephen chucked into the back of a truck, then drove it all off to the tip.

Amongst all this, there was a large fireproof cupboard filled with many of my father's pictures. There were also many files containing my father's diaries and records, year by year, from the 1920s. These were on shelves of papers my father had dated and stored. I put together most of these and offered them to the West Sussex Record Office in Chichester. Thankfully, since my father had been so much a Sussex artist, these records were unique and the Record Office were happy to accept them. Indeed, the office sent a large van to pack them into and drive them down to Chichester. I have to say that this was a huge relief to me. I'd had a carpenter to build a large cupboard exactly like the one my father had in his studio. I knew it was going to be a huge job emptying it!

Obviously, I knew I was going to have to find somewhere to live while I searched around for a permanent home. I therefore contacted the Country House Company which I knew were specialists in renting properties. One of their local staff, Rachel Turner, came back to me saying she was in charge of renting a pleasant flat above the High Street in Petersfield. She showed me round. It had a good kitchen and bathroom, a spacious sitting room and two bedrooms. It was, in fact, situated above Marks and Spencer and being at a high position was remarkably quiet. I hardly noticed the noise from the traffic in the High Street. It also had an excellent car park at the rear for residents of nearby flats, so I always had space for the car. Beyond the park was an extensive view of the South Downs and Butser Hill. All in all, perfect for my needs while I searched around for a home.

I moved into the flat on November 15th, 2013, and was very happy with the move. Sara had told me about a man called Sam Hughes-Stanton who had a removals business and was most competitive. I got in touch and we arranged the date. I was most impressed by the way Sam and his partner, Tom, carried an amazing amount of heavy furniture, including three beds up two flights of stairs. I was still on crutches at that time and was no help at all!

Sam had also told me about a good storage facility at East Meon, and a huge amount of stuff from Clouds Hill had to be put in store there. Tom was a marvellous packer and managed to squeeze everything into what was, actually, just a very large 'container'.

Time with Sara

I was now seeing a lot of Sara, me being somewhat disabled. In the months before my accident we had enjoyed many things together; walking on the Downs, going to the Yvonne Arnaud Theatre in Guildford, going to films at the New Park Cinema in Chichester (and holding hands all the way through!)

Sara and I also went to see some performances by my dear friend, Janie Dee, such an amazing and hugely talented actress. We went up to Leicester to enjoy Janie starring in 'The King and I' at the Curve Theatre. As always, she was wonderful, and we all had time for a coffee together after the matinee. We also went to see Janie, acting with her husband, Rupert, in Noel Coward's 'Private Lives' at the Nottingham Playhouse. Another triumph! I have followed Janie's profession for some 20 years. Indeed, she knew Iona in the early days. Now of course, I go with Sara.

By now I had met a number of Sara's friends, including Jenny and Richard Abbott who lived in Guildford. Sara was amusing about Jenny. She said she admired Jenny because she was always so smart and well turned out. Sara was really happiest with her hands in the soil, or working in her large allotment at the end of the garden, which she filled with rows and rows of delicious fruits and vegetables.

But I'm back to present days…

Sue Clegg (who's most kindly typing chapters of my book) kept horses for local friends and had a huge dung heap near the large field where the horses cropped the grass. Sara was adept at feeding the ground in her allotment and I helped her barrow huge sacks of horse manure from the dung heap, which we heaved into the back of her car. On one occasion, when I had helped Sara come back with sacks of manure, her daughter Lucy, came over from the family house across the street, and Sara said how thrilled she was at having such marvellous amounts of dung to feed her allotment. With a sideways glance, Lucy retorted: "Mum, I really can't get excited about manure!"

I had a jolly good laugh! It seemed such a timely and apposite remark.

I now visited all the various estate agents in Petersfield leaving them instructions for exactly what I was looking for; preferably a cottage with character in a quiet position with a good view and, if possible, with a nearby stream. It was a bit of a tall order, but now I was happily ensconced in the flat, I wasn't in a hurry. The other happy fact was that I was a 'cash buyer'. Of course, I was sent all manner of properties, but none of them on inspection was in the slightest what I was actually looking for. In a way it was quite depressing, but I knew I could be patient.

Once in the flat, the first property I heard about was an old mill cottage by the River Lavant at East Lavant, near Chichester, which was advertised at a price of £600,000. It offered much that I was looking for, including having the river nearby and quite a large garden. It also had a super view over the Goodwood land away to the Trundle Hill. I went with Sara to view the property and even made an offer. I was quite keen on the place. It had several bedrooms, a large sitting room and kitchen with an Aga cooker.

Sara, however, was definitely not keen. She advised me against it, saying it was miles from her house at Liss, and the train service from Chichester was nothing like as convenient as the Portsmouth line, which she used from Liss. Also, and this was important to me, the River Lavant always completely dried in the summer. Even so, I was stupid enough to make an offer of £550,000, but it wasn't accepted. I tried again at £575,000. Still not accepted, but thank goodness! Sara was so right, it would not have been a good place for me. There was also minimal parking and a steep track up to the main road, which would have been dreadful in snowy conditions in the winter. So Sara saved me from making a seriously wrong decision!

So life went on. I liked Petersfield as a town and the flat was well positioned for the shops and I often went to the 'George' pub in the Square for a morning coffee. I had originally wanted to find a place in West Sussex, but by now had a pretty open mind.

One day, I had a call from an old friend of mine, Charles Oswin, whose parents had lived next door to us at Four-Winds, Petworth. Charles and I were of similar age and we used to go biking together. His father had been a Commander in the Navy and was a great character. My mother thought he was most attractive and loved his naughty humour! Charles went to Dartmouth when I went off to Stowe. Charles now told me that his daughter, Suzanne, had married a man named David Harding who had a business called 'Premier Properties'. Charles thought they might help me to find a home. It was good to make contact with them as they lived close by in Petersfield. We met in 'The George' which I believe David once owned. They were most kind and drove me around various properties they thought might suit me, but without result.

The Brussels Episode

Sara now told me that in October 2013, Patrick Quanten had invited her to help him present a weekend workshop near his home at Hasselt, not far from Brussels. Sara accepted the invitation and asked if I would like to go too. Over the two days, Patrick would be presenting some detailed lectures (though in Dutch) about his work and research into the natural way of dealing with disease. Sara, of course, was much in tune with this, though completely lost as I was, not understanding the Dutch! Thus, it was that I followed them, taking in an important NEWAYS meeting which happened to be taking place in Brussels on the same weekend. I went by Eurostar and was in time for the NEWAYS meeting; (somehow being allowed on board, as I've explained earlier having forgotten my passport!) then went on to stay with Patrick and his wife, Martine, at Hasselt. Sara was already there, having driven over with them the day before after Patrick's stay for his treatments at Liss. And so began the event which takes me right back to chapter one of this book! If matters had taken a different turn, I might not even be here to tell the tale!! That terrible day happened on Monday, October 28th, 2013. Sara and I had hoped to have an enjoyable day looking around the sights of Brussels. Things developed rather differently…

Sometime before, Sara had announced she was finished with caring. She said she'd looked after other people all her life, now it was time to take care of herself! Well, that was her idea. It didn't quite work. Almost immediately, I had my dreadful accident in Brussels having fractured my left leg and broken the small toe on my right leg, an unhappy scenario. Naturally, on our return, I went back to Sara's house, having to heave myself up the stairs to the bedroom backwards on my behind, step by step, it was the only way, my beloved Sara having told everyone she was giving up caring, now found herself caring for me!

She was, of course, absolutely marvellous, giving me treatments every night, massaging my leg most professionally. My leg was now swollen about the ankles and I noticed in the mornings, after Sara's massage, that the swelling was much reduced. I was so grateful to her. She took me to St Richard's Hospital, in Chichester (I couldn't drive) for X-ray and a general check-up. The nurses and consultants had a meeting to assess the need for a plaster cast. It took them ages to decide, and I thought I might get away with it. But in the end, the decision was to fix my leg in a plaster cast. This made my leg stick straight out and I found it quite difficult working my way into the back seat of Sara's car.

I was advised to go back for another check in a month. Meantime, I looked at flights of stairs, literally, with horror. There were two flights to negotiate to get upstairs to the flat, so it was clear I was going to have to stay with Sara for some time. Luckily, I only had to keep the plaster on for a couple of days, and it was quite a relief to have it taken off and was given a more flexible brace. I felt pretty useless not being able to help Sara in the garden. Up until then, I had at least been able to weed and mow the lawns for her. But when, after the month, she took me back for another check up at the Fracture Clinic at St Richard's, it was found that my leg had healed very well. This was good news.

The state of my toe on the right leg was a different matter, however. An X-ray showed it was quite badly broken. It had certainly been very painful. The consultant offered to put a pin in it, but said that over time it would probably heal by itself. I was definitely not happy with the idea of a pin.

It was quite some time before I was able to get back to the flat. Meantime, I'd been pretty busy, though getting around on crutches, and was even able to go to London for a couple of jobs Rhubarb had booked me for. I had also been able to take Sara as my guest to the Maritime Media Awards dinner at the Institute of Directors. On that occasion, we stayed with Rob and Sue White at their house in Finchley. Rob had made another film, with me presenting, to introduce the Awards. I thoroughly enjoyed working with Rob, the consummate professional.

After six or seven weeks, my leg was much better and with the aid of just one crutch to help me balance, I was able to get up the stairs to the flat at last giving Sara a break from caring! I was still singing bass with the Haslemere Choral Society and much enjoyed performing the Carol Concert at the Haslemere Hall.

Clive had recently written a delightful carol, 'Shepherds, Shake off Your Drowsy Sleep', which had won him an award in a 'Carol Contest' in the States. I suggested to our Musical Director, James Ross, that we might sing it at that year's Carol Concert just before Christmas. He agreed, and it was wonderful to hear Clive's music performed.

After Christmas, it was great fun to join the audience for yet another Lynchmere Pantomine – Michael Tibbs was as always the dedicated producer. I believe there has been a pantomime in the Hardman Hoyle Hall there since 1945. When the Dimblebys were at Lynchmere, the boys, David and Jonathan, used to join in.

So, the year rushed on. Looking through my diary, I'm quite surprised at what I managed to pack in. Weekly choir rehearsals, joining a French class, NEWAYS meetings, several recording jobs for Rhubarb, singing the Verdi Requiem from 'scratch' at the Albert Hall, and another stay in Somerset with Sara at the Coomb's cottage. Then, amongst it all, there suddenly came a highlight…

Just What I Was Looking For

One morning in late May 2014, Rachel Turner rang me to say: "I've seen a cottage which I think might be just right for you!" I lost no time in dashing round to the estate agents, Chesterton Humberts, in Lavant Street. A young agent, Matthew, took me round to the cottage in Mill Lane, Steep, and I knew within moments, that it was just what I was looking for. Now, how to acquire it? Apparently, I was going to have to act pretty smartly. I allowed myself to get a bit excited. The brochure made it look quite charming, and I was really keen on what I saw.

Millstream Cottage.

The cottage, about 150 years old, had been improved. It offered a modern and spacious kitchen, a sitting room with a delightful sunroom adjoining, 3 bedrooms upstairs and an en suite bathroom for the main bedroom. There was also a study downstairs with a door opening onto decking outside. The garden looked exactly the right size for me and, most exciting, a beautiful chalk stream, the 'Ashford stream', ran by the bottom of the lawn. There was an extensive view over a sheep field beyond and woodlands beyond that. It all looked almost too good to be true! The stream even had trout in it! Also, the old millstream ran down the side of the cottage, a wonderful sound of waterfall, which I knew would give everlasting pleasure.

By extraordinary chance, it had been the Ashford stream, further down the river, on which Tim had built his fish farm. When I later met the farmer, Terry Cook, who lived with his wife, Pauline, a few yards beyond the cottage, (which I fervently hoped would be mine), he'd said in his slightly country drawl: "Oh, yes, I remember old Tim!"

Meantime, I was still waiting and I now found that my patience would be greatly tried once again.

Rupert and Kate Day, I gathered, were selling the cottage because they were finding it too small for a growing family. They had two delightful little girls. Robert at Chesterton Humberts arranged for me to meet Kate and discuss some details with her. I was delighted to find that Kate had been in television and that Rupert produces films. So we got on rather well! Kate told me that there would be some delay, as they had to sell a flat in London before they would have enough funds, together with the sale of the Steep cottage, to buy another larger property. So, for the moment it had to be a patient wait.

Weeks and months went by until I was told that the Days were beginning to think of renting somewhere as they hadn't so far been able to sell the London flat. If they rented, they would be able to move out of the Steep cottage. So, the 'clock' was still ticking. I was hoping to get everything sorted by the end of the year as my current contract for the flat would run out in December and another short-term rental might not have been possible.

Another Busy Year

This was certainly turning into yet another busy year. If I look back at my diary I can see a good deal more than I've already written about, such as my golf. I had managed to play quite a bit with friends and also taken some lessons. These were certainly helpful, though any golfer will know just how vital it is to keep your head still and your concentration totally fixed on the ball! After heaven knows how many thousands of shots, I still sometimes lift my head! Disaster, of course, and the ball can vanish into the rough. Funny game, golf, everybody says so.

I've also enjoyed my weekly sessions of yoga. I've always admired how our teacher, Lorraine Grocott, can remain so supple. At nearly 83 myself, I'm afraid I have to work on that!

Another great enjoyment for me is the monthly luncheons we have as members of the Keats Club. Excellent fare and always a good speaker at the Vicar's Hall in the precincts of Chichester Cathedral. Our speakers recently have included Donald Sinden no less, Peter Sallis, who told some wonderful stories, and the Artistic Directors of the Chichester Festival Theatre among many others. The name Keats originated from the early days of the Club which held its meeting in the Keats Room at the Dolphin and Anchor pub.

Meanwhile, I had organised a viewing of the Steep cottage with David Harding. He was most impressed and said: "Buy it, Martin, and if you don't want it, I'll have it!" That certainly encouraged me to have the place surveyed and the report was good.

I was also thinking of changing the car and considering a Mercedes. My BMW had been very low to lift Iona into the front seat, and by doing this many times, I found I'd been creating strain in my shoulder. It had become quite painful.

I was also very involved as a member of the Maritime Foundation Media Award judging committee. This involved many hours of viewing CDs and DVDs from the various entrants. I took Sara to the 'Members' Concert' which is organised every June at the Garrick. Great fun, and most amusingly introduced at that time by Donald Sinden. I greatly enjoy the Garrick (I was elected as a Member in 1994) and it has become my London base. Most valuable.

Now, as I waited for news of the Steep cottage I was able to see a certain amount of Sara. She was most generous at giving me meals. I am definitely not a cook. For Sara, it was just one of her many attributes! Back in March, after 'Completion' on Clouds Hill, we had even managed a short break in Malta which was a wonderful respite.

At last, news came from Humberts that the Days had found a place to rent at South Harting. However, there was one more hurdle to get over – or a concern, anyway. Kate Day had promised a friend to let her have a look at the cottage before they could release it to me, so once again I was on tenterhooks! We were now in to November, so not long before I had to give a decision re the contract on the flat.

But after the weekend, I went in to see Robert at Chesterton Humberts and he had a broad smile on his face. "The cottage is yours," he said. Imagine my joy and relief all merged into one. It was a fantastic moment. We could now go ahead to completion. That came through on Friday, November 15th, so I was able to tell Sam Hughes-Stanton to start moving me out of the flat.

A week earlier, I had given a cheque for £513,750 to my solicitor, Bryan Farley, in Haslemere, that cleared my mortgage on Clouds Hill. Things were coming together, so at long, long last… I had a home!

Chapter 21

Some Family Affairs and an 80th Birthday

I find it hard to express just how I felt having a home again and 100% what I'd been looking for. Quite amazing. I can only say I felt such gratitude every morning as I looked down from my bedroom on the garden. I gave deep thanks and have continued to do so.

There were quite a few things to do to make the cottage my own and I engaged Michael Vaughan, a wonderful craftsman, to work on various improvements. Some were just details, others more important, such as the wooden panels all around the extension which were definitely in need of refurbishment. Michael carried out a painstaking job on this but it necessitated expensive scaffolding to enable him to get at it. Back at Clouds Hill, he had converted our very basic garage into a beautiful Sussex-style timbered barn. Now at Millstream Cottage, there were things to do in the garden, too. For instance, he built us a flagstone base under the pear tree for the garden seat so that I, or anybody in the family, could sit there with a glass of wine or cup of coffee and study the stream! David Harding had suggested this and it was a perfect idea. He also strongly advised me to get a big enough garden shed – 8ft x 12ft at least – or I would always be wishing I had a bigger one. It was interesting how quickly it was soon packed with garden tools and my bike! The tiny shed the Days had used turned out to be rotten at the base when we removed it. They'd probably inherited that from the former owners anyway! So I quietly thanked David for his advice.

Another thing I was keen to do was buy the area of bank on the opposite side of the stream from Terry Cook, the farmer. The Days had wanted to do this but had found it too expensive.

One evening a man called Paul Garstin came to see me. His company was involved in building a large house next to my cottage and he came to ask me for any comments I may have. I was keen that they kept the hedge as a screen between us. I was also concerned that one of the windows high up on the building would overlook my garden. But he assured me it was only going to be a small bathroom window and would be screened anyway.

For some reason, we got talking about bees and it turned out that Paul was a beekeeper. I asked him if he could put a hive in the garden and he was happy to do so. I also mentioned wanting to buy the bank. He said he'd worked with Terry Cook for years and offered to act as middleman in negotiating a price. I said I would certainly offer £15,000 (thinking even that was a lot) and Paul said he'd speak with Terry to see what he might have in mind. So all in all that was a useful discussion.

In fact, it all turned out very well. Paul encouraged Terry to let me have the piece of land at a price quite a lot lower than the figure he'd asked the Days. It was still a great deal of money, many thousands, but I felt it would enhance the property and in time increase its value anyway, quite apart from the fact that it gave me ownership of the stream. Before this, the boundary had run down the middle of the stream. So I was happy with the outcome and plan to make the bank into a bit of a flower garden. But it is not particularly good soil at the moment so will need lots of feeding.

Another development that happened this year (2014) was my beginning to learn bridge. It was not something I'd been in the least interested in but Sara had started to learn and with her excellent mind was beginning to do rather well. Not so for me. I found I was a slow learner. I was driving everyone mad with my 'grumbles'. One morning as we were playing and I was 'going on', feeling I was doing badly, Jan Gavin who was often with us said: "Get off the stage, Martin!" I felt awfully hurt but, of course, she was absolutely right; I was being a pain and I had to learn to keep quiet.

The fun bit for me though was the social enjoyment with a gathering of friends, making up a 'four' and having a great tea! We all got together in Anne Langton's house in Liss – Sara, Jan (usually), Anne and me. Anne was a special friend of Sara's. As time went on I was spending time being given lessons by Anne. She was really good at bridge and helping me a lot. I was even beginning to enjoy it. But I began to be worried about Sara as she was by now suffering from pain in her hip. She was so stoical that I don't think any of us realised just how much she was suffering.

So the weeks and months of 2014 went on with many fairly mundane happenings. I was seeing my osteopath from time to time to keep in good shape. I also had acupuncture about once a month with Tamara Kircher in her home at Haslemere. Again, she was someone recommended to me by Sara and was brilliant. I hardly felt the needles. I was keeping up my music and was invited by Sara to join the choir at Warminghurst Church (near Storrington), close to her aunt and cousin Rachel's house. We sang the Faure Requiem which I much enjoyed on Saturday, 21 June, a beautiful summer day, and we were treated to a spread of wonderful food.

Clive and Dulcie had come back to the UK in mid-June and of course, as usual, had much arranged. Dulcie always has so many friends to see and Clive makes sure he sees something of the boys. So, this time I only had half a day's golf with Clive!

My 80ᵗʰ Birthday – 17ᵗʰ July 2014

But there was a big day in the diary for me. I had arranged a special party at the Garrick for my 80ᵗʰ birthday. I chose July 18ᵗʰ, (instead of the 17ᵗʰ, the actual day) as it was a Friday and with the weekend coming up I thought it would be a more convenient day for most people. It happened to be the hottest day of the year so it was 'jackets off' for the men.

However, I kept mine on for the short 'entertainment' which I performed with William Godfree. We sang some Flanders and Swann and Richard Stilgoe songs and I told a few Sussex stories. I reckoned it would be more fun to have a bit of entertainment rather than just a lunch. Anyway, it went down really well as did the super Garrick food. We all felt spoilt! It was a wonderful occasion and grand to be surrounded by so many close friends.

There was another very special occasion which was being mooted. Jane (my first girlfriend, her mother was my mother's best friend) had met an ex-Brigadier, John Pownall, at a dinner party and in talking with him discovered he was thinking of getting together a performance to pay tribute to those who had lost their lives in the First World War. November 20ᵗʰ was, of course, exactly 100 years since the start of the war. My name came up as apparently John had been wondering if I would accept the job of getting a team together for the exact day. Jane promised to ask me and naturally I was happy to help. It's funny how the world goes round, as it happened Sara had been carer for John's wife, Sylvia. She was unwell for many years and had ended up in a wheelchair. Apparently, John was fantastic in looking after her. He was truly dedicated.

So we started to pull together some ideas and I had meetings with John. He was keen to have the show performed in the Milland Village Hall which could hold an audience of at least 100. The very fine hall was literally just down the road from John's house at Milland.

I asked William if he'd do the music for us and approached my longstanding friend Roden Richardson to ask him if he would write the script. For many years Roden and I had a business we worked together, Canopus Communications, producing videos and CDs. As part of the business, we had created a system for making tapes to help choral singers more easily learn their notes. It had been my original idea as I badly needed help learning the music and words we performed in the choir! So I had telephoned my friend Lloyd Silverthorne, to ask if he could help. Lloyd had worked in radio production as a Senior Studio Manager with the BBC for decades, and I wondered if he and his wife, Sue, could assist in building the business. Lloyd had been totally brilliant and recorded a huge number of works and the big oratorios on a computer with separate notes for sopranos, altos, tenors and basses. Roden suggested a name for the product 'ChoraLine' and another name for the business itself 'Music Dynamics'. ChoraLine has, in fact, become famous and even now is helping many hundreds of thousands of singers more easily to learn their notes. Roden was key in this business as well as in Canopus Communications. He was a highly professional and creative writer and designer and he had won awards for major examples of extremely elaborate and hugely effective video presentations for some big clients including British Aerospace and Glaxo. He also won special awards for his complex presentations for the Financial Times and Rolls Royce Aero Engines.

Using the business before we closed it down, we made a film with Bev Smith (on camera) for the Chichester Harbour Trust. Roden did a terrific job writing and project managing the film, even getting a helicopter to fly low over Bosham and the channel leading up to the Harbour. Sir Jeremy Thomas, the Chairman, and the trustees were delighted with the film, which they were going to use for marketing the Trust. The mission was to prevent nasty development around Chichester Harbour and to retain the Harbour unspoiled for future generations.

But I return to the business of getting Roden to write the script for our 'War to End all Wars' performance. Roden took a bit of persuading, he knew all too well what such a job would entail! But I brought him round in the end so I'd made a good start with the team. John asked me to present which I was very pleased to do.

My next job was to find an actress to join us. Naturally, knowing her well, I approached Janie Dee. She is incredibly talented and would have been perfect, but sadly she would be extremely busy in November and couldn't commit to us. However, she promised to think about it and finally suggested a young actress called Fiona-Jane Weston. She already had her own show 'Wartime Women'. Janie gave us a number and I got in touch with Fiona-Jane. She happily agreed and I soon introduced her to John. We were getting there.

There was one more person I was keen to involve – Hugh Bonneville. He had, of course, become extremely famous because of his leading role in 'Downton Abbey'. It so happened that I had for some years known Hugh's parents, Pat and JP (as his father J. P. Williams was always known). They lived in Fernhurst, so John and I went to see 'JP' to find out if he could put in a word for us! He said he would 'see what he could do'. It wasn't long before I got to know that Hugh actually lived in Milland, very close in fact to the Village Hall, which now has a very good shop which Hugh, indeed, had officially opened. John knew exactly where Hugh lived with his family and we decided to make an approach. The upshot was that Hugh would be pretty busy in November but if we could be flexible with the date he'd try to fit us in.

Meantime, there were all manner of household matters that had to be dealt with. I kept up my golf and fishing in the Hamble and spent several enjoyable days on Hayling Island with Jan and Sara. Jan's uncle, who had a home there near the beach, had recently died and Jan had the job of clearing the house. 'Tucker', as he was always known, had been a brilliant pilot and had flown bombers on several missions over Germany during the War. He had many effects which all had to be carefully gone through. A big job for Jan.

Sara and I, together with Jan, joined a group of friends for a meditation together on Sunday mornings once a month. We each offer our houses and take it in turns to host the meditation and provide a wonderful breakfast. One of our members, Heiner Thissen, whose wife Diane had created a country house in Portugal with local materials, invited us all to Portugal to see the house, enjoy a concert there provided by musical friends and to stay in the local hotel. Unfortunately for me, I had the most frightful cold and cough which certainly took the shine off the visit for me. I felt pretty dreadful and very nearly didn't go, but I thought I was being 'weedy' so decided to make the best of it.

It was May so I thought it was pretty bad luck to have such a rotten cold in the summer. However, after a couple of days I began to feel better.

Later, in October, Sara and Jan booked up for a group tour in Turkey. This did not bode well. I took them to the station for the train to Gatwick but when they got to the airport, horrors! Sara found she'd left her passport behind, most unlike her as she was usually so efficient with such things. Jan had to go ahead on her own while Sara got in touch with Son-in-law Misha telling him where her passport was and asking Misha if he could drive it to the airport in time for the plane. He nearly made it, but in the end Sara had to take a flight next day. Then it was a matter of linking up with Jan, but which hotel was she in? The whole business became extremely stressful. They got together in the end without much help from the tour operators, apparently, so their stay in Turkey was not the enjoyable time they'd hoped for. To add injury to what was a pretty difficult situation, on an ancient site they went to visit, a woman fell over near the edge of a precipice and Sara threw herself onto the woman to save her.

In doing so, Sara banged her knee badly on the stone ground and of course there was no first aid box to help her bathe her very painful wound. She was incredibly good about this.

Concerns for Sara's Health

We wondered later if Sara's health was beginning to be affected by the problem in her right hip. It was particularly bad luck that it was the right knee which had been damaged by the fall. It was certainly the beginnings of trouble she had with that hip for many months to come. Though she made nothing of it and followed the advice for doing things the natural way which she received from Patrick Quanten, Sara had absolutely no time for the medical profession and refused to take even a mild painkiller saying she didn't want chemicals in her body. I have to say, I was concerned that she would do nothing to ease the pain.

Lots had gone on during the year. More jobs for Rhubarb; there were AGMs for the UK Film Studio and the Chichester Area Talking News; I hosted another Fernden old boys dinner at the Garrick; attended another Maritime Foundation Awards dinner at the Institute of Directors and in November, there was a final meeting in Germany of some of my NEWAYS downline distributors, before

NEWAYS was taken over by the new business Modere. I'd also managed some golf, particularly with my friends Robin Lee (actually, my Counsellor), Peter Hawley who'd been a top surgeon, and Chris White who lives at Lynchmere. His wife, Bronwyn, had spoiled me with her delicious teas after rounds of golf with Chris! So, these were merely a random collection of notes from the diary.

Now, we entered another very significant year, 2015. As one gets older the time seems to go faster, everyone says so! Indeed, the months flew by, packed with incidents. But since so much was more or less mirrored by earlier months I will only briefly go on and relate a few particularly significant ones.

As one gets older the more funerals I seem to have to attend. A sad time came when Sara and I had to go to the funeral of Pat Williams, Hugh Bonneville's mother – a very special occasion in Milland church. The packed congregation, including a full marquee behind the West Door, was a tribute in itself. 'JP' related a most moving personal tribute to Pat, and in a strong voice without so much as an emotional tremble. Having had to do some of these things myself, I was most impressed.

I took Sara to a super St Valentine's Day dinner at Langrish House with her being beautifully dressed up in her 'glad rags' again! That night she joined me at the cottage. I hoped everything looked OK, but she sometimes berated me for not having things ready enough for her visits. Sara was a master herself at noticing what other people needed. I don't have quite the same natural gift!

On 12th March I went to the Optega Eye Hospital in Guildford for a cataract operation, one eye at a time. The second eye was done a week later. This operation has literally changed my life. I had been getting worried that I couldn't easily see the road signs ahead in focus. Quite different now. The ops were performed by Miss Gilvarry (very Irish) a brilliant surgeon who had operated on Iona, so she knew my name. I found her quite a sexy lady, and one of the nurses said to me, "She always wears a smart dress and high heels. We often say to each other – which shoes today?"

As the result of a recommendation from my granddaughter, I went to France (La Rochelle) for a week to stay with a woman who, in her home, gives private lessons to help people with French conversation. That certainly helped me, but I wish I'd had the chance to keep it up. I actually found myself speaking some French at the airport when I got home!

I attended several concerts including another Members Concert at the Garrick again with Sara as my guest. I kept up the fishing and golf, including a day at Cowdray with Clive over from the States.

This year, Sara and I much enjoyed a performance of the Beethoven Ninth on September 26th, at the Royal Albert Hall. The conductor was Hilary Davan Wetton, who was the music master at Cranleigh when Tim was there. He got us excellent seats. Hilary is a fellow member of the Garrick.

In another completely different professional area, I worked for a dozen years at the Game Fair.

Commentating on the fly-casting demonstrations at the Game Fair in front of a packed Grandstand.

I was commentator for the casting demonstrations given by fly-casting experts. The Fair visited many of the 'Stately Homes of England', including such famous places as Chatsworth, Blenheim, Harewood House and Broadlands, as I've mentioned earlier. The Fair was hugely supported by many thousands over the three days and, though enjoyable, I found the job pretty exhausting. I set up a system of microphones between the demonstrators and myself which enabled me to talk to them and ask them questions as their demonstration progressed. I used to announce each coming demonstration. These announcements could be heard on speakers around the fishing stands and were a great help in filling the grandstand with spectators.

One year, the Fair visited Scotland and at Kelso we sloshed around in deep liquid mud after heavy Scottish rain. Much ladies' footwear disappeared into the mud that time!

Talking of 'Stately Homes', one of the jobs I'd had over a number of years was researching, writing and presenting the 'Souvenir Series' an extensive series of videos telling the stories of many of the great houses. The films also included visits to Blenheim, Tower Bridge and Westminster Abbey. I must say, this was all most interesting, but meant a very great deal of painstaking work! The videos were sold in the shops at the various venues for a 'knock down' price of £5.00.

These, then, were just another random collection of my varied experiences over the years. Until, later in 2015, there was a dreadful event which was, as it were, 'waiting to happen'…

One evening in early October I was in the kitchen preparing some supper when the doorbell rang. I went to the door, opened it and saw a young policeman standing outside. I thought maybe I had damaged somebody's vehicle in the car park… or been caught speeding.

"Mr Martin Muncaster?" asked the policeman.

"Yes."

"We've had some difficulty finding you, there's another Millstream Cottage in West Harting."

It had apparently been quite a story. Somehow, the police had got in touch with the orthodontic practice in rooms below mine at the flat. Sandra Roke, who cleans for them and incidentally for me too, had my mobile number and had left me a text giving me the message that 'the South East Police want to get in touch with you most urgently' (the wrong Police County as it happened, the West Sussex Police should have been the actual message, which was puzzling). The text message had, naturally, not only been puzzling, but really worrying.

"Can I come in?" asked the policeman at my door.

"Of course."

But before I'd even had a chance to sit down, he said, grimly: "I'm afraid I have some very bad news for you!"

Chapter 22

Finality – Twice!

It was October 9th, 2015…

Very early that morning, on a quiet country road near his home in Tunbridge Wells, my son Tim had been killed in a car accident. As I heard this I went cold. What was I hearing? How does one cope with such news? Apparently, he had for some unaccountable reason, skidded and hit a tree! The policeman couldn't tell me more. He said that a Police Family Liaison Officer would be in touch to explain in more detail.

Then, with words of understanding and condolence, he quietly left.

By now, all manner of horrific pictures were racing through my mind. How could that possibly have happened to Tim? He was a highly experienced and excellent driver. It didn't make sense…

I rang Sara: "Darling!" she said… a brief silence… then: "What has happened?"

I explained what I knew. She was simply wonderful, so supportive and gave me what words of comfort were possible in such circumstances.

I then had to ring Miranda. I really find it hard to describe how the news hit her. Ollie happened to be staying with her at the time, so she had the horrid task of passing on the news to him. It was drama upon drama.

The next morning, Miranda and Oliver walked to the site on that quiet country road. As they approached the place where Tim had hit the tree, two deer came out from the very spot and crossed the road. That said everything to them, and when they told me later I was sure that Tim, probably picking up speed, had seen two deer crossing his path. That brought me to a memory of a nasty happening to Tim years before, when in the early morning he was driving to his fish farm at Steep, and a deer leapt out of the woods and landed with a resounding crash on the bonnet of his car, which was a write-off as a result. Tim, luckily was quite OK, but it was a huge shock to him, of course, and it was quite impossible to drive the car – now a complete wreck.

I must say, it occurred to me that in this case, he suddenly had a mental picture of that fateful moment, did his best to miss the deer this time, skidded and lost control of the car, with the resulting explosive crash, and his precious new VW car a tangled wreck. The police told me that the engine had broken away from its bolts and landed many yards away amongst the trees. The Police assured me that Tim would have known nothing, which was a blessing in itself.

I don't want to make all this sound over dramatic. I am simply reporting the information the Police had given me. They also told me that the car had spun round and smashed into a second tree!

I went to visit Miranda and Oliver a day later and asked them to take me to the spot. Indeed, there was good evidence that Tim had tried to miss, we are certain, two deer, as there was a long tyre skid mark for many yards way back along the road.

It was all so hard to take in. So final.

But instead of the inevitable shock and deeply felt sadness, we had to look at the blessings; there were several.

First, as I've already said, the Police gave me absolute assurance that Tim would have known nothing. He must have been killed instantly. Second, he was quite alone, there was no one with him in the car, there were no witnesses and no other vehicle was involved. It was far, far better, not only for him, but also for the family, should he have survived, that he did not henceforth live the rest of his life as a vegetable, an appalling thought.

So, after the obvious period of grief, we had to look on the positive side. It was most important, healing indeed, for us all to do that and appreciate that life just has to go on, whatever the trauma we had all experienced.

Now, it was a matter of organising a funeral and memorial. Miranda and Oliver did a marvellous job getting all the detailed business of probate sorted out as well as the complex organisation of the release of bank accounts, etc. Some of this took many weeks.

The funeral, including cremation at the Tunbridge Wells Crematorium, was a most moving and, it has to be said, very amusing occasion, with Gareth, Miranda's husband, making a really funny speech giving us a wonderful insight into Tim's character. Oliver, too, gave a most moving and insightful speech about his brother, including showing a film he'd made on the fish farm, with Tim's collie, Ben. Tim had the idea of entering this little film into the TV programme 'You've been framed' with the possibility of winning £250 if the clip was broadcast. The idea was to show the dog getting extremely wet as he jumped up biting the water as it poured out of the pipe being pointed at him by Tim; Ben was thoroughly soaked of course. However, Ben got his own back. Tim had taught him to jump up and bite the starter key thus turning on the pump, while Tim was kneeling nearby repairing a pipe. When Ben bit the starter key and turned on the pump, water poured out of the pipe Tim was holding, and he was suddenly completely drenched! This caused howls of laughter!

We all then repaired to a local pub, the 'Brown Trout', where we were treated to a delicious lunch. Tim would have been proud of his sister and brother, and Gareth, for all the organisation and work that had gone into making the day so memorable. A highlight had been that Clive's five boys had all come to the funeral. It must have been a long time since they were all together in such a way. It was a shame Clive and Dulcie couldn't be there.

Getting on with Our Lives

With Tim's departure finally complete, we all had to get on with our various separate lives. Even now, it was hard to appreciate that Tim was no more. He had been such a leader, and he was dreadfully missed.

For my part, I was much comforted at being able to spend time with Sara. We spent hours in each other's houses and helping each other in many ways. I always felt she did much more for me than I ever managed to do for her.

In fact Sara could be very direct, and sometimes said things quite sharply. I found this difficult. I tend to go 'round the edges' a bit myself not wanting to hurt feelings. But when Sara was direct, I often felt criticised and got really cross. She always went quiet when this happened, then would say later: "That's just relationship darling!"

But I was quite good at getting her lawns mown, front and back, and having to haul the mower through the house to enable me to do the front lawn. I also did a lot of weeding out of dandelion and plantain roots with a special pronged fork. Most effective, and with some help from Sara, we got a lot of her lawns clear of weeds. We went to films together at the New Park Cinema in Chichester and hugely enjoyed a special 2015 Valentine's dinner at Langrish House, with Sara, once again, looking gorgeous, and I told her so! But by now her leg was giving her much pain. I was glad, though, that it didn't appear to spoil her enjoyment of our evening and dinner.

I was also able to take Sara to another Maritime Foundation Awards Dinner in November at the Institute of Directors. However, a great concern was beginning to loom. Sara was now suffering even greater pain in the hip area of her right leg. She was so stoical, and hardly complained about it, that I didn't realise just how much of a problem it was becoming. She also had some lumps along the left side of her stomach, of which we should have taken much more notice!

We all began to be deeply worried, family and friends alike. Several were urging Sara to see the doctor, but she seemed fixed on Patrick's advice. He was even giving her his special massage which she found very painful. But then we all found Patrick's massage painful as he worked so deeply to try to release 'stuck' muscles and ligaments. He was obviously helping many of his patients who came for treatment at Sara's house, as they kept coming back for more. I had a number of treatments from Patrick myself, hoping it would help the various places in the bottom of the back which were often rather tender. When he hit particular points with his thumb it was all I could do not to shout out! But I felt I just had to be brave!

As I've intimated, Sara was most generous in giving him, and his wife Martine, when she came, a room in her house. They were kind in bringing food, and Martine used to provide delicious soup.

For many months and on into the New Year and the Spring of 2016, this worked well. But now, with Sara obviously suffering dreadful pain, friends and family were trying to get her to understand that she really must see a doctor. There were two friends in particular, whom I knew well, who tried to 'get through' to Sara. But she got very cross, saying to me: "Why do people keep fiddling with other people's lives?" With one of her yoga friends who loved her and was only trying to help, Sara shared with me that she was furious with her for 'interfering'.

'Leave Me Alone'

"Why can't people leave me alone to make my own decisions?" she said. But quietly, I have to admit, I agreed with them and was sure they were right.

So time went steadily on…

Then, suddenly one day, standing in her kitchen, Sara said to me: "I think I should go to the surgery." I was absolutely delighted. Had we, at last, got her to change her mind? The pain was obviously excruciating. It had come to the point when it was just too painful to walk at all and she certainly couldn't make it up the stairs. She began lying downstairs on the couch she used for her healing work. It was so sad that she was unable to heal herself.

Finally, she phoned the surgery in Liss and an appointment was made for the Monday.

I took Sara to the Surgery on the Monday morning and the very kind lady doctor looked carefully at the problem. Lucy was there too, and we were both amazed to see the doctor gently moving Sara's leg up and down without a sound from Sara. Lucy said anyone else would have yelled out in agony! The Doctor said (I imagine not to frighten Sara) she thought it was possibly mainly a muscle problem, but she also said it was vital she had an X-ray. So I immediately took Sara to the X-ray department at Havant (separate from the Queen Alexandra Hospital in Portsmouth). There, the radiologist who took the X-ray was clearly most concerned by what he saw. "I'm not moving you," he said, "we must call an ambulance."

In the event, we waited for an hour before an ambulance came, with all the other poor patients having to wait for their appointments, and the paramedics, both young women, moved Sara most carefully on a 'pat-slide' keeping it level and onto the ambulance stretcher, then drove her to Q.A. I followed on behind. I got to the hospital A&E Department to find Sara had been swiftly moved up to the front of the queue as a most urgent case. Quite soon a middle-aged consultant came along, Polish, I think, to examine Sara. Very quickly, he said: "I could fix you up tonight and get you walking again, but I must talk to my team first." This meant that Sara's case was, in effect, being discussed by committee and everyone had a different idea for the best route for treatment! It led to inevitable delays and it was some days, following a series of tests, before Sara could be operated on. The biopsy taken from the lumps along her tummy showed that she was suffering from cancer and there was obviously concern about it going to the bone in her leg. This was not good news and clearly an operation was necessary. At last, after several delays, the operation was eventually carried out on Easter Sunday, 2016. A pin was inserted into the bone to give her the ability to walk again, and it was necessary for her to stay in hospital for several more days before she could be released.

Meantime, a number of us had been to visit her. I went most days myself and it was sad to see her so confined and now in the very medical system of which she so much disapproved!

At last, after about ten days, she was released from QA, and I was so very touched to see many of the nurses congregated around the Nursing Station to say an affectionate 'goodbye'. She was obviously much loved as a very special and highly regarded patient.

So, after her sojourn in hospital, I was able to take her back home, and to do what I could to ensure that she was looked after by family and friends. Lucy was particularly good as she lived right across the street and would see that Sara was all right. She would also bring the girls, Anna and Lois, to see their granny or 'Ba', as they called her, short for the Russian 'Babushka'. I played my own part as best I could to help my beloved Sara back to health. She was certainly able to walk better without that dreadful pain in her hip. I was also able to give her massage on her leg when she went to bed to help it be more comfortable.

After about a month, I took her back to QA for a follow up. She saw a really kind surgeon who showed us the X-rays, saying he was delighted with the result of the operation. "It's all worked perfectly," he said, "But we must keep a careful watch on it." I had brought some hospital equipment which Sara had to return to the hospital and which I had forgotten to take in. It was still in the car. So I said to Sara I would collect it from the car to take in to the hospital, asking her to wait for me while I dashed out.

It so happened on the way back that I saw her consultant again in the corridor, and quickly asked him for his real opinion. I'd rather felt I hadn't 'read between the lines' of what he'd said to Sara about needing to 'keep an eye on things'. I quizzed him a bit and he gave me to understand that they didn't want the cancer to move into the bone. This worried me, of course, but I didn't pass any of this on to Sara. She had quite enough to worry about already.

But most unhappily, she started to show signs of going downhill and began to spend long periods in bed. Daughter Zoe was wonderful and planned weekly rotas for family and friends to go in to ensure that Sara was looked after, had companionship and proper meals. This worked well, as we were only too keen to help.

However, after a few weeks, even this wasn't enough, and nurses from the Rosemary Foundation (which Sara had always supported) were called in to help

Sara be comfortable. By now, it meant the administration of 'morphine' to help the pain. It was so desperately sad to see Sara in such a state.

The Last Kiss

Before she got too bad and was still very much with us, I was able to lean over the bed and share a long kiss. It was the last time I was ever able to share a kiss with her again, and she looked so happy to have had the connection. Her face really lightened. It was such a special moment.

She was now going rapidly downhill and the Foundation nurses did a wonderful and most caring job, coming in night and morning to make Sara as comfortable as possible.

I sat with her for several days, holding her hand under the sheets and hoping she knew I was there. I was pretty certain she did, though there was no reaction. I even spoke to her hoping she would feel my love wafting towards her. One time, as I sat with her, my mind went back to a happier, romantic time. Before the War when I was quite little, my parents used to go to the beach at Climping, a short way along the coast to the west of Littlehampton. Clive and I had a great time playing in the sand. I was remembering now of the time I took Sara there for old time's sake, and we sat on the rocks holding hands, listening to the steady rhythm of the sea and watching the waves rolling up the beach, then gurgling back leaving bubbling froth on the sand.

Then on the afternoon of September the 23rd, when I was on my way to sit with her again, I called in to Lucy to tell her I was going in to see Sara. Lucy came to me from her kitchen and said quietly: "Sara died this afternoon." Her dear friend, Jan Gavin, had been with Lucy and just missed the actual moment. I was two hours too late, but went over to sit by Sara anyway and pray that she was now at peace and happy to be released from all the pain. For the last few days, her mouth had been open, almost in an expression of agony, as I heard her quiet breathing getting gradually slower and quieter. But now all that was gone and her face was quite relaxed. I was so pleased for her and spoke, sending streams of love to her, yet myself being flooded with sadness.

Somebody said later that 'when Sara died, a light went out in the world.' It could not have been better said… But Sara had gone the way she had chosen and we all had to respect that. It had been her 'journey'.

Lucy organised for the funeral directors to come. They took away Sara's body in a white shroud. Sara had never wanted a coffin. I didn't think Will was involved, but Sara's three girls (as I will call them) together organised probate and all the many details necessary for the funeral.

Sara had chosen to be buried in a grave at the Sustainability Centre, high on the hill above East Meon. It was a most beautiful October morning, Tuesday October 11th, with the sun shining upon some 150 of us, as we sat or stood around, with a warm fire in the grate under the extensive canopy. Sara's body in the white shroud had been brought to the site by the Funeral Directors on a handcart which was touching in itself. The funeral was officiated most sensitively by our dear friend, Robert Gussman, who had once been a vicar. He brought everything together quite beautifully.

The three girls, Lucy, Zoe and Rosie, with Will beside them, all spoke most movingly, as did Will, and with much humour. They all gave us a lot of laughs about their mother, her remarkable life and her eccentric character. It had been a life of such service to so many hundreds of people over the years. I was invited to read the insightful and most moving passage on 'Death' from Kahlil Gibran's 'Prophet'. I'd had to hold on to myself as I read. I was on the verge of breaking down with deep feelings, but managed OK; at least people said most kind things about my reading afterwards when we repaired for a celebratory lunch at the nearby Langrish House Hotel. This particularly meant a lot to me, as I had been there several times for meals with Sara, and also, as I've mentioned, for two delicious Valentine's Night dinners, the last one in February this same year.

Today was a great celebration and we felt we gave Sara a wonderful 'send-off'. Thus closed an era with, I have to say, a beautiful life ended far too short. Sara was just 76.

Sara, how I like to remember her.

Epilogue

It is almost self-evident to state that I felt bereft, in effect for the third time, Iona having died three years earlier; and the shock and sadness of Tim's departure from this world only adding to the overall sense of grief.

But I am determined to end these chapters of my life on a happy and positive note. For me there is still so much to enjoy and be thankful for, my good health to start with. I have a beautiful home, I have my golf with friends to enjoy at Cowdray, which must surely be one of the most beautiful courses in Britain with its stunning views along the length of the South Downs, often in certain lights, standing out in deep aquamarine blue.

I have my trout fishing on the Upper Hamble, that delightful little stream chuckling along in an oasis of quiet in the valley running between Bishop's Waltham and Botley, in Hampshire. Times with my rod and line have given me great solace. Indeed, on occasion I have been able to leave a brace of trout on Sara's doorstep!

My visits to the Garrick Club always give me special pleasure, meeting people who are becoming friends, particularly my dear partner, William Godfree, with whom I tell my 'silly Sussex' stories in the dialect, and together singing Flanders and Swann and Stilgoe songs. Such good fun, and audiences love William's brilliant expertise at the piano. Some say he is 'more Swann than Swann!'

I have also much enjoyed being part of the romantic, comedy, thriller movie, 'Blue Iguana', now complete and premiered in London. That was really exciting. I made good friends with the writer and the producer, Hadi Hajaig, a man of immense talent and charm. He has made several films and did a brilliant job with this one too.

The film, had some great stars in the cast, including the famous actors Sam Rockwell and Simon Callow, with whom I enjoyed working. We were all thrilled when Sam was awarded his Oscar.

Another venture into film for me has been a part in the now famous movie 'Darkest Hour'. I must be one of the last broadcasters left who can remember what it was like reading the BBC Radio News soon after the war. We read the bulletins differently then. We had to be very clear with our enunciation and we spoke at a slightly slower speed. This style was what was wanted for my part in the 'Darkest Hour'. The Churchill family was sitting listening to the wireless and the bulletin I was reading about the Germans marching through Holland and Belgium. They were listening to the very first days of the war. I was excited to be asked to perform that very special role.

And, of course, I have the family who are so precious to me. But I really don't see enough of them, except Ollie, who is staying with me at the moment. He is brilliant behind a camera and has made some delightful films, together with a catalogue of very fine stills. Miranda takes after her mother, with no doubt influence from my father, in her artistry, in writing and illustrating books for children.

As I record these final thoughts, I am staying with Miranda, Oliver and my granddaughter at an excellent hotel at Port Charlotte on the Isle of Islay. As I've written, we stayed on Jura as a family at the old lighthouse station for some 12 years each summer, starting in July 1969, just after we'd moved to Clouds Hill. We had come now for a bit of a holiday for old times' sake, but also to say prayers for Tim and his life at a favourite spot of his on Jura.

It is now, as I write, the evening of June 28th, 2017. This morning, we took the ferry to Jura from Port Askaig on Islay, drove along the road to Craighouse, past the shop there and further on down the long, rutted track to Ardmenish Farm, which we knew so well during our visits to 'The Lighthouses' (as the house was known by the locals). It was originally a Trinity House property, surrounded by stone walls, built for the Lighthouse keepers and their families. Following on from the Shaws, who we knew, Ardmenish is now owned, I believe, by the Craig family.

On this day, the weather was beautiful with plenty of sunshine. We walked the track to the house, then up onto a high gully between the rocks with a magnificent view across Lowlandman's Bay to the three Paps of Jura beyond. This was the favourite spot of Tim's, and I have cine film of him stalking the stag there which, as I mentioned earlier, eventually eluded him, dropped into the sea and swam across the Bay.

The Stag.

It had been such a happy time.

After our intimate and very private ceremony, Ollie took this picture of us, my granddaughter, Miranda and me, pondering the beauty of the expansive scene before us – Lowlandman's Bay and the great Paps beyond.

Now, as we sat quietly meditating, looking across the bay with the sleeping Paps in the distance, the peace and silence were tangible, only broken by the calls of a pair of oystercatchers as they skimmed low past us along the rocks, their sound echoing back from the hillside.

I felt sure Tim was happy and undoubtedly close by – if you believe in such things.

May he be well, happy and now at peace. That was our fervent prayer as we quietly trudged our way slowly back to the farm…

Appendices

Biography of the author

Memories and letters of BBC days

Eulogy to the author's mother.

"Let the Peoples Sing"

"Fernden Time"

Holiday Property Bond printed brochure

Martin Muncaster studied at the Guildhall School of Music and Drama, but before starting out on his ambition to be a broadcaster, he did his National Service in the Royal Navy, becoming an RNVR officer. Then after a spell being tried out as an announcer on the BBC's General Overseas Service (now the World Service), he was advised to "go away and get some experience". Taking this advice seriously, he took a ship to Canada where he worked with CBC on a range of radio assignments as well as appearing on the stage.

On his return to London, he became an evening host on BBC-tv – in the days of Michael Aspel and Sylvia Peters, later presenting a range of programmes including *Come Dancing* and *Songs of Praise.*

When ITV began in the 50's, he was recruited in 1958 by Southern Television in Southampton as their main newsreader, announcer and reporter. He was the newsreader who opened the station, assisted by none other than Ian Trethowan, down specially from ITN. But when BBC South was created in 1960 to compete with Southern's evening magazine, Day by Day, Martin was delighted to have the opportunity to move back to "the BBC" as the regular presenter of South Today. After some four years, he returned to London and the national scene to become one of the news-reading and presenting team for a decade, first on the old Home Service, then on Radio-4.

Martin also had his own video company, Canopus Communications, Ltd., and was busy working on films and videos for commercial clients. He also took part in special events at many of Britain's stately homes and castles, as narrator accompanying Caroline McCausland, a fine singer with a beautiful soprano voice. She was also expert on the guitar. Martin accompanied her musical presentations acting as reader of poetry and prose.

He pursued his abiding interests in sailing, fly-fishing and the countryside generally and was regularly engaged as commentator for the fly-casting demonstrations at the annual Game Fair at various prestigious venues around the country. He was a regular contributor to the BBC Radio-4 "Waterlines" series with Cliff Michelmore, and also presented features on the famous "Countryside" programmes for more than 20 years. He found time, too, for a special interest in alternative and complementary medicine and was Chairman of the Working Party which later became the NCC (National Consultative Council of Alternative and Complementary Medicine).

Martin was born in Sussex and was educated at Stowe. His father was the famous landscape and marine painter, Claude Muncaster, who went round The Horn in a sailing ship as a deckhand. He went on to paint several commissions for the Royal Family in the 1940's including an impressive landscape commissioned by the King, which now hangs at Balmoral. Martin wrote a book, The Wind in the Oak, relating stories of his father's fascinating life.

Now in his 80s and living in Hampshire, Martin has found yet another career by investing in new film productions and thereby appearing in a minor role or as an 'extra' in a thriller named *Cleanskin*, starring Sean Bean. He was recently delighted to take part in a much larger production, *Blue Iguana*, a romantic, comedy thriller, with a 'star' cast, shooting scenes with no less an actor than Simon Callow.

This was given to me as a reminder by my Producer (Gordon Randall).

In my day the closing captions were made up on cards with the letters stuck on individually. The cards were then put up on a stand in front of the camera and the studio manager would lift each card off one by one. That would seem archaic today. But it was how we did it at the time.

When I left "South Today", I received some warming tributes from various of my colleagues, and another, later, from the Head of Presentation (radio) Rooney Pelletier, who sent me a very kind message about the occasion when I read news of Churchill's death.

There are other additions I thought interesting and relevant to include.

Bristol 32211

BROADCASTING HOUSE
WHITELADIES ROAD
BRISTOL 8

Dear Martin,

Thank you for your personal note. I am naturally sorry that you are leaving Southampton, as you have done a first-class job for us in a very pleasant & happy way. I need not tell you how much you will be missed because I'm sure your colleagues will leave you in no doubt of that. However I think you are wise to make a change, & the London experience should be valuable.

I certainly intend to see you before you go & can deliver my good wishes for your future then.

As ever —

Desmond.

Desmond Hawkins

THE BRITISH BROADCASTING CORPORATION
Southampton Studio Centre, South Western House,
Southampton

TELEPHONE AND TELEGRAMS : SOUTHAMPTON 26201

22ᵈ October, '64.

My dear Martin,

Thank you so much for your very nice letter, and for all you did for us during your four years at Southampton. We all gained enormously from having you here during this very important, exacting and exciting period. All the hard work that went into setting up a new station is an investment for all time.

I attach a few more letters which you may like to reply to yourself. Could I have them back again for our programme correspondence files, please?

Our thoughts will be with you on Monday. Good luck to you — I know you will keep up Southampton's reputation for turning out winners!

Yours,

(Peter.

P.S. There's an item in tomorrow's programme (Friday) that will appeal to you! P.

Peter Marshall

Langham 4468
Broadcasts London-W1
Telex 22182

BROADCASTING HOUSE

LONDON W.1

My dear Martin,

I heard you on the
Home Service this morning &
realised that you have taken
up your new job. Here's
wishing you a most happy
& enjoyable spell in Bristol.
You are most welcome. We
shall be meeting face to face
before long I hope.

Yours,

Frank.

Frank Gillard

THE BRITISH BROADCASTING CORPORATION

Broadcasting House, Whiteladies Road, Bristol, 8

TELEPHONE AND TELEGRAMS : BRISTOL 32211

14010/SFW/MBA

15th October, 1964

Dear Martin,

This is your last week in Southampton and I write to thank you most warmly for all you have done for us there.

I know that the Staff feel that working with you has been a delightful experience - quite apart from admiring your professional approach to the job.

I do hope you will find happiness in London - and I am glad to know you will still be with the Corporation.

With our thanks and every good wish,

Yours

(Stuart Wyton)

Martin Muncaster, Esq.,
c/o Southampton Newsroom.

BROADCASTING HOUSE

WHITELADIES ROAD

BRISTOL 8

11th November 1964

Dear Martin,

As I motored back to Bristol this morning from the BBC Symphony Orchestra's concert at Exeter, I listened with great enjoyment to "Morning Story", but the enjoyment was twinged with conscience when I remembered that I should have written to you long since to tell you of talk at our last Advisory Council meeting about your translation to London. The Rowridge section of the Council wanted to record their appreciation of all your performances in "South Today", their deep regret that you should have left the programme and their good wishes for your new job. Their enthusiasm was so contagious that the whole Council wished to be associated with "an appropriate message" to you. This is it - but some twenty-six days overdue!

I do hope all goes well and that you feel the change was a wise one at this particular point in your BBC career.

No acknowledgement please since this is only fan mail - though at the highest level.

Yours
Lobby

Martin Muncaster, Esq.,
London.

Seymour Joly Lotbiniere

From :   Chief of Presentation (Sound)

Subject :   DEATH OF SIR WINSTON CHURCHILL: SUNDAY, 24th JANUARY

To :   Mr. Martin Muncaster   Copy to: Chief Asst., Pres.(S)

                                               27th January, 1965

                                                  <u>PERSONAL</u>

      I did not hear you read the 6.00 p.m.News last Sunday,
but I am told by someone very senior, whose opinions I usually share, that
your performance was truly excellent. Thank you very much.

HRP/PW

                                          (H. Rooney Pelletier)

AS/20/P

Please turn over

325

17th July 1991.

Dear Martin,

How very kind of you to have taken the time to write to me. Indeed, I feel much honoured by the Muncaster family, since your mother also, as you say, wrote me a most generous letter earlier.

I must say, your news reading talents are much missed nowadays on the morning bulletins. I'm sure you're happier & freer and better off now, but the quality of news reading seems to me to have dropped off sadly. However, when I catch your voice I am always delighted, and remember with pleasure the days when we worked together.

Many thanks again.
Yours sincerely,

John Simpson

Along with my brothers, sister, and cousins, I knew the gracious lady whose life we have gathered here to celebrate as "Aunt Prim".

Oddly enough, it only struck me when I sat down to prepare this address just how inappropriate that name was. For there was nothing "prim and proper" about Prim.

I remember her as young and vivacious. She had a wonderful sense of humour. She was full of fun and energy, not least on the tennis court where she really excelled.

And it was here -----on the tennis court and still only 18 ----- that she met Gray, her first husband.

Tanned, handsome and totally irresistible after his epic voyage from Australia before the mast as an able seaman on the Olive Bank ---- one of the last grain clippers.

Gray played tennis but preferred golf, once described by a sergeant-major of my acquaintance as " 'ockey at the 'alt ".

Now unlike tennis, golf is ideally played in total silence. Alas, this was not Prim's strong point.

Having converted his drive into a divot (or whatever golfers do) because she burst into speech at the crucial moment, Gray hurled his club in the air in frustration. Alas again, it stuck up a tree, and he had to climb up and fetch it.

Another enduring quality associated with Aunt Prim was her kindness, and generosity. My first distinct memory of this was in 1940, during the run-up to Dunkerque.

Our home in Maidstone was perilously close to the front line. Prim welcomed into her home in Petworth her elder sister, Evelyn, with two unruly sons aged nine and six.

Unruly, perhaps, because my father was a career officer in the RAF, spending years at a time abroad while we ran riot at home. Whatever the reason, Martin and Clive were scandalised by the way we fought each other.

But Prim was ever ready to help anyone in trouble. Jane Tinley, who has read [will read] to you, and her sister Bridget were left behind as young teenagers when their mother went to South Africa.

When they more or less turned up on the doorstep unannounced, Prim it was who took them in and saw them through difficult times.

And much later, when my mother Evelyn died in 1967 and the family house had to be sold, Prim took my sister Jennifer in and provided a home while she took a nursing course at Chichester ---- and got back on her feet emotionally.

Prim was an excellent cook, inspired at flower arranging, and very house proud. I confess to being a trifle nervous when visiting with my own youngsters lest some priceless ornament should shatter in a dozen pieces

There was that unfortunate episode around 1970, I guess, when some evil-minded boy -----who shall today be nameless ----- persuaded my Colin aged 7 to jump onto a pile of grass cutting that was actually a thin covering over a pile of very mature compost.

We had come by train with no spare clothes ---- and the day was warm. Prim took it in her stride, and all was well.

But then Prim was very much involved with her family, which on the Balfour side was extensive.

She was the youngest of Lord and Lady Riverdale's five children --- two brothers and two sisters.

Every one of the five children married, buried their first spouse, and married a second time, producing a total of 13 grandchildren.

And Prim was also the last to go, bringing that generation of my family spanning precisely the whole of the 20th Century to a close.

I guess it is a tribute to the cohesion of this clan that six of the nine surviving grandchildren are with us today.

So in closing I would just like to say "Thank you Aunt Prim".

Late in life you had a tough time, with much physical pain and mental anguish. Now, all of us here wish you peace, amid God's love and care.

"Let the Peoples Sing"

For many years on the World Service, I introduced the BBCs worldwide choral competition. Entries from amateur choirs came from all manner of countries around the world to be judged by well-known conductors, such as Sir David Willcocks and John Alldis. The winning choir was awarded the coveted *Silver Rose Bowl*.

"Fernden Time"

Because of 'double summer time' during the War, all the clocks at Fernden were timed to be ten minutes early. This can be read in an excellent book "Fernden Time", the story of an English Prep School, by Johnnie Brownrigg.

I notice that my name is mentioned several times in the book; also, those of my grandparents, Sir Arthur and Lady Balfour.

On one memorable morning, a particular small boy got the Fernden timing badly wrong and arrived terribly late for Assembly. As he crept in, Miss Joan Napier, our formidable School Secretary, yelled out in strident voice: "Boy, you're late! The entire school has been waiting for you."

Miss Napier also had charge of a special bowl of sweets, donated by parents, which she kept under lock and key. On Sundays, because of rationing, we were only allowed to choose just one each!

This was a long series I performed for the Holiday Property Bond.

HPB The Video

Just completed is a super new video on the HOLIDAY PROPERTY BOND and you can own a copy. It is introduced and narrated by television and radio personality Martin Muncaster.

The video tells the Bond story spelling out the unique benefits Bondholders enjoy and describing how the Bond works. It visits all the current locations some at which you may have already holidayed. With this one handy package you can recall those happy days, and at the same time show your friends what you have discovered with the Holiday Property Bond.

The HPB video runs for twenty two minutes but we've recorded it for you on to a two hour tape. So you can reuse the tape whenever you wish.

Bondholders: Remember there are £1,000 bonuses to win and £50 cash rewards to enjoy when you introduce a friend to become a Bondholder. The HPB video will help you!

HOLIDAY PROPERTY BOND

THE VIDEO

TV's Martin Muncaster presents the Holiday Property Bond

OFFERED AT COST PRICE!
VHS or BETA
£5.80 including post, packaging, and VAT

For overseas delivery please add £1.50 to the above prices.

Index